Commonly known as the 'Queen of Common Sense', Maggie Dent has become one of Australia's favourite parenting authors, educators and podcasters.

Maggie is the author of nine major books, including the bestselling 2018 release *Mothering Our Boys*, her 2020 release *From Boys to Men* and her 2022 release *Girlhood*. She hosts the award-winning ABC podcast *Parental As Anything*, and in July 2021 released a book of the same name. Maggie is also the host of *The Good Enough Dad* podcast.

Maggie's experience includes teaching, counselling, working in palliative care/funeral services and suicide prevention. She is a dedicated advocate for quietly changing lives in our families and communities. Maggie is an ambassador for Telethon in WA and a champion of the Telethon Kids Institute. She is also a proud ambassador for mental health not-for-profit Gotcha4Life Foundation, mindfulness app Smiling Mind, and The Sanctuary, a crisis shelter in the Sydney Hills District for women and their children who are fleeing domestic violence.

Maggie is the mother of four sons and a very grateful grandmother to a growing tribe of precious little boys and girls. She lives in the South Coast region of NSW with her good bloke Steve Mountain and their dear little dog, Mr Hugo Walter Dent.

Also by Maggie Dent

From Boys to Men
Girlhood

MAGGIE DENT

help me help my teen

MACMILLAN
Pan Macmillan Australia

First published 2024 in Macmillan by Pan Macmillan Australia Pty Ltd
1 Market Street, Sydney, New South Wales, Australia, 2000

NATIONAL LIBRARY OF AUSTRALIA

A catalogue record for this book is available from the National Library of Australia

Typeset in 10.5/16 pt Sabon LT Pro by Midland Typesetters, Australia
Printed by IVE
Illustrations: Katharine Middleton (pp22, 153), Kylie McCaffrey, Lantern Designs (pp36, 37 and 41) and Depositphotos (pp46, 65). Image on p341 used with permission from NeuroWild.

I wish to acknowledge and pay my respects to Australia's first peoples and to the traditional custodians of this amazing land. I especially pay my humble respects to the Noongar peoples of south west Western Australia, the custodians of my homeland, the country of my childhood, which I carry deeply within my heart every day of my life. This book has been written on the lands of the Wodi Wodi peoples of the Dharawal nation, and I also acknowledge and pay my respects to elders, past, present and emerging.

The ancient knowledge and wisdom that our Indigenous elders have known and shared for thousands of years still has value for our modern world. May we all find ways to walk gently and compassionately on these ancient lands and come to a place where every child ever born is respected, valued and has a strong sense of belonging.

As I dedicated my last book, *Girlhood*, to my granddaughters, I dedicate this book to my precious grandsons, Alfie, Arthur and Solly. I hope I am still on this earth when you are teens crossing the bridge to manhood. Thank you for the hours of fun and laughter and may you always know you will always have a loving family to turn to, no matter what, no matter when, we will always be here.

All my love, always and forever,
Nanny

Contents

Breakout Key

Keep an eye out for the following breakout boxes throughout the book. They each mean something different.

TEEN SURVEY

This box contains a quote from two surveys: a teen survey conducted online in 2023 as research for this book, and an earlier survey of teen boys from 2019.

MAGGIE TIP

This box contains important takeaway points and suggestions from the Queen of Common Sense.

Foreword

In my more than 25 years of practice as a psychologist and parent educator, I can say without question that the most overwhelmed parents are those of teenagers.

After all, adolescence is an extraordinary time of development. Our children's brains and bodies are going through incredible changes, all while they attempt to understand enormous coming-of-age questions like who they are and how to make a go of this thing called 'life'. When the wheels fall off during this rollercoaster period, it can seem like things are going all sorts of sideways, and quickly. Yet parents who look for support find it increasingly hard to come by, waiting weeks and months for professional care, even in dire cases.

This challenge has weighed heavily on my heart in recent years, and a single word has continued to push its way into my consciousness – *adaptation*. When we find ourselves in circumstances that cannot be changed, it is sometimes on us to come to terms with the futility of that situation, and then to summon the courage to find a different way through. To adapt. But what might that look like?

As I've learned through illuminating conversations with many experts over the past several years, the way through has quite possibly been staring us in the face all along: we can epically empower parents to help their teens. After all, a professional may be available an hour every week or month, but a parent is there 24 hours a day. And knowing how incredibly parents can and do show up for their kids, what if we were to harness that collective will and wisdom with expertly and compassionately delivered knowledge?

Imagine my exuberance when the one and only Maggie Dent called me up one afternoon and said her heart had been called to pen one last book, on just this topic!

The result is a masterpiece. It is as though Maggie Dent (and the numerous world-renowned colleagues she cites throughout) have stepped right into your living room, and over a cuppa, are there with you – the parent – as you take your place, confidently and with swagger, in guiding your teen through their journey of becoming.

Maggie has taken on every single topic with wisdom and depth, leaving you knowing that you really can do this. You really can help your teen, no matter how daunting that might feel at the outset. And if you should waver at all, Maggie will be right there at your side, lighting the way forward, chapter by chapter.

Help Me Help My Teen is the answer we have been waiting for. Let this be the start of a movement that sees parents empowered, and most importantly, teens supported.

Dr Vanessa Lapointe
Parent supporter and champion,
bestselling author, educator and mum

Introduction

I don't take the decision to write a book lightly, as it is an enormous commitment. I really felt that I was finished after writing *Girlhood*. Genuinely, I felt that I had explored all the things that burned a fire inside me in my nine books.

Then, unexpectedly, the concept for this book started wandering through my mind and my heart. Clear messages were coming from worried parents, concerned high-school teachers and health professionals that so many of our teens were floundering and struggling. The waiting lists to see both school and private counsellors and psychologists were getting longer and longer.

One parent shared her concerns about her daughter, who had been hospitalised after a suicide attempt. Once she had been stabilised, she was sent home and the earliest she could see a psychologist was three months after being discharged from hospital. I shared her deep concerns that her daughter was left without significant support following a suicide attempt.

In my local community, there was a suicide cluster in 2020, and on consulting with teens in the months that followed, many shared that when they reached out for help professionally, the earliest appointment was five months away. For teens who live in rural and remote areas, the situation is even more dire and telehealth opportunities are equally in short supply.

I believe no one really wants to die by suicide. What they want is for their pain, anguish and deep sense of despair to end. From the moment you read the introduction to this book, if you live with or work with teens, I want you to start reassuring them that no matter how difficult things may seem, no matter how awful it feels to be them, there is nothing too big that can't be overcome without the support of one good human.

I have focused this book on the parents of teens. However, it is often the significant adult allies – whom I call lighthouses – who are equally as important in guiding our teens over that bumpy bridge to adulthood. These allies can be even more skilled and capable than parents at shining an essential light into the darkness many teens experience. I seriously doubt that I would be here today if it were not for a couple of significant lighthouses who brought me hope and support when I was a troubled teen.

The statistics I will share in the background chapter will capture a bigger picture of how difficult it is to be a teen today. More evidence is coming through of the harm that the negative influences and dark side of the digital world have caused. One glaring statistic has come out recently, showing that the earlier a child is given a smartphone, the more significantly they are impacted by poor mental health in the ages 18 to 24.

I don't believe we can solely blame the arrival of the smartphone. What children and teens need to thrive has not changed, but the world around them has changed. I have been concerned for over 20 years that we have become overly focused on the education of our kids and teens, especially in the pursuit of high grades, rather than the nurturing of the whole child. My key message has been – stop stealing childhood in the name of education. American psychology researcher and scholar Peter Gray has been exploring the decline in mental health in American teens and the increasing suicide rates of teens, and he believes that not only has an over-concentration on academic performance, especially with testing and grades, been a contributing factor, so has the changing nature of childhood. Children play less, especially with groups of multi-age children, and less frequently without significant adult supervision. Gray argues that when you totally focus on test performance, you negate creative thinking, problem-solving and social and emotional competence. Kids are growing to be less resilient and less able to navigate the challenges of adolescence, which have always been there for every generation ever born. That is serious food for thought and yet another reason why we can't sit silently back and let teens flounder and struggle with education systems that are failing many of them and putting too much pressure on all of them.

This message is from a teen who completed a survey I conducted for this book:

> Young people now are suffering more than others think. Elders look down on us as if we are spoilt, addicted to our phones and more. The truth is, you see us on our phones as we make more friends on online platforms than actually care in reality. Elders tell us we're lazy and lock ourselves in our rooms when in reality our rooms are the only place we feel safe anymore without being judged. We lack motivation nowadays due to the standards and expectations others have set for us. We feel pressured and unheard. We overeat, under eat, don't shut up or shut up completely, have bursts of energy only to be shut down by others, feel confident in our bodies only to be told we're ugly and it's not just our generation telling us this, it's older generations, it's fake magazines, it's photoshopped models, it's peer pressure, etc. And when all this pressure finally pushes us to our breaking point, it causes us to take drugs, it causes us to vape, it causes us to be rebellious and even causes us to suicide just to escape this cruel reality and the world we stand on.

Our 21st-century world has created many additional risk factors and potential dangers for our children. This has impacted today's teens, who, I believe, are less able and less equipped to manage the unique pressures and challenges of the post-COVID world, increasing youth violence and crime, global uncertainty and huge pressures on the cost of living. Even though the main focus of this book will be the teen years, much of what I write about will apply to tweens and emerging adults right up to 30. The capacity to make thoughtful, logical decisions needs a fully developed executive function in the brain, which usually happens by the mid-twenties. However, some research suggests that with digital natives, it is closer to 30.

As these concerns kept mulling through my mind, I remember a conversation with Associate Professor Mat Coleman, a practising psychiatrist in a rural community and a former commissioner on the Australian National Mental Health Commission. He was kind enough to participate in an episode about suicide on my ABC podcast, *Parental as Anything*. Dr Coleman expressed his wish that parents could be empowered and educated to know how better to support their troubled teen. Maybe I need to blame him for me devoting months to writing the book I didn't think I was going to write!

Technically, our teens have always needed rails on the bridge as they transition from childhood to adulthood. To be honest, the digital world has stolen much of the connection time with caring parents. Teens no longer need to come and ask their folks questions as previous generations may have because they just ask Google or Siri. If we can keep in mind that every human, especially our teens, needs to be seen, heard, accepted and loved exactly as they are, not how they could be, it can make a world of difference.

As our teens are gaining autonomy and personal competence, there is meant to be friction with their parents. Psychologist and author Dr Lisa Damour explains this beautifully, saying that pushing up against boundaries and different perceptions is part of how our teens develop their own sense of self and control of their own lives. It is a difficult dance; however, it is important that parents see that experiencing conflict is normal rather than something to be avoided at all costs. Overcoming adversity is a key way of building resilience and confidence. If there are no boundaries for them to push up against, it is like crossing a bridge with no rails – so much more dangerous. When they struggle, when they fail, when they muck up – they are not weak or bad. They are being human and experiencing life as best they can. Heck, with four sons, I had many of these moments. Some of the toughest moments were when they failed important exams, lost mates in car accidents, or had their hearts broken, or they made a lousy choice that cost them dearly. My approach was to allow them to know that it takes time to feel better and that some things will help, while others will quite simply make it worse.

My role as a counsellor was never to fix a teen who was struggling. It was first to allow them to feel seen, heard and validated. Sometimes, a teen who was drowning in angst and sadness would sob on my shoulder until there were no sobs left. Then, we would work to get some clarity around the challenge they were experiencing, and they'd figure out possible choices they could make that would help them move forward. Often, our teens see the world so differently from grown-ups. I will explain the why of this and why lectures (and unsolicited adult advice) can have the opposite effect than is intended. In my years as a full-time counsellor, I often found that when working with a teen who was struggling, asking quite simply, 'What things could your parents do to help?' as well as 'What things are they doing that aren't helpful?' could make a huge difference.

Given that I'm writing a book about teens, I wanted to include their voices. When I wrote *From Boys to Men,* I conducted a survey that captured the voices of many adolescent boys, and I've included some of their responses in the pages that follow. I also conducted a new research survey for this book asking 13–25-year-olds the following:

- Who is your 'lighthouse' – a safe, adult ally who you can turn to, not your parents?
- What have you found most challenging about being a teen (if you're older, what did you find most challenging)?

- Think of a time you have recently felt you were struggling emotionally in terms of your mental health. Can you describe how that might have been for you (i.e. trouble sleeping/getting angry or sad/feeling anxious)?
- What (if anything) did your parents do or say during this time that you thought was helpful?
- What (if anything) did your parents do or say during this time that you thought was NOT helpful?
- What would you have liked your parents to have said/done differently during this time you were struggling?
- And is there anything else you'd like to share that you think might be helpful?

Of the 1,153 responses, I was surprised to see that teens from around the globe had responded. The main countries they came from were, unsurprisingly, Australia, New Zealand, the United States, the United Kingdom and Canada. However, we received one or two responses from Austria, Romania, Philippines, Kenya, Italy, India, Bahrain, South Africa, Slovakia, Oman, Nigeria, South Korea, Israel, Ireland, France, Czech Republic, Cambodia and Angola. I am beyond grateful for every teen who responded because the journey from child to adult happens in every culture, in every country and to every child.

It was important that we get a reasonably fair representation of how this journey is for all of our kids, regardless of gender. I was so happy to see that we had a good, fairly balanced response to my survey, with 55.5 per cent of responses from girls, 40.9 per cent from boys and 2.5 per cent from those who identify otherwise.

Even though we have come to know that gender is more fluid than fixed, there are some statistically significant differences in how many girls and boys transition to adulthood. I will attempt to add some gender-influenced information, however, to cover the material for all parents and lighthouses, I will be unable to do this in depth.

- This may sound stupid but making comparisons to your generation (parents) helps no one. 'Back in my day we had to do xyz', 'when I was your age we didn't get (insert new thing)!', 'my (mum/dad) wasn't even alive when I was your age!'. Saying these things is harmful. Extremely. You're trying to gain sympathy from your child by saying you had it harder. That's crazy! But they can't do anything about that. Please don't compare your very different upbringing to today's world. Also, some parents TRULY forget this kid didn't ask to be born. It's YOUR job as the parent to take care of the kid you brought into this world! Some people are of the opinion that kids 'owe' their parents this or that for raising them. No???? You're the one who wanted to have kids.
- I'd imagine that there are similar people to me out there, and that the thought of having a one-on-one conversation with your parents could be daunting, but it can be the most eye-opening experience you'll have. Parents are special people and you learn a lot from them even if you don't believe it.

As I am known as the Queen of Common Sense, I figured that if I helped parents better understand why this journey of adolescence is bumpy, unpredictable and incredibly stressful at times, it could help them with their own teen. No teen *wants to* struggle or become confused and stressed. Every young person is unique. Some teens who were surveyed wished their parents had checked in on them more, while others wished their parents hadn't checked in as often. There were teens wishing their parents had had more time to have deep conversations, even if they were awkward, and then there were those who wished their parents had left them to work out stuff by themselves! The most important thing that can help you as a parent is *to understand why your child changes and how these changes impact them so that you can help them understand why this transformative stage of life can be tricky*. Then you can better meet your child's needs and wants.

In the survey, I had many messages about how parents can help more:

- Sometimes I will just need a hug.
- Just say 'we love you and are here for you'.
- Hug me more.
- More hugs would have helped.
- Just simply asked if I was okay.
- I would like them to really listen and then hug me.

Below is an important message from the teen survey that needs to be kept in mind.

Yeah, every teenager is different, so whatever you write in your advice for parents is probably not going to apply to that parent's teenager. BUT you should consider telling parents to make sure they know as much about their child as possible, even simply observing can work. A teenager who stays in their room all the time and doesn't like to talk to their family probably won't be helped by being asked a million questions about their mental health. Instead, they may benefit from silent acts of kindness, e.g. helping them clean their room, buying their favourite food. You can't generalise mental-health improvement.

So, the first part of the book explores – *what the heck is happening!*

The second part of this book is *How can I help?* This section explores what to do when something big happens – such as when you find a vape, a bong, or a used condom in your teen's room or your teen just can't get to school anymore. In the second section, I will explore ways to help you be the informed, calm, safe base your teen needs so that you can work with them to explore the options they have going forward. Having correct, up-to-date information plus an ability to communicate without judgement are the keys to helping our teens navigate the bumpy ride to adulthood. I will provide suggestions about where you can find reliable information, resources and guides from respected experts in that field. This can save hours of online searching, especially when you are distressed or extremely worried. Given that our teens' world is so different from the world when you were a teen, it is important to be as curious, compassionate and kind as possible. They are living in a very confusing, overstimulated, noisy, instant, mainly digital world with an immature brain driving a very mature body seeking a way to find out who they are and how to feel they matter.

HOME MATTERS – having a safe base to come to rest, restore and fill their cup is one of the most important protective factors for all children, especially our vulnerable adolescents.

This book explores how we can walk beside our developing teens and young adults – not leading out front, not pushing from behind and certainly not carrying them. Walking beside them allows them to grow in autonomy while they seek an identity that fits them well and a way to be in the world that is meaningful.

I was a troubled teen. I totally hated myself as a teen. I survived a suicide attempt. It was not until I stepped into a classroom as a teacher that I truly found a place that gave me self-worth and purpose. I tried to be a lighthouse to many, and it's been my great pleasure to hear from some of my former students over the years that they saw me that way, too. Every teen needs a safe, guiding presence on the unpredictable journey to adulthood – every single one needs rails on the bridge. They simply can't do it alone.

My hope is that this book will help more parents, extended family members and lighthouses learn how to be what a troubled teen needs. Judging by these voices from the survey, I am hopeful it will make a difference.

- Thank you for doing this and I hope it helps some people have a better experience than I am having right now.
- Thank you for asking for the input of those you are writing about, rather than coming to conclusions yourself from personal experience/limited sample size!

PART 1

WHAT IS REALLY HAPPENING FOR TODAY'S TEENS?

It is incredibly important to capture an authentic picture of how our teens are navigating these times. Often, I come across articles that quote statistics from before 2010, which is before smartphones and before COVID-19. As both these things have had an enormous impact on everyone's lives, I worry that research might be missing a piece of the puzzle. Given that longitudinal research, in particular, takes time to collate and analyse, many of the statistics I am going to share come from prior to the arrival of the global pandemic because they are the latest available. However, some research is coming through, and there is plenty of anecdotal evidence to show that the pandemic and the impact of massive restrictions and change hit our adolescent population hard. Many are still struggling in different ways, although some of the patterns of anxiety, especially social anxiety, may not be at the level of clinical identification or in need of professional support. It is commonly accepted that around 75 per cent of mental-health issues occur before the age of 25; indeed, half of all mental-health conditions we experience at some point in our lives would have started by the age of 14. This is seen in the statistics: according to the 2023 Mission Australia Youth Survey, the 19,500 teens surveyed listed the following four issues as being of most personal concern (the figures in brackets are percentage of respondents who said they were *extremely* or *very concerned*):

- Coping with stress (38.4 per cent)
- School and study problems (37.1 per cent)
- Mental health (31.9 per cent)
- Body image (29.0 per cent).

Stress, anxiety and mental health impact all areas of a teen's life, and when it runs untethered, it can contribute to poor physical health and even poorer mental-health outcomes. Also deeply concerning is the fact that the number one killer of 12- to 25-year-olds in Australia continues to be suicide. This statistic is beyond sad and tragic; however, I hope it can be a catalyst for everyone reading this book to step forward and create light in a teen's life.

Let's start by looking at anxiety among our teens in a global context

Australia

- According to self-reported data from the Australian Bureau of Statistics National Health Survey, rates of high or very high psychological distress in young people increased between 2011–2012 and 2017–2018, from 12 per cent to 15 per cent. The pandemic had a big impact on these figures. In 2020–2022, almost one-third (31.8 per cent) of young people aged 16–24 years had experienced an anxiety disorder.
- Two in five females (40.4 per cent) aged 16–24 years had a 12-month anxiety disorder in 2020–2022.
- Based on the Australian Child and Adolescent Survey of Mental Health and Wellbeing (also known as the Young Minds Matter survey, undertaken in 2013–14) around 14 per cent of children aged 12–17 met the critical criteria for one or more mental disorders in the previous 12 months.
- In the LGBTQIA+ populations, individuals experience anxiety conditions at almost two and a half times the rate of the heterosexual population, and 44.7 per cent had a 12-month anxiety disorder.
- A WA-based report into the decline in wellbeing for Australian girls found that while almost one-fifth (19.9 per cent) of all people aged 11–17 experienced high or very high levels of psychological distress in the previous 12 months, for females aged 16–17, this was significantly higher at 36.2 per cent. These findings are consistent with international research that finds adolescent girls report poorer wellbeing and mental health than male adolescents.
- In the Mission Australia Annual Youth Survey for 2023, almost a quarter (24.9 per cent) of young people indicated high levels of psychological distress, and one-fifth (20.8 per cent) said they felt lonely all or most of the time. In the 2022 survey, more than half (53.4 per cent) of all respondents also said they had needed support with their mental health at some point in their life.

- In an Australian longitudinal study of male health, for boys aged 10–14, anxiety was the most commonly reported mental-health disorder experienced by about 9 per cent of boys.
- Untreated anxiety disorders have been linked to depression, school failure and a two-fold increase in risk for substance-use disorder.

USA/Canada

- Anxiety disorders are the most common mental-health condition to affect teenagers.
- The National Institute of Mental Health reports that 31.9 per cent of teens have some type of anxiety disorder (38 per cent female/26.1 per cent male).
- Around 8 per cent of young people meet the criteria for severe anxiety-related impairment.
- Seventy per cent of 13–17-year-olds surveyed by Pew Research Center said anxiety and depression are a 'major problem' among their peers in the community where they live.
- Between 2008 and 2018, there was a rise in healthcare providers' recognition of anxiety in young people, including a 17 per cent increase in anxiety-disorder diagnoses, according to a Child Mind Institute report.
- The same report says that, at some point, anxiety affects 30 per cent of children and adolescents, yet 80 per cent never get help.

United Kingdom

- There is evidence of increasing anxiety and depression among young women aged 16–24 in the UK, with nearly 31 per cent reporting some evidence of anxiety and depression in the years 2017–2018.
- The UK Mental Health Foundation reports that in 2021, young people aged 16 to 29 were most likely to have some form of anxiety (28 per cent likely).
- One in six children aged 5–16 is likely to have a mental-health problem. This figure has gone up by 50 per cent in the last three years. Between 2021 and 2022 alone, the proportion of older

young people aged 17–19 in England with a probable mental-health disorder jumped from one in six to one in four.

- A 2023 survey of 6,000 UK adults by the Mental Health Foundation and Opinium found of young people (18 to 24 years) surveyed, 86 per cent had felt anxious in the previous two weeks. For over half (58 per cent), this had stopped them undertaking day-to-day activities.
- Half (50 per cent) of LGBTQIA+ young people report they have had or currently have an anxiety disorder.

The statistics for depression are also pretty eye-opening

Australia

- Beyond Blue reports that among Australians aged 12–25 years depression causes more burden than any other physical or mental illness. Around one in six young people will experience depression during adolescence. Rates are much higher among young females than males.
- One in seven young people aged 4–17 experience a mental-health condition in any given year. 13.9 per cent of children and young people met the criteria for a diagnosis of a mental disorder in the last 12 months.
- 38.8 per cent of people aged 16–24 years surveyed in the National Study of Mental Health and Wellbeing (released October 2023) reported having had a mental disorder within the previous 12 months.
- Young females were twice as likely as young males to report not feeling happy with themselves, feeling unable to achieve their goals or being unable to deal with things that happen in life.
- Female young people are significantly more likely than male young people to have anxiety and depression, lower self-esteem and some evidence suggests lower resilience.
- In 2015, 19.6 per cent of Australian females aged 16–17 years met the criteria for a major depressive disorder compared to 8.2 per cent for males of the same age.

- An Australian survey of LGBTQIA+ young people aged 14–21 reported very high levels of psychological distress, and 48 per cent had received a diagnosis for depression in their lifetime.
- Three in 10 people who identify as LGBTQIA+ are currently experiencing depression, which is four times the rate of heterosexual people in Australia.
- During the COVID-19 pandemic in 2020, 23.4 per cent of children showed clinically significant depressive symptoms.
- Research suggests that indicators of depression for First Nations people are often quite different to those of other Australians, and so the gathering of accurate data can be problematic. Despite these differences, there have been no visible improvements in First Nations people's social and emotional wellbeing. Indeed, some evidence indicates it is worsening, especially for adolescent First Nations girls, as indicated by the escalating rates of self-harm hospitalisations seen between 2008–2021.
- According to the 2023 National Study of Mental Health and Wellbeing, more than one in four females (27.9 per cent) aged 16–24 years had self-harmed in their lifetime.

A note about the pandemic

- The Black Dog Institute conducted a rapid review and meta-analysis of whether rates of depression in children had risen in recent years. *While rates of diagnosed depression have not increased in children over the past two decades, their research showed an 'alarming spike' in depressive symptoms during the pandemic.*
- An Australian Psychological Society survey of 1,000 psychologists (covering their experiences with clients from 2020 to 2022) showed that kids aged 13–18 had the highest increases in mental-health disorders with depression (65 per cent), social anxiety disorder (60 per cent), general anxiety disorder (60 per cent), suicidality or self-harm (50 per cent) and peer relationship difficulties (48 per cent) reported most by psychologists.

USA/Canada

- Over one in 10 young people in the US are experiencing depression that is severely impairing their ability to function at home, school or work, as well as with family or in their social life.
- 16.39 per cent of 12–17-year-olds report suffering from at least one major depressive episode in the past year.
- 11.5 per cent of the same age group are experiencing severe major depression (over 2.7 million young people).
- In 2019, 13 per cent of adolescents reported having a major depressive episode, which was an increase of 60 per cent from 2007.
- A Centers for Disease Control and Prevention (CDC) survey showed that 57 per cent of teen girls experienced persistent sadness or hopelessness in 2021, up from 36 per cent in 2011. For a more comprehensive analysis of teen anxiety and depression since 2012 in the USA, explore Jonathon Haidt's latest book *The Anxious Generation*. Statistics are available at www.theanxiousgeneration.com.

United Kingdom

- In 2009, just 9 per cent of 16–25-year-olds disagreed with the statement that 'life is really worth living'. By 2019, that figure had risen to 18 per cent.
- In a survey of more than 2,000 young people by YouGov for the Prince's Trust, more than a quarter of young people disagreed that their life has a sense of purpose. Levels of youth happiness have fallen most sharply during the last decade when it comes to relationships with friends and emotional health, the survey found.
- Seventy-five per cent of 18–24-year-olds had looked for mental-health support in the last two years, along with over half of the under-16s and 71 per cent of 16–18-year-olds.

New Zealand

- The Youth19 Rangatahi Smart Survey of 7,721 Year 9 to Year 13 students in 2019 found female high-school students were much more likely to have significant depressive symptoms (29 per cent) compared to males (16.5 per cent).

- The survey suggested that young New Zealanders' emotional and mental health had significantly worsened since 2012.
- The proportion of high-school students reporting significant depressive symptoms increased for girls from 14.5 per cent in 2001 to 17.4 per cent in 2012, and then by 2017, it had risen to 28.9 per cent. For boys, there was no increase between 2001 and 2012 (both 8.7 per cent), but the figure almost doubled to 16.5 per cent between 2012 and 2019.

Now to some good news

When we read the statistics above, we can think that everything is doom and gloom. However, statistics can be read in different ways. When a statistic reads, 'almost one-fifth of all people aged 11–17 experience high or very high levels of psychological distress', we can miss the perception that 80 per cent of young people surveyed were not experiencing high or very high levels of psychological distress.

Even though I write about the chasm that exists between teens and their parents and that things can get difficult at times, especially with the impact of the global pandemic, things are not really as bleak as the statistics are showing.

A whole new world

We still need to acknowledge that the world we live in now is so very different from the world parents of teens lived in when they were adolescents. With 24/7 world news of every disaster and crisis being poured into our homes, our children are marinated in more trauma than ever before. The digital world – while I acknowledge that it has brought many benefits – has created some additional challenges, particularly for our emerging adults and how they see the world and themselves.

One of the things that makes my blood boil is the fact that the largest tech companies in the world have deliberately created algorithms that marinate us in more negative content.

It seems the more negative the content, the more people stay engaged, and that means the more advertising that they are exposed to and the more money the companies make. Why are we more drawn to negativity? Well, it's all down to a function of our evolution called 'negativity bias', which means we're designed to look out for threats to our survival.

But what can parents of teens do right now, living in the world as it is?

As I have stated clearly in the introduction, not only do our teens need rails on the bridge, they need caring humans to help them. Sometimes, the best thing we can do if we are raising a teen or teaching a teen or working with teens is to have them share their life through their lens while we listen and observe with compassion and curiosity.

When I worked as a counsellor, that was exactly how I approached the time I spent with teens who were struggling. I wanted to hear their story without judgement and to help them find a way to understand and then navigate a better way of being themselves. To be reassured that you are not broken, or dumb or not enough and that you are *simply experiencing one of the most turbulent times of transformation in a human life* can be a real lightbulb moment for a teen.

So often, they simply hear all the messages about how they are disappointing people, they're not working hard enough, they lack focus and motivation, and they seem to always have their eyes on a screen, especially a phone.

Statistically, both our boys and our girls are struggling with poorer mental health in our homes, schools and communities. Given that the journey over the bridge to adulthood is such a stressful and tumultuous time of change, feeling stressed and overwhelmed needs to be recognised as quite normal. I remember being a really moody teenager, and I wrote very dark poetry, and yet I had moments when I was happy.

Dr Lisa Damour, an American clinical psychologist who specialises in teenagers, wants us all to know that mental health isn't just about feeling good or happy. Rather, she would like to see mental health be more about having the right feeling at the right time in the right context and then having the ability to manage that feeling in a way that doesn't hurt anyone else and actually brings a sense of relief. This makes such good sense to me because, as a moody teen, I would often take myself on long walks in nature when I was having big, ugly feelings, and this helped me manage my emotions. Interestingly, I still do that today. We all have moments when we have big feelings because we are human. Learning how to notice and then respond to them in unharmful ways is an important life skill and can be learned as a teen.

The upside of this generation

Today's teens are drinking noticeably less than their parents' generation. We are also aware that smoking has also drastically decreased over time (although vaping is, of course, a rising problem!). Some research shows that the use of cannabis has also dropped except in countries where it is legalised. Overall, in a recent research study that considered countries around the world, it was identified that there has been a significant decline in the risky behaviour of adolescents in general.

This has to be the best news possible given that we know:

- Adolescence is a time when many teens yearn for their own autonomy and want to have the freedom to make their own choices.
- Teens have a tendency to avoid the wisdom and guidance of parents and teachers as they strive for that autonomy.

- Teens often make impulsive, poor choices due to the fact their prefrontal cortex is still developing, and their impulse inhibitor capacity has been turned off (see Chapter 2 for more on the brain).

In a comprehensive study, the researchers found that across the developed world, there had been a dramatic decline between the late 1990s and approximately 2015 in adolescent smoking, drinking, underage sex and juvenile crime. Now that is seriously good news!

I found the decrease in juvenile crime and underage sex quite illuminating given that the media seems to portray a very different picture. In Australia, youth crime has become problematic in many communities, and we need to question whether it is just the bad behaviour of 10 per cent. Yes, we need to remember that bad news (often sensationalised) is what the media tends to focus on. There's that negativity bias again!

Why the change in risk-taking behaviour?

The research found that the most significant reason for some of the reductions, especially around alcohol and smoking, has been the extensive education about potential harm. Many parents came to realise that giving their teenagers alcohol early was extremely problematic not only for physical health reasons but also due to the link to mental illness. If our teens are drinking less, they are also likely to make less risky decisions in social situations.

Given the increasing rates of young people using e-cigarettes and vaping, with the dangers of developing nicotine addiction, it is obviously time for a major education focus in that direction.

There has been a significant decline over the last 10 years in face-to-face socialising among teens, and in Europe and North America, this has been linked to a significant drop in adolescent risky behaviour. Given that teens are prone to being influenced by peers and friends, this makes sense. For example, research is very strong around the influence of driving at night with friends in the car versus driving without friends in the car. And in some places, there are laws in place around this.

It is much more dangerous to have your friends in the car with you as you are more likely to be distracted or choose more risky behaviour in terms of speed. Sadly, there have been some tragic multiple deaths of young people in car accidents in the last few years in Australia.

If, like me, you thought this shift in risky behaviour was because the digital world has replaced the real world, it seems it's not so simple.

Much is written about the 'displacement effect' of the digital world, which basically means that engagement in the digital world stops other activities that have been a normal part of childhood and adolescence. Several studies showed that heavy Internet users, particularly social-media users, were more likely to smoke and drink than those who rarely use the Internet! One study hypothesised that a rise in computer gaming was empirically linked to declining adolescent binge drinking in six Nordic countries but found that there wasn't an association. (I have to say though, I have spoken to young gamers who said they felt they were safer in their bedrooms gaming, rather than being out on the streets with their mates being tempted to make poor choices.)

Even before the pandemic, research showed there was a significant decrease in the amount of unstructured time spent among teen friends. Our kids are not playing as much with other kids outside, and the decline in resilience, coping skills and capacity for self-determination has been well documented. Vital social and emotional skills are learned through the dynamics of human interaction, especially through play. We all need practice in learning how to lose, how to cope with disappointment, how to be creative to form strategies, and how to negotiate with others. In Jonathon Haidt's book *The Anxious Generation* he writes significantly about the harm that 'social deprivation' is causing young people. Being digitally connected rather than connected in real life (or as teens write, 'IRL') is contributing to the sense of loneliness that many are expressing. Healthy connectedness needs an 'embodiment' experience – face to face, physical touch and conversation – to nurture genuine friendship and intimacy. Jean Twenge's research has shown that the more teens use social media instead of building real life connectedness, the more likely they will struggle with their mental health.

The double-edged sword of a less risky adolescence

The last 20 years has seen a massive decline in risky play for children in many parts of the world. Jonathon Haidt calls this 'safetyism', where our society as a whole has created an experience-blocker for kids to avoid experiencing any discomfort at all. We have created a risk-averse society where parents are hyper-vigilant and monitor their children much more than previous generations. Could this be also contributing to the decrease in risky behaviour? Absolutely yes. I'm not saying it's a bad thing that adolescents are taking fewer risks – I'm just saying some of the reasons behind this may indicate that it's a double-edged sword. Sometimes, as emerging adults, we must take potentially big life risks – to leave home, get a job or dive into an intimate relationship – so some risk-taking is necessary.

More good news is that the shift in parenting from strict authoritarian styles to more connected and respectful styles has meant there has been less teen rebellion. Being emotionally closer to your parents means that more adolescents are spending time with their families rather than their friends, and they seem to be more compliant with parental expectations, which ultimately results in less risky behaviour. Hallelujah, that is fabulous news! This result from the study was not found in all countries, however, it became evident in many.

Another important factor is the role of rites of passage in adolescence, where young people experience markers of transition that help them prepare to become adults. In many parts of the world, there have been delays in these markers, like getting a driver's license, getting a job and leaving home. Some of these have been driven by financial challenges. However, it is becoming more and more common for these things to be happening later. There is some argument that these delays may mean that risky behaviours are happening later and given the growing maturity of the executive function of the brain, they may simply be making better choices as a consequence.

Another possible influence that is a double-edged sword is the increased pressure to succeed in school and beyond. There is evidence that some young people see drinking and partying as not being compatible with their ambitions in academics, sport or career. Sadly, this increasing pressure is impacting the wellbeing of many students, especially with heightened levels of stress and anxiety.

Over the years, it has become more difficult for young people to get into the workforce, and then with the global financial crisis, followed by a pandemic, many have less disposable income to be able to afford alcohol and cigarettes. They just don't have enough money to spend! There is conflicting evidence to this idea, however, it may be applicable for some.

We know that young people are far more aware and concerned than previous generations were about the environment, equity and discrimination, and wellbeing. Some scholars and researchers have proposed that a decline in risky behaviours may be a shift in youth culture where healthy lifestyles are becoming more fashionable.

To be honest, I am finding many of our teens and young adults more aware, more concerned, more passionate than previous generations. They are worried about the environment, they do tend to embrace equity and diversity more openly, and they are finding ways to become better informed, and to be a part of the solution to the problems they see. I guess one of the positives of all the technology is they can share their views more widely too.

I hope this is giving you food for thought and possibly giving you an opportunity to refresh the lens with which you view our teens. They have always needed significant, caring adults to guide them, an opportunity to have a voice and to be heard, and we can all make a difference by leaning in with compassion and understanding, not judgement and shame.

Some of the things our teens are struggling with despite the optimistic statistics:

- Just being a teen.
- Figuring out what's normal and what's not in your life.
- Navigating family issues by being at home, and the difficulties that conflict with stepparents (while well loved) brought.
- Keeping up with trends and trying to fit in.
- Other people telling me who I should and shouldn't be. Being made to feel I'm not enough.
- I'm currently at the stage of being a teen, and I think being confused with myself and who I am, but I know I can get past it and become a better me, and also stress of school, such as my friends and the work getting harder and realising that I'm in control and I can do the work.
- HIGH SCHOOL! Unrelenting stress mixed with relationship struggles, both platonic and romantic. It's all very exhausting, especially since I have no idea what I'm doing.
- Friendships and relationships.
- I think the most challenging part of growing up for me is the stress that school, particularly homework, is putting on me. I want my time at home to be for whatever I want to do whether that be going for a ride with friends or a walk with my dog or playing video games with mates but almost all of the time I spend at home after school I feel like I am consumed by homework and can't find any time to do those things that I want to do and love to do. The worst thing about this being that I can't do anything about it. I can complain all I like but nothing is going to change.

1

The biological drivers: what's supposed to happen

Adolescents, especially teens, are learning how to manage their rapidly changing minds, bodies, hormones and emotions while navigating their way through some important years of their education. They are developing key skills that will enable them to manage life and, at the same time, are exploring their identity and potential. The strong drive to become independent is matched in intensity by the drive to belong with their peers, as well as wanting to step back from parental influence while they undergo what psychologists call individuation. In many ways, the world around them today offers so many more stressors and a lot less support than 20 years ago. However, the main drivers of adolescence are still the same as they always have been. There are five main drivers of adolescence that are bubbling away under the surface of your growing child, and the same drivers would have been impacting you at the same stage of your life.

Five main drivers of adolescence

1. Seeking autonomy and independence

As a child gradually grows bigger so too does their need for more autonomy and freedom to make choices. The tricky bit about teens and choices is that they are biologically wired to make more risky decisions. Often, they will exaggerate the benefits of a choice and disregard the possible negatives. For boys who are being flooded with testosterone and who are wired to be more impulsive, these poor choices can cause injury to themselves and others. More recently, we've come to understand that GABA (Gamma-Aminobutyric Acid) is drastically reduced during adolescence. Given that this amino acid acts as an impulse inhibitor, we can better understand why the young adolescent brain tends to make poor, irrational choices impulsively.

There are concerns that the influence of screens is impacting how our teens make choices. Children who have had a wide variety of books read to them will tend to develop a wider multifaceted understanding of things in the outside world and a deeper sense of self. Essentially, the more connections that we create in our brains in childhood, the greater our capacity for understanding more complex things later in life. It is like a basic building block.

Another concern of children who spend unhealthy amounts of time on technology is that they are often navigating a world in which there are limited options because of the directory system of arranging information that is prevalent online.

If we want to encourage our children to be independent thinkers, problem solvers and highly creative humans, they need to be practising freedom and autonomy as often as possible within their childhoods – not spending hours in a highly orchestrated environment that is shaping the way they think and experience life.

When parents offer their children genuine opportunities to contribute to conversations, to family decisions and to be problem solvers in their own right, they can make a huge difference to the growth and development of their child's authentic sense of self. Even if their point

of view is radically different to yours, allowing them to explain why they believe what they do without judgement can help them in their search for their own voice.

The big part of the learning around more autonomy is *that every choice will have a consequence of some kind* – sometimes positive and sometimes negative. The role of good parenting is to help our teen in the exploration of making choices with an understanding that decisions may have far wider consequences than may seem evident at the time. Teen girls are often more capable of making enlightened decisions that can explore both choice *and* consequence than teen boys, however, they can still make poor choices often.

Teen boys can even repeat the same risky or dumb decision within the same week for the same reason! I can remember boys in my classes repeating words and actions that I had told them were inappropriate in the classroom – in the same lesson. Sometimes it can help to balance their need for independence and choice with some safe adult guidance on what behaviours are appropriate (or not) for different settings.

> Avoid asking a teen who has made a poor choice, 'WHAT WERE YOU THINKING?' or 'WHAT WERE YOU TRYING TO DO'?

I have worked with parents who have threatened to ground a teen for the rest of their life when they broke curfew or deliberately lied about where they'd been. This may not be the best way to help a teen learn from that experience because it can damage the connection between them and their parents, and it won't help them make a better decision next time. They may just become angry and resentful, which tends to make them rebellious.

Remember, every experience will have a learning opportunity, especially the failures, disasters and muck-ups.

Discipline is where we teach and guide our kids when they make poor choices and this is far more effective than punishing them. When we punish them, we make them feel like they were wrong, and we hurt them, but they don't learn how to explore how to make a better choice next time. It may be time to remind them that every choice will have a consequence and that as the brain matures, they will tend to make better choices.

Another thing that helps teens make better choices and exercise their independence is to give them a few days to ponder a problem if possible. Thinking deeply over time has become more difficult for today's digitally connected children and teens, but they need that time for their minds to truly understand some of the complex realities of life.

The good news is that if your teen is questioning you or disagreeing with you, it is not a sign they have suddenly lost love and respect for you. It is a sign that they are developing exactly as nature intended!

Some things teens told us in the survey that they would have liked their parents to have done/said differently:

- [I would have liked them to say] That I am struggling. And while yes it will be over soon, it's hard right now. And that where I am at mentally is really common for students and teens, but I am also not alone. There are people who can help. There is a future for me but there is also a present.
- . . . that the teens are a difficult transition into adulthood. Hang in [there] and things will change. I will always be here for you no matter what.
- I would have liked to have heard that struggling and having mental-health issues doesn't make you broken; it's doesn't make you less of a person; it just means you need some more help and support and that's okay.

2. Identity searching

The search for identity is one of the most important jobs that teenagers have, and in order to complete this search, they need to step back from their family – especially their parents. Every child is a unique one-off and helping them discover who they are and how they can be themselves as authentically as possible has become even more difficult with the influence of technology.

In the pre-digital world, especially in our classrooms, well before Wikipedia and Google, students had to find things out the old-fashioned way with careful research, often in the library and also through meaningful conversations with mature elders such as parents, teachers or community members. This allowed a wider scope of possibilities than happens when you do an online search. This may be getting even more complicated as AI continues to sweep the digital space.

Fake news abounds on the web, and even well-educated adults can struggle to find authentic, evidence-based information. Consider the impact of fake news in recent presidential elections and also around the COVID-19 pandemic. Without an understanding or capacity to critically question information, we can be led to believe anything and that has created a massive industry for spammers, conspiracy theorists, sexual predators and unscrupulous influencers and advertisers.

The teen years are when our kids are most easily influenced, either positively or negatively.

We must always remember they are creating a sense of their own identity in this window, and every success and every failure and the narrative they have in their mind is shaping that identity. I once worked with a juvenile justice inmate who had a long history of delinquency. We explored his possible natural strengths and talents, and a place he could use them in the world. This was like creating a new map for him to navigate his life. He expressed his surprise to learn that there could be a different way of being. Before that, he had believed that he was basically bad, and that he would continue to make potentially dangerous, risky choices that were outside the law. If we keep in mind that a teen can't be what they haven't seen, it can help all grown-ups appreciate how important we can be in shaping the lives of our emerging adults.

How do we shape our sense of authentic identity?

In basic psychology, there is an understanding that we have three layers to our personality. One layer is our ego mind, where endless chatter invades our brain randomly – this is our inner critic. Then, we all have a shadow where some of our darkest emotions are contained. At the centre of who we are is an inner compass, the core of a decent human, which I often call the higher self. When we are able to access this quiet voice of wisdom and self-compassion, we have the best opportunity to become our best selves.

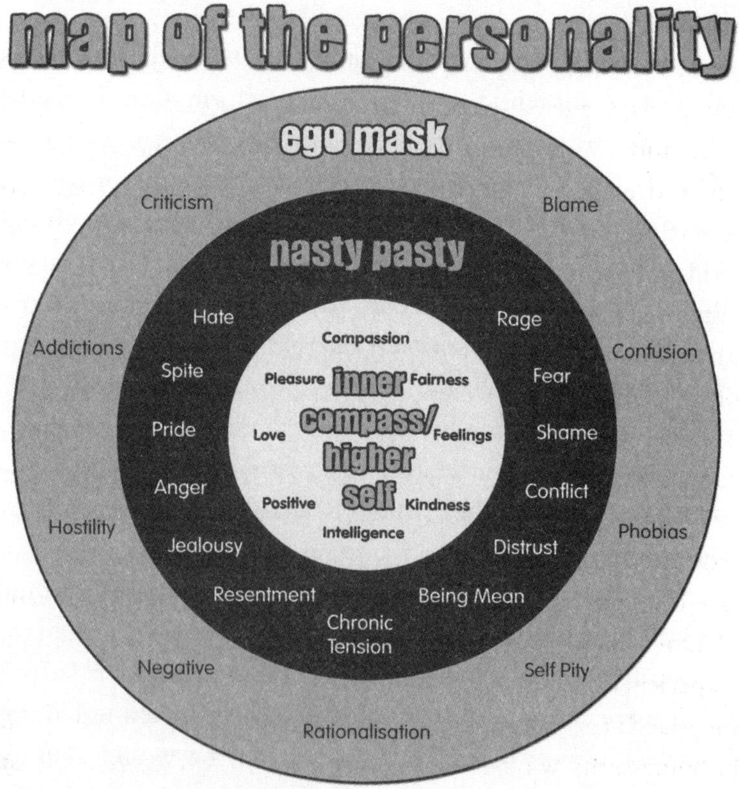

In her book *ID: The Quest for Meaning in the 21st Century*, Baroness Susan Greenfield explores how access to instant digital information is changing the brain architecture of today's children. She explains that around 50 per cent of who we really are does come in on our DNA. It is the other 50 per cent that is concerning in the digital age, especially when there is so much negative bias built into the algorithms.

We are all shaped by the experiences that we have from birth to adolescence. The music we listened to, the holidays we had, the books we read, the games we played, the trees we climbed, the kites we flew and the deep conversations we had with interesting grown-ups, the failures we experienced, the illnesses and the play opportunities we had as children.

Today's children are more passive and play less in the outside world and it is causing harm – something I am constantly advocating that we need to change. This is a key message in Jonathon Haidt's book, *The Anxious Generation*. Our kids and teens are struggling more mentally and emotionally not just because of the impact of smartphones and endless digital access, but also because of the massive changes in childhood.

If kids are spending hours and hours in the digital world, they are spending much less time interacting with the real world in real time, and that is one of Greenfield and Haidt's biggest concerns – as well as how it is changing our children's brain architecture. Consider that there is now a significant number of children who play the same apps over and over rather than reading books. Their neural pathways will be very different from those of children who've been big readers. It is harder now for our kids to become unique, authentic individuals because they are being shaped by the digital world instead of coming into contact with a wide range of real-life or even fictional influences and experiences.

The search for 'Who am I?' is a huge part of the journey to adulthood. Some teens want to follow the tribe at any cost, while others want to follow no one.

Masks

Those who live with or work with teens may be familiar with the notion of 'masks' – the ways teens can hide or shield themselves from the world, which can appear physically and metaphorically. Often parents may be unaware of their teen's mask as they often remove it when they get home.

Physical masks can appear via body piercings, fake eyelashes, tattoos, heavy makeup, interesting hairstyles and choices of clothing – and also an absence of these! I can still remember the goth fad when I was teaching. Sometimes, these teens are deliberately testing the world around them. They simply want to be different from who they had been before, and they are curious how the grown-ups might treat them differently because of how they look *rather than for who they are.*

Remember, the things they do with their hair, no matter how bad it looks, will grow out one day. Hold your tongue and breathe deeply when they do strange things – although it is helpful to let them know that some forms of personal expression are preferable to others. One mum told me that her daughter had her upper arm tattooed with 'I love Ross'. Unfortunately, Ross dropped her three days later. It was a painful way to learn about how some choices can be more permanent than others.

> The louder you complain about their hair, clothes or makeup, the longer it will stay.

The metaphorical masks tend to turn up via behaviour and the choices that teens make, especially around others – mostly peers and friends.

Teens do a lot of work around trying on identities, especially in classrooms. When they are feeling confused, dumb and not good enough, they often create a mask to cover their vulnerability.

When they feel inadequate, disliked, and that they don't belong, they need their mask to hide behind. Often, they try to conceal their true sense of identity, too, in case it is rejected by others. This is why it is so difficult for many LGBTQIA+ teens and why coming out can be so hard when they are unsure how their family, friends and the community around them, for example, may react.

Some other masks that adolescents may try on include:

1. **The invisible mouse.** The teen who doesn't want anyone to notice them and seldom speaks in class. They often have a long fringe over their face, wear earphones or look towards the ground. Often these can be ND teens masking their unmet needs in a neurotypical world.
2. **Princess Nasty.** She wears makeup, jewellery and 'cool' clothes and acts as the fashion police – also very good at 'tsk-tsking' and eye-rolling and much worse online.
3. **The jock.** This is the sports freak who just loves wearing tracksuits and playing sport. They can use sport as an excuse for not being studious!
4. **The smart Alec or smart Alice.** They usually try to disarm teachers and big-note themselves to be seen.
5. **The drama queen.** Oh my God! *Everything* is *always* a negative drama or a potential moment to perform, so *everyone* notices ME!
6. **The clown.** Always trying to make people laugh, although usually at someone's expense – slightly less painful than the smart Alec.
7. **The bully.** Deliberately shoves their power around either physically, verbally or psychologically.
8. **The people pleaser.** Always sucking up to adults to make people like them.
9. **The victim.** Everyone else is to blame, and they have a 'poor me' mask.
10. **The giggler.** Usually, girls who avoid being taken seriously and just giggle instead of being involved in real interaction.
11. **The affluent spoilt I-Have-Everything brat.** Always bragging about the latest tech they have, as well as other stuff money buys.
12. **The confronter.** Argues about everything, disagrees with everything, and always challenges the teacher's authority.

We all wear masks to a degree – it is a role of the ego. It helps us belong in a wider social circle because we don't want others to see our 'shadow' or our worst character traits. Teens need them to help them survive in their chaotic worlds – especially in high school – and many will adjust their mask to fit in. The ego mask is also a form of protection for our higher self. Imagine if we shared our innermost being with someone who then rejected us. It is easier to cope if we share our ego mask and keep our most sacred inner self hidden. True intimacy in relationships occurs when we are able to share all layers of ourselves and still be accepted and loved. Sadly, the teen years can have us believe we are our ego, and that can be problematic in our twenties, thirties and even forties.

The more uncertain and threatened they feel, the stronger their need for the mask. The more respected and safer they feel, the less they feel the need to armour themselves and the closer they will be to their authentic selves.

Sometimes, an adolescent may want to drop their mask, but others find it difficult to accept the change. For example, a student may want to stop being a bully, but their reputation makes it hard for others to trust them. A mask can help create mindsets that can then feed negative thoughts followed by difficult emotions. 'I am not good enough' is something even many adults struggle with at times, and they have the maturity and an executive brain that can help them overcome being stuck.

I have worked with teen boys who wanted to stop fighting and bullying younger students, but it was difficult for them to drop their mask and so they went back to using the mask they were known for. Their peers often find it hard to accept they have changed, and they could end up becoming socially excluded or friendless – and that is a scary place to be.

Sometimes, teachers and other significant adults find it hard to believe someone can change. *This is partly because we form concepts and beliefs that influence the way we think and behave.* These concepts become unconscious, and it takes time or a powerful new experience to change them. Sometimes, it's easier to just keep playing the game if an identity appears fixed.

So, while masks can be frustrating for parents and teachers, they are important in helping our teens navigate the uncertain journey they are treading until they develop the full capacity of the executive functioning of their brain. Know that under that mask is a unique, emerging individual yearning to be independent, accepted, respected and valued by other people, especially their family and friends.

When a teen feels connected and safe in their home and at school, they can take their mask off.

As parents and educators, we must be careful not to believe that teens are defined by the mask they wear in the classroom – the same as they are not defined by their grades or the clothes they wear. Our teens are so much more than that, and it is our responsibility to guide them to grow in independence while supporting them to discover who they really are in the busy world of their friends and peers.

3. Needing to belong: The importance of peers and deepening friendships

Those parents who have warm, connected relationships with their kids prior to adolescence often struggle the most when their teens turn strongly towards their friends and peers. This is yet another biological drive that comes from the DNA going back to the earliest kinship communities. One evolutionary biologist explained it as being linked to the survival of the species. The reason teens turn towards their own age group is because they will soon become sexually mature, and for the healthiest survival of the species, it is best not to breed with your parents. Makes sense really!

In the pre-digital world, teens and their friends met more often in real time. They hung out in each other's bedrooms, they met socially more often outside of school and parents tended to know their teen's friends better. Being connected to friends and peers has the added advantage that a *teen will be in touch with the parents of those friends.* These friendships help develop social skills, help modify the 'dark moods' of adolescence and usually enhance moral development. Through friendships, teens learn unspoken codes of conduct that they will take with them throughout life. Much of today's teen friendship dynamics happen online, and while, of course, it is often positive, it can be incredibly destructive. There is an enormous difference between saying something hurtful and demeaning to someone's face and doing it online in front of many others.

Friendships can be tricky at the best of times, especially girl friendships, which are often very complex. Being sanctioned by peers can be one of the fastest ways to create the catalyst for a teen to change an unhelpful behaviour or uncaring communication. However, it can create a lifelong scar that can impact the way that they see themselves and value themselves right into adulthood.

Positive friendships are a powerful protective factor that will help adolescents avoid unlawful, risky behaviour, especially those involving addictions. Negative friendships can have the opposite impact.

Positive friendships help young people develop a sense of belonging. This builds their inner sense of acceptance, as well as their extrinsic sense of 'I am acceptable'. Research shows that 90 per cent of teens reported that being positively connected to peers was the second most important protective factor during crises and times of challenge (the first being a stable and committed relationship with a supportive parent).

Friendships also deepen after 16 years of age when boys catch up with girls and stop being 'so immature'. Things change when they start to bond, even across genders, based on shared values and interests. It is helpful for boys to develop 'girl mates' that are not their girlfriends because they can help boys decode the 'girl world'. The reverse can happen as well, and these friendships are particularly beneficial in the transition years as an adolescent prepares to leave home and stand on their own feet.

As they continue to spread their wings by trying new experiences, starting new jobs and becoming sexually active, having secure, predictable friends or extended family can be incredibly important. Teens are not really supposed to share the intimate details of their first sexual encounters and/or disasters with their parents. This can be much healthier with someone their own age whom they know and trust.

This is one of the reasons why it is helpful to keep teens engaged at school for as long as possible, even if they are not performing well academically: leaving school early can alienate a teen from their key friends, and they can miss this deepening of the friendship process. I have worked with many teen boys who fell into depression during this vital window because they were feeling separated from peers by being in an adult work environment with no one their own age and definitely not any friends. These more deeply committed friendships often create a lighthouse effect for teens who are leaving home, especially.

Despite raising digital teens, parents and community members who create opportunities for teens to hang out together in real time can create not only opportunities for fun but also environments where teens feel connected, seen and heard. Joining clubs, whether sporting, music or adventure-driven, is an excellent way to enable young people to feel connected and valued. Create a space like a garage or a den or make a fire pit to encourage your teen to invite friends over. They will hang out together, plus it is much safer keeping them around your home than it is to have them wandering the streets. It is a good idea to get to know your teen's friends' parents so that you can take turns at having 'overs' (that's a sleepover without much sleep!). Often, a teen will listen to a friend's parent's advice more than their own parents' – even if they say the same thing!

> If your teen plays sport or does dance or karate, make a habit of offering to drive other teens home. It's amazing what you can learn with a car full of teens chatting away – completely forgetting that you are in the car!

4. Immature brain driving a mature-looking body

When a tween develops early, many parents believe they are automatically more mature than their less developed friends and peers, however, their brain and hormonal changes still haven't happened. They are equally as immature in cognition and emotional awareness. There is no doubt that puberty is happening earlier, especially with girls, and many tweens and teens look much older than their years, but do not be fooled! The changes taking place in their brain have not moved at all. Many will be like an L-plater driving a Porsche, which is why they need to have vigilant, loving care in their adolescent years.

5. Separation from parents

When a teen steps back, it is a sign that the child-parent relationship is fading (as it should), and a new relationship with your teen is forming. It is healthy for them to question your values and beliefs because they are searching for their own way of interpreting the world. This is where the friction is meant to happen, and it is a sign that your teen is developing well! No, really, it is, and yes, they could be a bit kinder sometimes in how they tell us that we don't know what we are talking about.

WHAT I WISH MY PARENTS HAD DONE:

- Ask what I needed.
- Be more supportive and listen.
- Just reiterate they are there for me and potentially ask what I would like them to do to help.
- I would have liked for them to say that even if I don't do well as long as I've tried my hardest, they are proud of me.
- Leave me alone for a little bit instead of babying me.
- Try to understand my point of view and spend more one-on-one time together.
- I don't think they could have said anything different. They have been very supportive, loving and helpful.
- Compassion, comfort and physical – cuddle.
- Give me space.
- Let me ask for help without feeling like a burden.
- Listen and validate my feelings without making me feel like a disappointment.

While stepping back from parents is healthy and normal, research shows that adolescents with positive parental involvement travel better on the bumpy ride. Rather than seeing this stepping back as a weakening of the parent-adolescent relationship, *it is better seen as a sign of a changing relationship*. There is no question they still need those guiding rails on the bridge. This is an extract from a longer blog post by psychologist and author of *Journey Through Trauma*, Gretchen Schmelzer.

> I know there is nothing inherently satisfying in this job for you. I know I will likely never thank you for it or even acknowledge your side of it. In fact I will probably criticize you for all this hard work. It will seem like nothing you do will be enough. And yet, I am relying entirely on your ability to stay in this fight. No matter how much I argue. No matter how much I sulk. No matter how silent I get. Please hang on to the other end of the rope. And know that you are doing the most important job that anyone could possibly be doing for me right now.
>
> Love, Your Teenager
>
> Gretchen Schmelzer, 'Letter Your Teenager Can't Write You'
> 13 June 2015. gretchenschmelzer.com

When a teen does not have someone hanging on to the other end of the rope, they can become untethered and lost. The increasing rates of adolescent crime and violence are fed by videos on TikTok and other platforms. These increasing rates are a sign of many untethered tweens and teens who are desperate to be noticed, accepted and to belong somewhere.

Another positive pathway for this tricky window of development is Rites of Passage programs. Traditional kinship communities would all have a rite of passage for young people as they ventured into adulthood to help them accept the ending of childhood. There are many excellent programs now being run in schools thanks to the wonderful work of Dr Arne Rubinstein (Rites of Passage Institute) and Andrew Lines (The Rite Journey). There are many others also being run at a community level like Fathering Adventures, Pathways, The Fathering Project, True North Expeditions, Raise Foundation, Zero2Hero and others. All teens can benefit from similar, excellent programs that help them transition with positive mentors and guides.

Many teens are often reluctant to want to learn from significant grown-ups, not just parents. Again, the digital world has given them access to information that previously could only be learned from another human. I spoke to a young lad one day about why it was important to develop life skills like learning how to change a tyre or what to do if you get bitten by a snake. He laughed and said that you don't need to learn that stuff, you just go to YouTube. I then asked him what he would do if his phone was flat or there was no mobile reception. He just said, 'Oh shit! Never thought of that!'

THINGS THAT TEEN BOYS WORRY ABOUT:

- I worry that I won't have my crap together by the time I'm an adult.
- Losing my sense of fun and becoming boring and sad in future. I worry that I might not be happy in later life sometimes. And that I will lose some of my friends, particularly my closest ones.
- Not knowing if I will find someone I love and not being happy.
- That we're not looking after our planet and that we prepare so much for our future lives but we don't even know if we'll have one because we might destroy the planet before then. Then I'd like to have kids, but is it moral to bring people into a life where their world is going to be destroyed? However, at the same time, we don't want to sacrifice anything that we already have, especially technology, which is one of the biggest contributors to the destruction of our planet.
- I worry about something going wrong that I can't control (parents fighting, unexpected illness, car crash, etc.).
- Being lonely and everything being harder than I thought it would be.

It is important to note that these five drivers are biological. They occur for adolescents and teens everywhere, regardless of ability, gender identity or sexuality, and they occur according to each individual's unique inner programming. Neurodivergent and LBGQTIA+ teens can struggle more during this stage of their lives as they are often misunderstood, judged and seen as 'difficult'.

We need to keep in mind that adolescents did not ask for these changes to happen, however, they need to happen to allow a child to begin the changes necessary to become an adult in the future.

Many teens are just as confused and stressed as their parents. Let's be honest: there has always been a generation gap between parents and teens, and the more we can build understanding and compassion, the better it will be for everyone.

WHAT'S DIFFICULT ABOUT BEING A TEEN?

- Lack of ability to fix the problems in society (e.g. climate issues) due to age. Additionally the examination system, which places unnecessary stress on students (with time limits of one to three hours), does not reflect the workplace (which will never give you an essay to complete in that timeframe) and which focuses only on memory instead of application of knowledge.
- Not being able to do what I want when I want because my mum and dad still think I'm too young – like if I go out after school and Mum tells me to be back by five. That's not fair as I could still be busy or having fun so I should be able to come home when I want, as long as it's before night time. And my mum always questioning me about school and also Mum ringing or texting me when I'm out with my girlfriend or friends to find out why I'm not where I said I was going to be because she checked where I was on find my iPhone. I don't think she should have to have access to all my stuff like my phone but if I don't let her, she takes it off me and that's not fair because it's mine and I'm old enough that she doesn't have to check up on everything all the time like she does my sister.

2

The teen brain: what is going on up there?

> . . . the teen brain shows us that adolescence offers perhaps a second chance – or at least an additional one – to unleash the enormous potential and possibilities that lie within a person's brain and to shape positively that person's social, emotional and intellectual development. It means that what happens during their adolescent years is very important and can have a considerable and long-lasting impact on their lives.
>
> Barry Corbin, *Unleashing the Potential of the Teenage Brain: 10 Powerful Ideas*

Even though the above quote is over 15 years old, it is still a profoundly important message for all those who live with or work with teens. What happens in this hugely transformative window, from the beginning of puberty until adulthood, has enormous, long-lasting impacts on the trajectory of a child's life – either positive or negative.

The significant brain changes that occur at different times for different teens can create changes in behaviour that are incredibly confusing and stressful. If we keep in mind that the child brain needs to be reshaped and remodelled to become a mature adult brain, we can get a sense of why these changes need to occur. From my experience as a high-school teacher and counsellor, there is no question that there is a significant difference in how these brain changes impact a statistically significant number of girls to boys.

In my classrooms, the difference between boys and girls was very noticeable . . . teen boys can easily forget when assignments are due, when there is an orthodontist appointment, how to get organised before the school bus arrives, and to take sporting gear on appropriate days. I have yet to meet a teen girl who has left her backpack on a school bus – complete with laptop and phone – though I am sure there are some. It can be helpful to teach our tweens that these massive brain changes are coming. One caring mum gave her 14-year-old son my book *From Boys to Men* so he could read the chapter on the changes in the brain. After he had read it, he grinned at his mum and said, 'Would have been really good to know about this before it happened!'

Given that the multiple and unpredictable changes that are occurring for our teens create stress in the body, and possibly a flooding of the stress hormone cortisol, we can understand why they are so desperate to make choices that make themselves feel better. They are hunting dopamine as it is the feel-good neurochemical. One of the best books to read if you are curious about the teenage brain and a hunger for dopamine is *Brainstorm: The power and purpose of the teenage brain* by Dr Daniel J. Siegel. He explores the importance of growing in the capacity for 'mindsight' when an individual can come to truly see or know their own mind. He argues strongly that as we walk beside our teens, we need to accept that even though we would love to fix all their problems, we need to give them what they need the most which is to feel seen, heard and connected to us. This means that whatever experience they are exploring, we recognise it is their experience and not our experience. One message you'll hear over and over in this book is to start a conversation by validating their experience, 'Oh that sounds tough,' or 'Oh no – that's a bummer.' Or if it's a positive experience, 'That sounds fabulous,' or 'how exciting for you!'. Then pause and tune in to where they will take the conversation next.

So, what are these brain changes all about?

Brain cells are called neurons, and when a new learning occurs, an axon grows from one neuron to another neuron, and fixes on to the other neuron via things called dendrites. It can be helpful to think of a neuron like a tree, and the dendrites are like the branches of the tree, while the roots are the axon. We have billions of these (maybe 100 billion) neurons in our brains.

Adolescent Brain Development

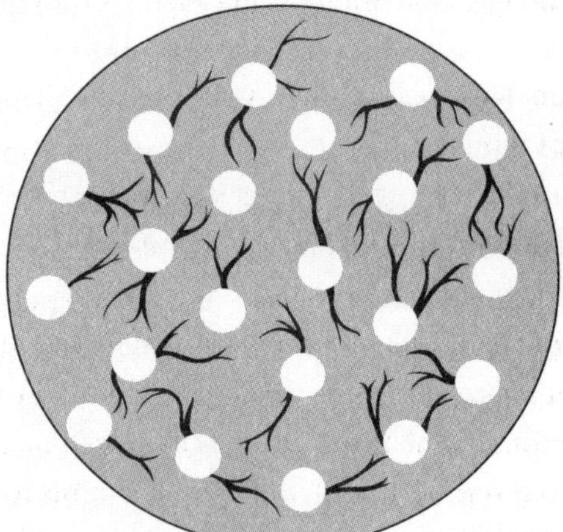

Key factors of adolescent brain development

1. Pruning – use it or lose it

There is a massive pruning of neurons that occurs in the brain during the early teenage years, anywhere up to 15 to 20 per cent. Information that is used often is deemed important and becomes stronger and is easier to remember. Information that is not used often is deemed unimportant and is forgotten.

Adolescent Brain Development

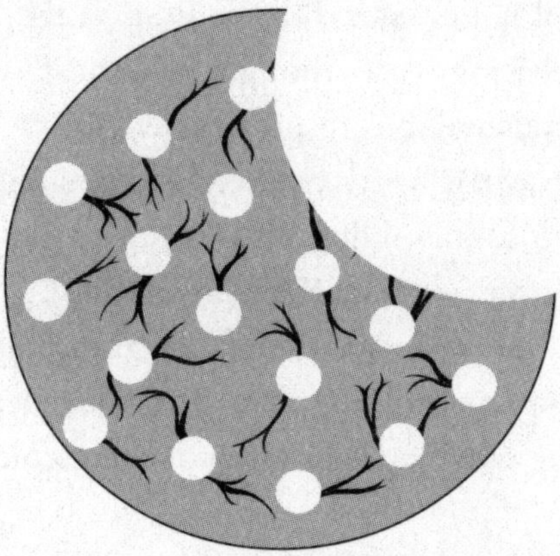

In adolescence, there is a 15 to 20 per cent pruning of neurons that prunes what is not being used. Use it or lose it!

This pruning can happen without warning, and it impacts in many areas of a teen's life. The brain is trying to upgrade by removing unused parts to make it more efficient. Remember these are unexpected changes that the adolescent did not ask for, and it can be confusing and stressful for them, as well as you. Generally, girls begin puberty earlier than boys (by approximately 18 months to two years) and their brain pruning does not seem to be as noticeable as it is for boys, although it is definitely happening to them too. Generally, girls' memories are more efficient (even from toddlerhood) and they also tend to have a capacity for reflection BEFORE choosing to do things. In my high school classrooms Year 8–10 showed the most glaring and significant differences.

This is a message I received from a mum several years ago that captures the change beautifully.

> 'The problem I am having is with my 14-year-old son who does not apply himself to his school work at all. He won't revise, study or plan at all. His grades are weak and failing in some major areas. He just won't apply himself and is lazy. In his own words he can't be bothered. And on top of that he refuses to acknowledge his body odour or wear clean clothes! Help!'

On top of the concerns already expressed are forgetfulness (left his backpack with laptop and smartphone in it on the bus for example), increased disorganisation (I thought the test was tomorrow?), mumbling and monosyllabic responses (whatever!), endless hunger (there's nothing to eat!), badly behaved penises (especially at breakfast), every excuse for avoiding chores and a passion for wearing favourite daggy clothes – preferably sans undies!

I have received many desperate emails from mainly mums asking me what could have possibly happened to their beautiful boy, some even contemplating whether their lad had been stolen by an alien and replaced.

The brain pruning can also impact a boy's capacity to speak articulately. This can happen quite suddenly where a boy starts speaking in very monosyllabic tones that are often difficult to understand. There were times in my classrooms when a boy would do an oral presentation, mumbling incoherently, where the students and I would look completely confused as we could not understand what he was saying. A key thing to remember in this window is not to tell your son to open his mouth so he can speak more clearly. It is not his mouth's problem; it's an issue with his brain that will gradually return to normal closer to 18. I hope that makes sense of some of the 'yep', 'nup' and 'whatever' responses that you get.

Another change for boys is the deepening of their voices. There are times that a boy's voice will almost come out like a squeaky mouse and three words later it will sound like a growling bear. Boys are easily embarrassed when these things occur just as they are when they talk very differently. No wonder some boys disappear behind a mask of indifference and apathy. Many boys struggle with feeling embarrassed, and then angry. We need to cut them some slack and help them understand what's behind these changes.

On the other hand, for many girls, brain changes in early adolescence often mean they can be drowned by the negativity of the inner critic. I have rarely met a girl who liked who she was in this window. More on this later.

We need to keep in mind that Mother Nature is preparing the child's evolving brain to become smarter, faster and to function with more maturity. In order to do that, it must prune those things that it decides a young person may not be using enough. Some pruning activity impacts across other competencies in an adolescent's life that can be unhelpful.

> Every area of the teenage brain is pruned [. . .] this may sound like troubling news but in actual fact it's just the opposite – the brain becomes more efficient discarding some of its inconsequential information.
>
> Sheryl Feinstein, *Parenting the Teenage Brain*

Another common unhelpful change that occurs alongside pruning is a decline in short-term memory – they become more forgetful. Even organised students can forget to hand in assignments or do homework. Both girls and boys lose clothes, shoes and smartphones during this time. Rather than just expressing our parental angst, maybe remind them this is their brain's fault and that it is working to be more efficient.

During this pruning window, a teen's organisation skills in general can go awry, and messy bedrooms are often a product of this. The arrival of the 'floor-drobe' is often a sign that they have lost the capacity to put things away. That's if they had it beforehand! They simply find managing their world harder and more challenging and will often seem to forget simple things around the house, like putting towels back on towel rails in the bathroom, putting the milk back in the fridge and when it is their turn to do the dishwasher! Many parents feel that these behaviours are deliberate, and they tend to come down quite firmly and even harshly, thinking that they can simply do things the way they did before.

It is so important to realise how much the brain changes are impacting these changes in behaviour, which are beyond their control most of the time.

WHAT (IF ANYTHING) DID YOUR PARENTS DO OR SAY DURING THIS TIME THAT YOU THOUGHT WAS HELPFUL?

- My mum made me an assessment calendar which helped me manage my assessments so I knew what I needed to do.
- Asked if I needed space or just if I was okay.
- Mum told me that if I am struggling with my classes I can always ask for help.
- That the teens are a difficult transition into adulthood. Hang in and things will change. I will always be here for you no matter what.
- That feeling is expected. No 'shoulds' – you are doing incredible for someone with your brain at this age doing the work you're doing. Enjoy this moment!
- Told me what I was experiencing was normal and gave me options for support. Mum reached out to my year advisor who helped a lot. Mum also surprised me at times by cleaning my room and not whinging about it. I liked that.
- Assist in getting me back on track, regarding school work.
- Your school grade isn't the most important thing in the world.
- Just told me it's normal for most teenagers.

2. Overproduction of dendrites and synaptic connections

There will be billions of synaptic connections in an adolescent's brain by the end of adolescence. Synaptic connections are created as learning occurs when neurons communicate with each other. The more you engage in an activity, the more dendrites grow and the stronger the synaptic connections become.

The early teen years are a particularly wonderful window of opportunity and potential because the brain gets extremely busy at growing synaptic connections and enormous numbers of dendrites.

Adolescent Brain Development

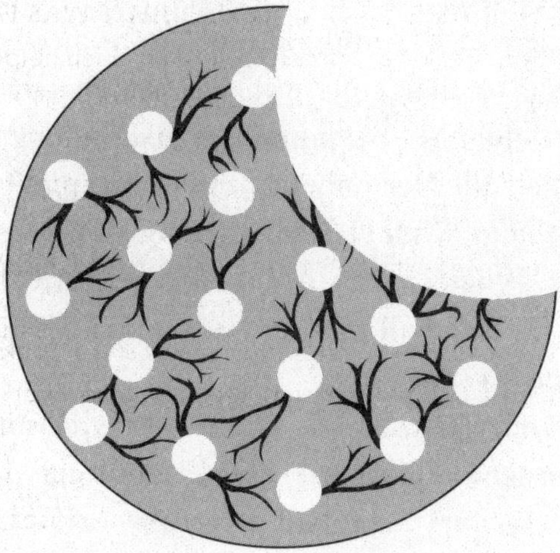

Massive overproduction of dendrites and synaptic connections – an 'enormous window of potential'.

Teens can learn skills and knowledge at an unprecedented rate. Evolutionary biology argues that this massive growth in the brain is linked to the importance of teens being able to survive in an unpredictable world. Boys needed to learn how to hunt and kill very quickly. Girls needed to learn how to find food, care for those most vulnerable and begin breeding! It makes sense that the brain was in a hurry to learn new things. It was either learn or die.

This window of opportunity is a vitally important window in the journey of human development. Learning, especially that which is based on real experiences, will happen faster than at any other stage in life (other than the first five years of life). If a teen throws serious energy into their studies, their sport or their favourite hobby, they will improve faster than any other time of life. They can pick up new skills like playing a guitar, learning a new language, or doing a triple flip on a skateboard so much faster.

This unique window is a kind of paradox because at the time when the brain is learning exponentially fast, it is often also the time that teens experience self-loathing and self-hatred, and they can struggle with feeling confused and a bit out of control.

A key message with this information is to be as warm and encouraging as possible so that your teen can get massively engaged in something they enjoy. My passion during my bumpy teen years was my love of basketball. Not only did I go on to play all through my university years and while I was teaching – I kept playing until my early forties. What I didn't realise as a teen was how important the enjoyment of basketball was, and how good the physical exercise was for my mental wellbeing!

This opportunity to learn fast is one of the reasons why Indigenous football programs have the degree of success that they do in Australia. The Clontarf Foundation started with 25 lads and now 20 years later they are working with 11,500 lads across Australia and have positively changed countless lives. Sadly, young Indigenous men are at much higher risk of suicide and more during adolescence than non-Indigenous boys. At a time that is full of risk and potential danger, young lads are given a tight structure in which they can play lots of football, be supervised by significant role models and still get to play rough and tumble in a socially acceptable way. Their rapidly improving ability builds their sense of being capable and competent, which also weakens the pattern of early adolescent self-doubt and self-criticism that many numb with alcohol and drugs. They also have a boundary they learn to respect – no school, no play!

There is, of course, a significant downside to this massive growth of dendrites. Of course, because you can learn faster than ever, you can also become addicted faster than at any other time in your life. This is why social media can become so problematic in the years up to 16, and why so many of our teens can become problematic gamers in the same window.

It is far easier to become addicted during this time of massive brain development.

Vaping has become incredibly problematic around the world, especially for teens. Nicotine is a highly addictive drug and, in this window with excessive dendrites, addictions can form fast and deep. In an episode on vaping that I did for my ABC podcast *Parental as Anything*, we heard from a parent who has chosen to home-school their teen because of their addiction to vaping. Another mother approached the school and asked if they could have a safe vaping room, because her daughter was in her final year of school and the only way she could cope with the stress was with vaping.

Research shows that becoming addicted in this window, whether it be to alcohol, drugs, vaping, gaming, watching porn or endlessly scrolling on your phone, means it will be even more difficult to overcome the addiction. A key message from neuroscientists is to monitor your teen's usage of anything that could be potentially addictive, until beyond the years of 16 when this massive growth has finished and they are starting to become more capable of making better decisions.

During this same window, GABA (Gamma-Aminobutyric Acid) is turned off. GABA is an impulse-inhibiting amino acid in the brain, and when it is turned off this increases the impulsivity of our teens, especially for our boys. Some girls can act impulsively from time to time; however, even as toddlers, girls are generally capable of pause-reflection, and this tendency continues in their teen years as well. This means teen boys are much more likely to want to try things that are potentially harmful no matter how bright or well educated they are. The biological drive to belong with your friends and peers, when combined with no GABA, means teens can make poor choices that can be a risk to their wellbeing. Much of the increasing youth crime in recent times has been fed by watching other teens participate in delinquent behaviour. In many communities, teens are encouraged to steal cars, to race cars and even to hang their bodies out of car windows while being driven at high speed. Some of the TikTok challenges call for others to see if they can do better. This hunger to be noticed, to be validated as someone worthwhile, and to do stuff that fires up dopamine, which makes them feel alive, has always been present. It is just now that the digital world has changed the dynamic, and sadly, not in a positive way.

When teens are not positively engaged in their education or in positive pursuits like music, reading, sport, creative arts or practical skill development, they may be learning things that can impede their development for the rest of their life.

This is why they need rails on the bridge and caring adults who help them navigate this bumpy and exciting window of development.

Stoke their spark

> 'Every teenager has a spark – something that is good, beautiful and useful to the world. Sparks illuminate a young person's life and give it energy and purpose.'
>
> – Peter L. Benson PhD, *Sparks: How Parents Can Help Ignite the Hidden Strengths of Teenagers*

I worked with struggling teens where it was like a light had gone out inside them. And there were times when simply helping a teen find what gave them a spark, what made them feel good, was just as important as navigating the challenges they were experiencing. Sometimes a spark could have been more obvious when they were younger. I once worked with a mum of a 14-year-old boy whose dad had died from cancer. She was concerned that his love of racing motorbikes might get in the way of his studies and asked for my advice. When I asked her what a normal day in her son's life was like, she explained that he got up early, had his breakfast and went for a ride before school. On returning home from school, he went for another ride, got his homework done quickly so he could get to bed early so he could get up early and go for a ride. I reassured her that her 14-year-old son was making some very sound choices! I suggested that she continue to allow her boy his passion because it was a 'spark' that lit him up. That spark was helping him cope with the death of his dad, and with being a 14-year-old boy.

A message from the teen survey that captures the importance of a spark:

As a teen I feel the number one thing that impacted me negatively was being unable to be great at something or achieve something. I was good at school but never great at it because it wasn't my thing, and that upset me because that's what I had to put all my time and effort into. And I wasn't interested in it at all and no matter how hard I tried I could never get incredible marks. And that killed any sense of purpose and my self-esteem. I completely understand why kids can go off the wrong path when they have to go through this. If you're terrible at school but suddenly really successful at fighting and dealing, then you're going to want to do that more. My life got infinitely better when I found passions and found myself goals that I could achieve.

If you have a daughter who loves to do competitive gymnastics, or loves Eisteddfods, or cross-country running, do everything you can to support her passion. If you have a son who loves the same, or who loves his sport, his music or surfing, do everything you can to support their passion. My sons became surfers, and while the last thing I wanted to do on weekends as a full-time teacher was to get up early and take them surfing, I knew that the boys who got out of the surf were always full of life and enthusiasm. It was so worth it. This spark may not be as obviously important for their future as good grades, however, those teens who have a spark that sets them alight travel so much better on this bumpy ride to adulthood. The spark increases the chances of your teen finding the feel-good neurochemicals in their brain, in ways that are dependable, predictable and often safer than the sudden risk-taking, impulsive choices they might make in seeking the same buzz.

The window when teens can have a lust for risking, playing, experimenting and exploring who they are is one that doesn't last forever. *Much more* at risk are the adolescents who are lost in virtual worlds in their bedrooms being numbed and distracted by the screen world. We need to keep an eye on our pre-teens to see where their interests lie and notice any experience that they seem very excited about, because it may be a clue to what they may like to pursue when the massive overproduction of synaptic connections occurs.

3. Myelination – insulating the neurons and synaptic connections

One of the most important things to remember about what's happening in your tween-teen brain is this – their brain is gradually maturing by growing myelin which will help them think better and deeper, but it takes a long time!

Adolescent Brain Development

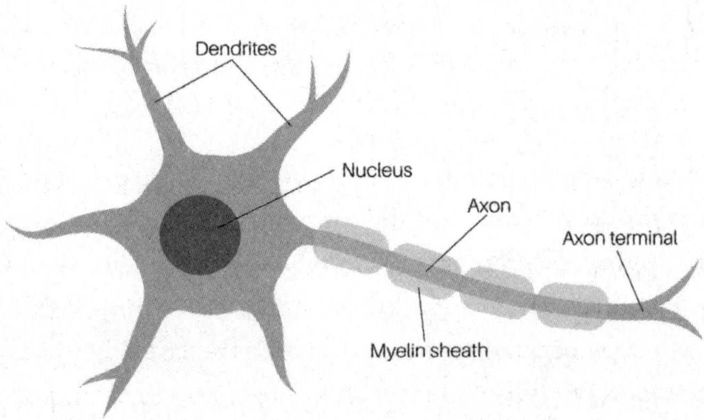

The process of myelination supports the completion of prefrontal lobe development, which results in an adult-reasoning brain.

If there's one thing that parents say often when their teen has made a poor choice, it's 'what were they thinking?' One of the most significant things to truly understand as a parent of a teen is that their capacity to understand the nuances of human communication and to make sound, logical choices depends on how much myelin is in the brain. It's not their age, or their size or their grades at school that help them make good decisions. They need myelin. Myelination is the final stage of brain development and involves the thickening of the white matter, or myelin, on the axons. This is the process of insulating the neurons and synaptic connections, which allows more connections and more efficient usage. This means the quality of thinking improves, and from 22 to 28 years of age the prefrontal lobe (the executive function of the brain) will be mature enough to ensure that improved decision-making can take place. This generally indicates less emotional unpredictability, more impulse control and better organisational skills.

The prefrontal cortex or the frontal lobes are the part of the brain responsible for abstract thinking, decision-making, analysing and problem-solving, and they are the last parts to receive myelination. As the frontal lobes finally mature, the quality of thinking increases. It is a gradual process, and you will gradually notice your teen making better choices or remembering more things. I recall my youngest son at 20 arguing with me that this was incorrect information. He said he was sure his prefrontal lobe was complete as he was studying physiotherapy at university and was managing his life in a fairly positive way. While he was talking to me, he took out a small bottle of ginger beer from the fridge and shook it up and then opened it. Of course, it went everywhere! He then agreed his prefrontal cortex still wasn't completely finished!

Dr Mari Swingle is a neuroscientist and researcher. In her book *i-Minds: how and why constant connectivity is rewiring the brain and what to do about it*, she writes that she believes that digital natives who have spent significant amounts of time online are experiencing delays in the development of the prefrontal cortex. She argues that from as early as 2005 to 2008, neuroscientists were aware that higher arousal and the dual nature of divided attention that was required for multitasking on multiple devices in multiple modes, often while doing homework, was putting the brain under stress and reducing its efficiency. The divided attention required for multitasking tends to thwart the development of deeper thinking and judgement, and also the ability to see the bigger picture. For these reasons she argues that it slows the development of the prefrontal cortex and that is why many young adults in their twenties are struggling in securing and keeping employment, achieving normal milestones like getting a driver's licence and why many have social anxiety that was largely unheard of 20 years ago.

It is important to keep in mind that the myelination process is negatively affected by alcohol and drug abuse. Marijuana is essentially a fat-loving substance and in the rapidly developing brain it can eat up the myelin and thus slow down the thinking and weaken motivation. Binge drinking can strip new learning from the brain – what a waste that would be in the final years of school! From approximately 22 to 24 years of age for girls, and 26 to 28 for boys (allowing for boy delay, although some may argue it takes much longer!) is when parents can start to breathe a sigh of relief. At this time there will be less emotional unpredictability, more impulse control and better organisational skills. This can only happen if the developing brain in that critical window of pruning and overproduction of dendrites has not been damaged by accidents, significant illness, trauma, addictions, or lack of positive experiences to grow positively.

Many adults wrongfully step back out of their adolescent's lives, thinking they need to develop autonomy or to work stuff out for themselves, or maybe they find their teen is just too hard to manage. They certainly need those opportunities; however, we now know that adolescents still need support and guidance well into their twenties. The perception that they will be fine after 18 years of age is a fallacy. You will know when the prefrontal lobe has finally grown because they will not only thank you for a delicious meal they will *offer* and *do* the cleaning up with a smile on their face.

On my bumpy journey through adolescence, I struggled and felt like the world was against me many times. I wished my ride had been smoother and that I had made fewer mistakes. Only as an adult did I realise it was *because* of my bumpy ride that I am who I am today. A wise 'lighthouse' (adult ally) gave me this saying and I have found it really useful throughout my life.

Life will throw you a curved ball from time to time.
It's what you do with it that makes all the difference.

Helping teens understand their brain

We can over-worry and keep our adolescents too safe and overprotected, and on their bumpy ride to adulthood they may never get a chance to find out what road they were meant to travel. This is the notion of 'safetyism' that I have already mentioned. But remember, teens have *an amazing capability to learn, adapt and cope.*

We need to keep in mind that the teen brain is highly malleable with a high degree of plasticity. This means it can change more easily than an adult brain. All these changes are happening at the same time as changes in hormones, physical maturation and the emergence of their sexual identity. No wonder it can be confusing.

When tweens and teens know what biological changes are happening in their brain and why, they can better understand some of the confusion they feel. It can empower them to know they are not alone and that Mother Nature is preparing them to become wise adults.

It is important to again emphasise that *these changes are not something adolescents asked to happen,* and they are often equally as confused as their parents. When I used to explain this stage of adolescent brain development to students, there was a noticeable sense of relief on their faces. Many parents think their adolescents are being difficult just to annoy them; however, confusion and frustration with things they have no control over is a perfectly normal response. There is very little *intentionality* in the adolescent world. They do not get out of bed in the morning deliberately planning to 'piss off' their parents – it just happens.

Lastly, we can teach our teens that their brain can be influenced by the choices they make, despite making many changes that they didn't ask for.

> Teen years are hard. We are learning how to interact with the world in an independent way for the first time in our lives. We learn from mistakes. Help us learn. Don't shame us for our stumbles.

Top tips for teens for getting the best from their brain and body

Researchers have been discovering more about the brain in the last 15 years than ever before. This information could fill a 500-page book so I am only going to cover the essentials.

Sleep is crucial for teens and for that reason, it has its own chapter. Otherwise, here are some more tips.

Essentials for teen wellbeing

Wonderful water

Eighty per cent of the body and brain are made up of water and it plays an essential role in keeping the brain working at its best. It also helps maintain a steady pH level in the blood stream, enabling it to carry essential ingredients to the brain. Your teen needs to be aware of becoming dehydrated – even without exercise, they can become dehydrated. They need to make drinking water a regular part of their day. Water also helps to keep stress levels down by cleansing toxins from the body. If water is restricted when a teen is stressed, they can have problems staying focused, and can feel unsettled, uneasy and may even get a headache.

Hot Tip: Fruit juices, soft drinks, alcohol, energy drinks, coffee and tea are all diuretics which help to make the body dehydrated. Water is the only fluid that rehydrates the brain!

Beautiful oxygen

Oxygen is carried via the blood stream to the whole body. In order to perform at an optimum level, the brain needs to convert glucose into fuel, and it needs oxygen to do this. The brain uses around 50 per cent of the oxygen in every breath we take! The more oxygen in the blood supply, the better the brain will function. Pausing to breathe deeply and often will help keep the oxygen levels up. A top tip for teens is for them to see how slowly they can breathe in deeply – count slowly as they breathe in. Then release the breath slowly. The more stress we feel the less we tend to breathe.

Hot Tip: Pausing to take three deep breaths often during the day can benefit your teen in many ways. A top tip is to try sighing three times for quick stress release.

Essential exercise

Exercise stimulates the body to oxygenate the blood better than anything. Encourage your teen to do vigorous exercise each day, and especially around study times and exams. It helps to release built-up tension from their nervous system, builds up oxygen in the blood and helps to burn off fat.

Hot Tip: Suggest your teen gets into a habit of walking the dog or walking after dinner to sharpen their brain for after-dinner study time.

Brain food – what is best for the brain?

Statistics show that a large proportion of all of us, adults and teens alike, do not eat well. According to dietary guidelines, for optimum health, young adults should eat a wide variety of nutritious foods from the five food groups every day, including fruit and veg, protein, grains and dairy.

If they don't feel like eating much around stressful times like exams, it would be advisable for teens to take a multivitamin tablet (and maybe try homemade smoothies with protein in them). This would ensure they are still getting potassium, zinc and magnesium – all essential for healthy brains.

When it comes to vegetables and fruit, you may have heard the expression 'eat the rainbow'. This is because it is best to aim for a variety of types and colours. Natural glucose is excellent for teen brain function, too – especially that found in apples, pears, strawberries, oranges and berries. Encourage your teen to try eating these fruits rather than cakes and biscuits before studying. These fruits will help your teen think better. Teen brains can also benefit from increasing the intake of anti-oxidants, such as berries, prunes, garlic, spinach, and both black and green tea. Teens can also benefit from getting more Omega-3 essential fatty acids found naturally in fatty fish like salmon, tuna, trout, herring and sardines, and also oils like canola, flaxseed and olive oil.

Excessive sugar can play havoc with teen blood-sugar levels and make a teen have huge mood and energy swings and a scrambled brain! Suggest to your teen that they avoid ice-cream, lollies, all energy drinks and sugary drinks when they need their brain to be working efficiently for them. If your teen needs a sweet fix, suggest they try some good low-GI foods such as yoghurt, bananas, dried apricots, cherries, strawberries, raisins or sultanas. Or if they're keen for a sweet treat, a little chocolate, honey or nut butter on wholegrain bread may be okay. A mix of nuts and dried fruits in the pantry is a good idea – but they need to eat in small handfuls, not by the jar!

With the huge popularity of energy drinks, a lot of young people are ingesting very high levels of caffeine. Although it may give them a temporary boost in energy and mood, caffeine can also cause anxiety, jitters, headaches and dizziness. It can also disrupt your teen's normal sleep patterns. Also, there have been reports of a US study that's linked the use of energy drinks to higher levels of risk-taking among teens – meaning the side-effects could be far worse than we imagine.

Lastly, your teen's brain needs them to have breakfast. Brekky provides the brain with vital nutrients and enzymes that stimulate the 'alertness chemicals' also known as dopamine and noradrenaline. It is best if they have protein with their breakfast and not just carbohydrates.

Hot Tip: Suggest your teen eats as much fresh and unprocessed food as possible to help their body and brain work at their best. Would you put cheap fuel into a race car?

Hopefully, you can see how incredibly important an understanding of what's happening in the teen brain is for all the grown-ups in their lives. This changing, adapting brain drives everything – from physical changes to emotional challenges. No matter how frustrating it can be when they forget things, argue with us, get stressed about stuff and struggle with their big feelings, it is all developmentally pretty normal. If we can help them to understand that this is a stage of growth that can be a bit tricky, and that they can lean on us for support – even if we don't have all the answers – it can make a world of difference.

The brain does get more efficient and effective, and we do need a lot of patience until that actually happens.

- Almost everything, for me my whole teenage experience, has been challenging. It's a never-ending battle for yourself, against your family, your friends and yourself.
- The most challenging thing would be having to be enough as in trying to keep up with everything that is happening in friend groups, at home, with sport and also trying to keep up with school.
- Comparison syndrome, constantly comparing myself to other weights, friendship groups, experiences. It's so challenging as people want you to make a decision for the rest of your life with career/uni and you put so much time into trying to figure it out that you forget to be a kid.
- Stop putting so much pressure on children to do well in school. It's not the end of the world if they don't do well and there are many different options and opportunities for them after they leave school.
- Also, stop forcing kids to make up their mind about what they want to do after they finish school.

3

Understanding the turbulent emotional world of teens

MESSAGE FROM A TEEN GIRL

If I could talk to my high school self now, I would give her a big hug and tell her that being herself and living her life the way she wants to is okay and exactly what she should do.

The development of the physical body, together with emerging sexual urges, novelty-seeking behaviours, rapidly changing moods and emotional states make adolescence a very challenging and interesting time. Change of any kind triggers stress, and even invisible changes can trigger stress and anxiety – especially for teens living in such unpredictable times.

Even though I am almost 70, I can still vividly remember the emotional rollercoaster of my teen years. I struggled deeply with low self-esteem, and I covered my poor sense of self with a mask when I moved into high school, as most teens do. I was an excellent student in my senior years, becoming a prefect and successfully completing my university entry exams. I took part in both school drama productions and became head girl of the boarding house – hardly the outward signs of someone with low self-esteem.

On the outside, everything looked fine, but on the inside, I was still deeply lonely and very negative towards myself. I kept people at a distance, even friends. To avoid the social scene, I spent a lot of time on my own, but little did I realise how unhealthy that was for a teenager.

These hidden insecurities came to a surface after I moved to the city for university. As I struggled to maintain my 'I'm OK' mask, I started self-medicating with Valium, which a doctor had prescribed for back pain as a teen. Fortunately, I did seek help from a counsellor at the university who helped me understand my emotions and that Valium was not a wise choice to manage my turmoil.

I would suggest that all teens can struggle enormously with their emotional world. Even teens who are living in safe, loving families with supportive parents can struggle deeply with the emotional ups and downs of the teen years. During my time teaching over the years, I sometimes wondered why a boy would suddenly punch a wall over something quite minor. I discovered in my counselling that teens could be drowning in the emotional sea of something that happened months ago, which others had already been considered to be resolved but was still troubling the teen. I also found that when I read a story from *Chicken Soup for the Soul* to a class of supposed tough students, they all had tears in their eyes and were moved by a collective emotion.

Emotion is a term that describes certain feelings and bodily changes that occur when the brain is aroused. Emotions are often aroused from an unconscious level of the brain. Biological changes during adolescence show a growth of the amygdala, considered to be the emotional epicentre or gatekeeper, especially around fear and anger. Adolescents rely more on the emotional part of their brains.

Let's be honest – we can all struggle with our emotions at times. The meltdowns that happen for teens are quite similar to those of toddlers. They are often a sign that their nervous system is overwhelmed and that they are struggling to cope. Discharging the cortisol, or stress hormone, to their safest grown-ups is a way for them to re-regulate themselves. When teens unload their painful feelings onto their parents, it may cause parents to worry more; however, often, it can help the teens to feel better. I have explained to many parents over the years that if you can pretend you are a duck, then you can let all the emotional garbage that your teen is dumping on you flow off you like water off a duck's back. When they are sharing their emotional pain with you, it is far safer than when they keep all of it from you, and it is a positive sign that they love you and feel safe with you.

We need to keep in mind that a parent will never see the full picture of their teen's overall psychological capacity.

There is some evidence that during the teen years, part of the limbic system increases in volume and reactivity in response to emotion and becomes more sensitive to factors such as failure and social rejection. This increased activity has been associated with an increased risk of anxiety, depression and behavioural problems.

> 'Various neurotransmitters (brain chemicals) that control and regulate such things as moods, impulse, motivation and emotional excitability are greatly influenced by sex hormones produced during this emotionally explosive time in an individual's life. Because of this, teenagers often experience emotional highs and lows more quickly and at the same time have less control over these emotions.'
>
> – Barry Corbin, *Unleashing The Potential of the Teenage Brain*

There is now significant research that has established that the teen brain interprets emotional expressions differently from the adult brain. They can seriously misinterpret normal facial cues that they had no problem interpreting before!

The cracked windscreen

Once the brain changes have started, the way your teen sees the world also changes. This can be one of the most frustrating things about parenting teens.

When teens hit early puberty, around the ages of 12 to 15, they start seeing the world through a different lens. I often use the metaphor of 'cracked windscreen' to explain this. Instead of seeing the world through a clean windscreen, as their parents do, the teen now sees a cracked-windscreen view, influenced by the biological drivers and changes in their brain we've already discussed. Now, when you ask your daughter as she leaves the house if she has her coat, this is seen as some form of criticism! Little things, even well-meaning gestures, can be blown out of proportion quickly and easily through the cracked windscreen. Your teen might see a student turning away on the bus as a sign of bullying. The tiny zit on their nose looks enormous, and many teens struggle as they compare themselves to others in negative ways, often quite irrationally. Some teen girls can despair that they have nothing to wear to a social event despite having a full wardrobe!

When teens look at themselves through this cracked windscreen, they see themselves in a much poorer light than previously. No wonder so many teens live in a haze of dark moods or grumpiness.

In today's digital world, where teens are desperately seeking acceptance and validation online, it is much harder to manage the big, ugly feelings of not being good enough. The tendency to compare-and-despair is particularly strong in this window – especially for our girls.

Research has found that as children reach puberty their ability to interpret and understand social situations and emotions in others can drop by up to 20 per cent. In one study, adolescents at 12, 14 and 18 years of age were shown photographs of facial expressions. At 12 the adolescents were accurate about 86 per cent of the time. This dropped to around 60 per cent at 14 and didn't return to the previous level of accuracy until 18. What does this mean? This means that in the window of 12 to 15 years of age when the brain does its automatic pruning, young adolescents often misread facial expressions and misinterpret body language that they could read much more competently before. They badly misread people including other adolescents. I have had teens say that someone 'looked at me like I was an idiot', or 'like I was a fat ugly slut'.

The cracked windscreen also explains why so many of your gentle reminders and well-intended explanations will go unheeded – you are expecting them to appreciate and understand logic or rational thought as though they have a complete prefrontal lobe. If a teacher growls at the class for poor effort, a teen may feel sure the teacher meant just them. Teens have told me that they're sure their mum hates them when she may simply be premenstrual or a little grumpy. This sensitivity, when combined with a few other changes, makes our confused adolescents very susceptible to self-criticism and self-judgement. They may look like an adult, however, their capacity to think and process information is still developing, and hence, lots of arguments will occur. Developmentally, these arguments are also showing that your teen is gradually developing their own sense of independence and autonomy, which is technically a good thing.

> In the moment, nothing helps. Even if my mum says something that I know makes perfect sense, I always find a way to poke holes in it or think about why it won't work.

If you as a parent can understand that your teen is seeing a very different world to you, through their cracked windscreen, then it might be easier to understand why they make the choices that they do. Sound decisions involve rationally assessing the risks, benefits and alternative actions that are relevant in any particular case. While teens are beginning to think more like adults than children, they often still need help from their parents or other safe grown-ups to make decisions that have serious or long-term consequences.

This is because the reality is that teens:

- are likely to be more impulsive
- lack rational thinking strategies
- are looking for novelty experiences
- are less concerned about risk
- are not thinking about the future

- are more susceptible to peer and friendship influence
- are more concerned about physical appearance
- are hungry to be accepted and to belong.

The underdeveloped prefrontal lobe also plays a role in the struggles that teens have with their emotional states, especially anger, frustration, fear, boredom, shame and feelings of worthlessness. Their way of thinking, which is strongly influenced by their negative inner critic, can see them frighten themselves with their imaginations rather than accurately assess the current situation. There is an increased reactivity and intensity in their emotional world that can be quite overwhelming.

We must keep remembering this is all completely normal.

The glitter jar

Even though it was almost 45 years ago, I can still vividly remember a 15-year-old boy who came into my English class after a maths class. Suddenly, about ten minutes into the lesson, he stood up abruptly, kicked his chair backwards and walked to the closest wall – a brick one – and punched the wall really hard! He then walked out of the classroom. I followed him and found him sitting on a bench with his head in his hands. Eventually, he explained that he had lost it because he had failed his maths test. He had actually broken three of his knuckles. This was the first time I had witnessed the incredible intensity of adolescent emotional angst as a teacher, and it was a sobering experience that I share often as an example of the depths of teen emotion.

I have also worked with a 15-year-old girl who had decided to run away from home because she was sick of her mother nagging her. Literally, one day, she just packed her bag and headed for the bus that would take her to the city. She had not planned it – she just made an impulsive choice to get away from what was causing her angst and stress. Fortunately, one of her friends mentioned her plans to one of the staff at the high school, who contacted her parents and they were able to collect her from the bus stop before the bus left.

Since then, I have seen these intense emotions often – in my classrooms, my counselling rooms and my home. Much like the two-year-old tantrum, I have come to see it as quite normal to have these enormous bursts of intense emotion that can be sudden, seemingly irrational and frightening for both the teen and the grown-ups nearby. It can be helpful to think of the metaphor of the glitter jar. When the glitter is all shaken up, it is the same as when a teen is upset and possibly venting. When they are in this state, the amygdala has hijacked their prefrontal cortex. Not only can they not hear you, they cannot respond to any reason or logic. It is best to simply let the glitter settle.

When your teen is in a storm, it is best to let the storm pass rather than join the storm.

Navigating emotional storms

We must not forget that teens tend to rely more on the emotional part of their brain to navigate their uncertain world. Many teens also struggle with negative ruminating loops, where they are unable to escape the constant voice of the inner critic. This can be one of the explanations for why they can appear moody, or they can be stuck in moods. We need to remember they don't enjoy being stuck in dark moods.

I tend to get frustrated and worked up if something doesn't work out (a lot of this stems from my ADHD and procrastination) and I feel so agitated and restless. I end up getting so upset and angry and it's such a horrible feeling as I often can prevent these things from happening if only I had started an assignment sooner (but really my ADHD makes it really difficult to do that).

As I mentioned earlier, Lisa Damour wants us all to know that mental health isn't just about feeling good or happy. Rather, she would like to see mental health be more about:

> '. . . having the right feeling at the right time in the right context and then to have the ability to manage that feeling in a way that doesn't hurt anyone else and actually brings a sense of relief.'
>
> – Lisa Damour, *The Emotional Lives of Teenagers*

This is such an important message for parents because there are times your teen will be feeling flat, sad or stressed due to something that is happening in their life. This is an appropriate response to their environment and not necessarily a sign that anything is wrong. They are merely being human. Parents can support them to help them manage these big feelings without making them feel they are a problem that needs fixing or that they are wrong or weak.

> Please please PLEASE if your child, teen, young adult or whatever seems off, do NOT guilt trip them. The worst thing to do is say things like 'why are you always sad', 'you never do anything', or 'why can't you be like (other kid)'. Trust me the kid is definitely aware if they're having a hard time, and you shouldn't remind them. Just be there if they need to talk.

In her book *The New Adolescence*, Christine Carter, PhD, reassures parents and educators that so-called negative emotions, despite how big they can be, are not necessarily going to be traumatic, unnatural or potentially scarring nor do they need to be avoided at all costs. Learning to navigate through emotional storms is an important part of maturing as an adult. This is how humans develop emotional buoyancy – learning through experience. When parents step forward and solve their teen's dramas and challenges, even though it may come from a place of deep love, they are not helping their teen develop life skills and important capacity, especially around conflict, that they can take into their later years.

Emotional intensity definitely **increases** in this window of change and *emotional contagion* is also common with groups of teens. I was once working with 500 teens in a school in rural NSW and I noticed that they were subdued, even sad. I quietly asked one of the girls if there had been a death in the community recently as everyone seemed sad. She answered me, 'No, but Noah died on *Home and Away* last night!' So these emotionally vulnerable teens were all grieving – for a character in a soapie! The emotional distress was very real. There was a palpable reaction recently too from kids and teens who missed out on tickets to see singer Taylor Swift live. It was such an issue that there were articles and interviews with experts about how parents could support their teens with the disappointment.

It can be easy for us older folks to think it's a bit silly, but we need to really accept that emotional intensity is much higher for teens, especially in early adolescence. This fact is possibly why they can slam doors or discharge verbal diatribes in very loud voices – it is an intense experience.

All emotions are normal and valid – it's what we do with them that matters.

Let's be honest, we can all struggle with big ugly feelings at times, which are triggered by events and thoughts. Mature grown-ups have a finished brain, which means their prefrontal cortex or executive functioning brain has fully developed, and we can make choices to soothe ourselves and change how we feel.

We might notice feeling stressed or even anxious and we choose to make ourselves feel better by, for example, making a cuppa, grabbing a Tim Tam or piece of fruit, doing some deep breathing, a downward dog or going for a walk and a stretch. As a mother of four busy boys, I have been known to lock myself in the toilet for some peace too – a strategy that worked for me!

Put simply, events – both real and imagined – and thoughts create emotions and feelings. The limbic part of the brain is where these thoughts become the emotional tension that can then flow through our bodies. Sometimes there seems to be many intense emotions happening at once and this can create a sense of confusion – which then can create even more unpleasant feelings. Without a mature prefrontal cortex, a teen's ability to make sense of what's happening and to calm themselves down is impaired!

WHAT I WISHED MY PARENTS HAD DONE DIFFERENTLY

- Maybe talk to me about it more at a different time because she hasn't followed up about it. I find it hard to start conversations like this.
- They suggested professionals like therapists, but I felt they couldn't understand why I felt so uncomfortable talking with strangers about my struggles. I wanted my parents to understand that they felt like the only people I could talk to, but I felt too shy out of doubt that they could do any more than they had tried.
- In the moment everything everyone says sounds like crap so I may get annoyed with their advice in the moment but otherwise they are good at helping me.
- My dad would sometimes come in and say 'It'll all get better; you just have to push through it'. I feel like saying this is telling someone with asthma to just breathe.
- My parents told me I just should be happy.
- Every time I've opened the emotional door to them – just a crack, they've responded harshly and negatively.

The adolescent response to threat

The adolescent brain has a tendency to be wired via the threat centre – the amygdala – rather than the wise mature prefrontal cortex. This means that teens are more likely than mature adults to be triggered by quite small things. The amygdala is part of the limbic system which also influences such aspects as hunger, thirst, sleep, sexual response and hormone production. The limbic system is particularly affected by the great surge of sex hormones.

So many of an adolescent's responses to their world are coming from the least developed part of the brain. The amygdala is supposed to have the capacity to size up situations and take control of them instantly. It works faster than the slower-thinking parts of the brain. For example it will quickly initiate pulling your hand away from a hot stove without you needing to actually think about it.

When confronted by a threatening situation, the primitive brain tends to respond automatically in one of four ways:

1. Flight
2. Flight
3. Freeze
4. Fawn.

We all have different spontaneous responses to significant threats; however, our teens can react incredibly strongly to things that are either not a significant threat, or a situation that they have misinterpreted as a threat when it is not. To them it feels valid and real.

Fawning is a lesser-known stress response and it means adapting yourself in order to avoid further stress or conflict. For example, this might look like people pleasing, over-apologising, rescuing others or putting other people's needs before your own. Kids and teens might pretend that they are doing okay when really they are struggling or experiencing the same levels of stress as others. This is quite common behaviour for girls and many neurodivergent students in our classrooms.

In a situation such as an alarm sounding loudly, in adults with fully developed prefrontal lobes, the brain will kick in with some strategies such as, 'Do I need to run somewhere safe?' or 'Take a breath and think!' or 'Maybe there's a number to call for the alarm-security people,' or 'Who would know the number?'

Teens do not have this capacity to reason well and do not have it until their mid-twenties at the earliest.

Adolescents struggle with situations of perceived threat. Remember, they can perceive threat where it may not exist because of the brain-pruning process, which means they can misread things.

David's story

I remember a 14-year-old boy called 'David' who had experienced a very tough childhood. He was always ready to fight over everything he was asked to do, even with teachers who treated him well. His brain had a habitual response to figures of authority because he had been subjected to many experiences that were painful. It takes time to change the core concepts or thinking patterns and this is one of the reasons why teen behaviour can be so challenging.

David did make some changes in my class because he finally realised he was safe. A sense of safety can allow the brain to come off guard and be less likely to react from an irrational place of threat. Unfortunately, he did not have the same good fortune in his physical education class.

The tough male teacher tried to make David more cooperative by shaming, yelling and using threats. He also would hit David with cricket bats as though it was a joke. One day, David snapped and punched the teacher to the ground. He came and saw me just after the incident and said he thought it was best if he left town because he couldn't take any more. Thankfully, these punishment strategies are no longer accepted in our high schools.

David did forge a positive pathway in his life. Later, after spending time in the army, he became a very competent businessperson and a very proud dad.

The emotional barometer

Emotions can continue to exist within our nervous system long after an event has triggered them. Anyone who has lost a loved one will know that grief and sadness, and sometimes anger, can last a very long time.

One way that I have helped teens, their parents and their teachers understand the emotional volatility of teens is through the use of the metaphor of an emotional barometer.

If we can imagine that there is such a barometer inside every teen, we can better understand when things suddenly become explosive. Imagine that at the bottom of the barometer, there are some emotions that are still in a girl's (or boy's) nervous system from early childhood.

Let's pretend that at one time, she was the baby of the family and loved being seen as special. Then along comes a sweet little sister who not only takes her place, she also appears to have become Dad's little princess. Colour in the bottom layer of the barometer.

Then, just before her second birthday, her older sister decides to cut off all her lovely golden curls while they are playing hairdresser. Now she looks like a boy in all the photos taken at her second birthday party. She's not happy about that! Girls tend to remember negative experiences very vividly, and they can experience the emotional intensity within the nervous system just by remembering the event!

Then, when she is four, her older brother steals her Barbie doll, cuts off its head and buries it in the backyard – and Dad never growled at him. She's very unhappy about that. It's time to colour in more of the barometer.

Now she is 14 years old and, on this particular day, she is finding it really hard to wake up. After three attempts, her mum has yelled at her to get up, which is not a good way to start the day. When she gets down to the kitchen to have breakfast, she finds Daddy's princess has just eaten the last of her favourite cereal. Then, when she gets to the bathroom, there is no hot water left. By this stage, she's very unhappy. Colour in more of the barometer.

Turns out, too, it's gym day, and as she forgot to put her gym gear in the wash last week after impulsively kicking it under the bed, she now has to put on dirty gym clothes. Then she needs to run for the bus, but she realises that she has left her completed maths assignment on her desk and forgotten her lunch. Every one of these setbacks adds more emotional tension to her emotional barometer!

Normally, her friends keep her a seat at the back of the bus, but today they didn't. The only seat available is next to the ugliest boy on the entire planet (in her view). He has food hanging out of his braces and hair so greasy that the grease is dripping on his shoulders, and his BO is so bad that she has to hold her nose. This day is unfolding in the worst possible way. Her emotional barometer fills up a bit more.

At school, she gets into trouble for leaving her maths assignment at home, and worse still, the teacher thinks she is just making an excuse and doesn't believe her. She just can't seem to win a trick and feels worse and worse during the school day – plus she's very hungry. She can't find her friends at lunchtime, and the negative self-talk in her head amps up – *Maybe they don't like me? Maybe they think I am fat, ugly and stupid? I have no friends, no one cares.* Then she sees someone who looks at her as if to say, 'You are a fat slut' (remember, teens misread facial expressions badly).

The downward cycle rapidly gets worse with an intensity that few adults can understand. So, when she accidentally bumps a small Year 8 girl outside the library and her books fall everywhere, she explodes. She calls the girl all sorts of names and makes a total scene. This is the explosive boiling point of her barometer – what I call the tipping point – and the incident with the Year 8 is the final straw. The final straw that overloads the nervous system can be quite small.

This metaphor shows how we all can become emotionally overloaded, and the tipping point can trigger a huge response that is way bigger than what the stimuli warrant.

- I felt like a volcano that had been plugged. Needed to explode but the pressure keeps building and nobody sees it – until I explode.
- I found I was constantly going from 0–100 very quickly and very easily. I felt very anxious, and like no one was listening and no one really cared about me while I cared about everyone else so much.

Teens have difficulty managing their emotional world and need to know that they can do things to help diffuse their emotional barometer. The tipping point for David was when he assaulted the teacher; however, it can be quite small too, as with the girl in the scenario I just shared.

We have real concerns for teens because mental illness commonly appears for the first time for many people during this vulnerable window. I remember speaking to a mother of a 16-year-old son at a suicide prevention conference. She said her son had walked in after school and eaten two biscuits out of the biscuit barrel. When he went to get a third, she asked him to put it back because dinner wasn't far away. Without her noticing, her son walked down the back yard and hanged himself from a tree. He had reached his tipping point and couldn't take life anymore. Impulsive suicides can occur without a teen struggling outwardly with significant anxiety or depression. His mother said if she had known he had reached his tipping point, she would have let him eat the whole barrel of biscuits.

What this poor mother didn't know was that her son had reached his tipping point and instead of hearing her comment for what it was – words of concern for his dietary choice – he heard something else. Perhaps it was rejection or a sense of failure. To a struggling teen the final straw can be tiny.

This young man's mind was probably raging in a storm of confusion, negative self-talk (or ANTs – automatic negative thoughts, which we'll get to later) and emotional despair.

From the outside, we cannot always see the signs that someone is reaching their tipping point (e.g. racing heart, dry mouth, suicidal thoughts, feeling frightened, struggling to sleep, to name a handful).

However, what we can all do is make sure that the adolescents in our lives understand that because of their developing brains, they are more likely to feel overly emotional, be forgetful, struggle with ANTs, feel self-conscious and make unsafe choices. And that we are here for them as a safe base.

We must always keep in mind the incredible fragility of our teens and the importance of explaining the concept of the emotional barometer. When I was presenting this concept to high-school students, a number of students sought help because the metaphor made sense and they felt they were near the tipping point.

We must be very aware of a teen's enormous emotional vulnerability and ensure we don't make assumptions about understanding what is happening inside their confused minds. Rather than making judgements about what is happening for our teen, *a helpful reframe is to become curious rather than furious!* Yes, it is much easier said than done. However, it is really important to come from this angle when your teen is struggling.

When you add other stressors like rejection, failure or lack of sleep, an adolescent can reach their tipping point quite quickly or unexpectedly. Many teens are looking for this relief in the digital world and sometimes through connecting with friends who are in a positive space this will definitely work. Unfortunately, the tech companies are using algorithms to ensure there is more negative content that will flood their feeds, so rather than find comfort, teens can find more distress.

- I didn't want to wake up. I didn't want to exist but I didn't want to die. It's a hard feeling to describe.
- Feeling emotionally overwhelmed but also empty at the same time. Thinking that I am not worth the life I was given. That I am always going to be alone. It gets really bad.
- As we near the middle of the year, due dates start looming, assessments start piling up, and exams get closer and closer. Sometimes having so much to do can drown you and you start to have a really negative outlook on everything. I know that I just get really overwhelmed and stressed, and everything sort of just seems slightly impossible or far more scary than it actually is.

Blocked, stuck or repressed emotions can stay buried in our nervous system for a long time and sometimes this can be problematic for individuals in adolescence and adulthood.

There is a lot of anger in adolescence. Understand that anger is a symptom, not the problem.

Many parents want their adolescent to stop being angry because they see the anger as the problem. The parent does not understand that anger is a response and is often a reaction to feeling disconnected, useless, powerless or out of control.

- Angry, really f*cking angry.
- Angry & disheartened, helpless.
- Explosive anger & frustration and disconnect from loved ones.
- I was getting angry at home because there was so much work to do for assessments and it was too much to manage. I didn't sleep properly because I was stressing about how to get my work done. And I felt sad because I was mean to my mum when she was trying to help.

It is important to remember that no matter how nonsensical and frustrating our teen's feelings may seem to us, **they are real and important to our teen.** Indeed, it is important that the safe grown-ups around our teens accept that *times of extreme emotional intensity are normal* and not necessarily a sign of a serious psychological fragility that needs professional help.

ANT attacks

It's sad that the worst enemy most teens (and many adults actually) have is themselves . . . they attack, blame and criticise themselves with their automatic negative thoughts – and these can sound like an endless negative chatter in our heads:

'I'm useless. No one likes me. I'm ugly and stupid.
I'm gonna fail the English assessment – what's the
point in studying? I'm too dumb to do well at school.
I'm never good enough. I'm a loser. My coach hates me.
My ears are too big. I am so fat. I just don't get it,
no one likes me. It's my fault we lost the debate.
No one understands me. I can't do that. I hate me,
I disgust myself . . .'

I call this sort of thinking an ANT attack – ANT stands for automatic negative thoughts as I mentioned earlier. Children and teens do not have the mental capacity to be able to catch an ANT attack and stop it using their rational mind. In my research, I have found that girls have a stronger tendency to get stuck in ruminating negative loops that they can find very difficult to escape from.

Teens can get stuck in an emotional state and often seem to make it worse with 'stinking thinking'. Teens tend to 'awfulise' and 'catastrophise', and the limbic brain can accelerate these big ugly feelings into becoming a threat that can then trigger an overload of cortisol. This can be made worse if their peers and friends are also in the same space as emotional contagion is very real.

That voice that is the inner critic inside us might always be vigilant, but it is not always reliable. Thoughts are not facts and just because we think something, doesn't make it true.

YOU CAN STOP ANTS AND CHANGE THE LOUSY FEELINGS THEY CREATE.

An easy technique to teach teens to interrupt an ANT attack is to have a simple repetitive, internal mantra that they repeat to themselves.

Your teen can choose one of the following phrases and repeat these words silently in their head. Their brain cannot listen to two lots of thoughts at the same time.

Circuit breakers for negative self-talk

- Delete, delete, delete (your teen can tap on side of head at same time).
- Go away – I have got this!
- I am okay exactly as I am.
- I am, I can, I will.
- My mum loves me.
- Relax and chill, puppy!
- Rack off, hairy legs!!!

Often well-meaning and loving parents and teachers can make things worse by overly reassuring our teens, minimalising their distress and telling them not to worry. It's a tricky balance!

- Super stressed and exhausted all the time. Feeing the need to sleep every waking second.
- I've always had insomnia since I was a young kid, however, when I'm stressed and going through stuff my sleep is definitely worse off. I also felt anxious and very down (& depressed) the majority of the time. It gave me bad thoughts and feelings about myself, and made me wish I was stronger, as well as made me more aware of what the recurring situation was for years before and wish that I'd stopped it long before it got to the point it had. I had deep hate and blame for myself, as if what was happening was really all on me (which I now know wasn't).
- I have recently been struggling a lot with anxiety and it has been one of the worst feelings that I have ever felt. The whole fact that I can't even help the pressure building in my chest and the bad thoughts running through my mind; it is horrible.
- I always have a problem where I think too much about something before I do it (over thinking). I expect too much of myself sometimes.

The map to joy

One of the techniques I used when counselling teens who struggle with big ugly feelings is to create a map to free themselves. The ability to create positive neurochemicals to counteract the negative ones like cortisol is such an important concept to teach teens. To create the map, we first explore the things a teen enjoys doing that bring a form of relief – and there is the long list of possibilities to explore. Many teens use unhealthy ways of shifting neurochemicals like consuming energy drinks, junk food or lollies and chocolates. These can create a temporary shift, however, this often ends with an even bigger flooding of ugly feelings because the sugar and caffeine crash can impact the brain and body negatively. So instead, we seek to identify the five best cup fillers – so five things that can shift negative emotions into positive ones. Your teen can create a colourful visual reminder of these five cup fillers which can be helpful to keep in an easy-to-see place.

The first steps are simple and might look a bit like this:

- Make themself a cuppa or get themself a cold drink.
- Find a semi-healthy snack – have some fruit, make some toast, eat a muesli bar, eat a couple of biscuits, or eat a small handful of nuts.
- Take five minutes outside – either with their snack and refreshment, or just for a short walk.
- If you have a family pet that they like and connect with, spend some time stroking it and talking to it.
- If they have a safe parent who is a good hugger, seek out a hug.

There are many different ways in which a teen can find joy, depending on their unique preferences. They'll often fall into these areas:

- **Athletic success & sport** – go for a run, shoot some hoops, kick a ball, practise some martial arts.
- **Artistic & creative expression** – drama, dance, music, art. Simply get up and do something they love.
- **Deep relaxation & stillness** – listen to a calming audio track, do some yoga, or spend some quiet time in nature.
- **Safe, honest human connection** – deep human connectedness, family, friendship. Seek someone who they know they can trust and who loves them and have a chat.
- **Significant immersion in nature** – walking, surfing, fishing, swimming, birdwatching, or gardening.
- **Acts of service** – helping others. Visit someone, bake biscuits for them, offer a gesture of kindness to someone.
- **Discovering new purpose & meaning** – start something new, such as a hobby or fitness program.

It is so important that this solution process is driven by your teen and not you.

So what else can safe grown-ups do to help teens manage the developmentally normal stage of emotional intensity?

1. **Do everything you can to make home be a safe base.** Sometimes leave the fight over the untidy bedroom and just close the door. If they discharge some of their emotional angst at you, breathe and choose not to take it personally. Self-harm in adolescence is at a disturbing level and it is seen as a coping strategy for big ugly feelings. Let them discharge these big ugly feelings safely at you (however, never accept them lashing out physically at you) because they love you and hope you can still love them as they work through huge feelings.
2. Almost in the same way that we care for toddlers who also experience the same levels of confusion and frustration, the most important thing to do is to **validate what your teen is feeling.**
3. **Become a trusted safe person in a teen's life.** Trust plays an enormous role for the developing teen. When their trust is broken, and they feel betrayed by the few people they have chosen to be trustworthy, teens become deeply wounded. Many teens do not allow their parents to help no matter how hard they try. Partly for developmental reasons, teens push back from parents. This is where teens can benefit from having a 'lighthouse' figure, a safe adult ally in their lives. Encourage them to find someone they can talk to safely. The only time adults can break a teen's confidence is when the teen is being harmed or expresses suicidal ideation, at which point duty of care must override confidentiality and a professional must be informed immediately.
4. **Become well-informed** about the unique developmental aspects of adolescence especially about the growth of the limbic brain and intensity of emotions, the cracked windscreen and the teen tipping point. These metaphors can be helpful for our teens as well as their parents.
5. **Understand that boys and girls tend to process emotionally intense experiences differently.** Girls can tend to respond very quickly

and can explore things verbally. Boys tend to internalise these huge emotional confusing feelings and often they come out via irrational behaviours, especially through physicality. Many boys have been conditioned to shut down their emotional world so that they can appear 'tough' or in control.

6. **Caring adults can help teens to make sense** of their emotional turmoil rather than deny it, make it wrong or minimalise it. Serious, active listening and caring communication are really important (more on this in Chapter 6).
7. **Model kindness and fairness above all else** while teens are walking this bumpy ride to adulthood – especially when they least deserve it. They cannot be what they haven't seen or experienced. Remember to ask your teen often, 'How can I support you on this bumpy ride?'
8. **Show your love unconditionally,** even if your teen disappoints you in some way. In our achievement-driven world we must be careful that teens don't come to believe that they are only worthwhile when they reach clear goals like passing exams or reaching a parental expectation. Being loved conditionally can cause problems later. Take the pressure off our teens and reassure them that you love them no matter what.
9. **Help our teens with how they see their world** and how to know what their individual top-five 'cup fillers' are when things get tough. When parents and other key grown-ups model self-care, it can also help our teens learn how to take better care of themselves – eventually.
10. **Choose to bring hope, light and fierce unconditional love into our teen's lives.** The world is often a big nasty place, and we need to reassure them that things can get better. I have found that teens are very easily influenced either positively or negatively. So please choose to influence them positively as often as you can.

'Having hope helps people from overwhelming anxiety, a defeatist attitude or depression. Optimism works like hope – it can lift performance in life. Hope and optimism can be learned just like helplessness and despair.'

– Christopher Peterson, Steven F. Maier, Martin E. P. Seligman, *Learned Helplessness*

Accepting that emotional turmoil and confusion is a completely normal part of this major life transition is the first thing parents and educators need to do. There are times in their confusion that your teens will have no idea why they are having the feelings they are having – they are simply having them. When we can normalise that, then we can seek to find how we can support them in that moment, knowing that it may be something different each time. When we *work with* our teens rather than *do to* our teens, we have a much better chance of being the guiding rails on the bridge that they need. Find moments in your home to create positive memories that matter and celebrate the small victories not just the big ones. Yes, you will need a good dose of patience, moments of laughter and lightness, lots of hugs and, if possible, find a supportive tribe of good humans who are doing the same thing – dancing the wonky waltz we call adolescence.

- Recently I had a bad day and it felt like the only way to deal with it was to take it out on myself. I was angry at myself and over thought what I could've done differently / better. Sometimes I try not to think about it, but this time I let my thoughts run away.
- Generally feeling sad and hopeless. Choosing to isolate myself with the hopes of regaining energy and rejecting the invitations of social activities (more than usual as an introvert). Irritable around family, and often 'wanting' to cry (especially at night) to relieve tension and stress from the day. Finding it difficult to get up in the morning and having more vivid dreams of stressful situations.
- Drama with my friends at school. This made me almost depressed. I would come home every day almost in tears. I found that I would snap at my siblings when I wouldn't normally. I became very quiet and sad most of the time.

4

The incredible importance of teen sleep

- I was really tired as I struggle sleeping at the best of times so when I was stressed it was extremely hard to sleep.
- I've had a lot of trouble sleeping recently due to my anxiety. When I don't sleep, I cry and I can't tell people why I'm crying because they will think it's silly. I haven't had a solid night sleep in over two months.
- My sleep schedule was mucked up to the point I couldn't go to sleep until two or three in the morning, which resulted in me having a lot of time off from school.

Let's be honest, even we grown-ups can struggle to get enough sleep. We all know how it feels to get out of bed already feeling depleted, tired and with a sense of dread for the upcoming day. The 21st century has created some unique additional pressures that steal sleep. It's not just getting caught up doom-scrolling; it's bingeing a great series on a streaming service (yikes, is it 1 am?). It is the lure of escapism from our worries that a screen can provide, and the irresistible temptation to keep gaming because you almost won. Of course, billions of dollars are invested in designing tech so it is hard for us to put down! It is also simply that we are living in an over-busy, overscheduled, time-poor world, trying to fit in too much stuff. Burnout was not a term that was heard very much in the last century, and the term 'parental burnout' was something I had never heard until recent times. When we adults whose brains and bodies have stopped growing and who are cognitively mature enough to make sensible decisions about our wellbeing are struggling, imagine how tough it is for our teens to get good sleep.

The science is very strong that teens need at least nine hours sleep a day from ages 13 to 18! The pressures on upper school students to do extra hours of study to achieve good results just create more stress and anxiety, and that means even less sleep. Many teens get into loops of procrastination and catastrophising when they have an assessment due that needs to be done outside class. Especially with the added challenge of digital distraction. As a teacher, one great strategy that I used after listening to student concerns was to have all major assessments done in class.

- I feel exhausted, drained emotionally and physically, absolutely filled with stress over deadlines and academic pressure but absolutely no motivation to do any of the work. Oversleeping, anxiety and severe guilt.
- I have trouble sleeping if there is a lot of stress at school.
- Trouble sleeping and had a lot of assessments – anxious, angry, annoyed easily.
- Have trouble sleeping and got constantly angry and anxious, stressing out about things I couldn't control.

Poor sleep impacts every level of an adolescent's health and wellbeing: it can make them sick, feel dumb, hinder learning, be grumpy, negative, overweight and depressed. Today's teens are struggling with chronic sleep deprivation at far higher levels than previous generations. When I interviewed paediatric and adolescent sleep specialist

Dr Chris Seton for an episode about teen sleep on my ABC podcast *Parental as Anything*, he said researchers have tracked this shift. Fifteen years ago, around 30 per cent of our teens experienced chronic sleep deprivation. Now, the figure is 70 per cent! I was pretty staggered when I heard that and that is why it needs to be a key area of consideration in supporting your son or daughter to be healthy during this incredibly tumultuous time of life.

Adolescents need more sleep than pre-pubescents or adults. This is a biological need due to the massive changes happening physically, hormonally and within the brain. With sudden growth spurts, particularly in boys, adolescents experience huge waves of intense lethargy or sometimes hyper energy with increased restlessness. Hormonal changes create more melatonin, which means, chemically, the body is demanding more sleep. Sadly, hormonal changes for women around menopause seems to do the opposite where they struggle to sleep. That makes for some family fun when Mum's going through perimenopause while parenting a teen!

The next big shift is with the adolescent circadian rhythm. Suddenly, they are more alert in the afternoon and evening and need more sleep in the morning. For approximately 75 per cent of adolescents, the body's sleep clock shifts by up to 1.5 hours, which means they are not ready for sleep until much later at night. Given this shift in the sleep clock for many teens, there have been some schools that have trialled later starting times for teens, with positive results. Sadly, it is impractical to have high school starting later than primary school. It would be a complete nightmare for most parents and teachers, however, it could help many of our teens with school concentration and engagement.

This changing sleep clock definitely impacted my sons, and I can still remember how difficult it was to wake up two of them and that was before laptops and phones. They staggered around the house in the morning, still half asleep, and were usually very grumpy as well.

- What I have found most challenging is not being able to sleep in! I now find getting up in the mornings and switching off at night time hard.
- Trouble sleeping, nausea, self-harm, suicidal thoughts/actions.
- Trash sleep. Waking up around 3 am almost daily. Unintentionally staying up all night. I felt that Mum and Dad thought I was setting alarms and going against them. This was NOT true, and I knew the sleep problem was real. I also used to run away from home and occasionally lash out at my teachers. I still have a very strong instinct to run away when confronted or scared.
- Trouble sleeping definitely. I would stay up daydreaming about both the good and bad outcomes and even the good outcomes would often get over-powered by bad thoughts

The impact of technology

The digital world has definitely impacted the sleep patterns of today's teens. Many of our teens are finding it difficult to disengage from their highly entertaining and stimulating digital worlds. With this shift in the body's readiness for sleep, something that was tricky before can very quickly become extremely problematic. Technology experts recommend at least an hour break from screen activity, particularly close screen activity, before bed. One of the challenges of small screens is the exposure to rapidly moving blue light, which is much more intense than light from a television screen. Technically, blue light is a sign for the brain to wake up, and that is what morning sunlight and blue skies do. The exposure to blue light suppresses melatonin release and that's another factor that makes it hard to fall asleep.

Often, to beat the frustration of sleeplessness, teens will go online to distract themselves, entertain themselves, connect or chat with their equally wide-awake friends. These activities all stimulate the neurochemicals that tell your brain to wake up and be alert. Without meaning to, teens can also get caught in a state of flow where time disappears, and before they know it, they have an angry parent expressing deep concern about how late it is, and why they should be asleep!

An additional challenge that the digital world has created is also impacting the way they see the world. In his excellent book *Stolen Focus,* Johann Hari explored how tech companies draw on our brain's 'negativity bias', which is a function of evolution that means we are wired to look out for threats to our survival. So, developers worked out that because we are wired this way people stay engaged online for longer when they see more negative content. Essentially, this means we see more advertisements, so the tech companies earn more money. They also manipulate the algorithms to keep people watching, so our teens are not only struggling with a lack of sleep, but their online time is drowning them in negativity and darkness. It is despicable and appalling behaviour to unashamedly make money off our children, all while knowing it negatively impacts their mental health.

- Social media is a massive influence on young minds. If your feed is filled with depressing stuff, you're gonna feel worse. Find some comedy to laugh at or share a funny cat video to your friends. I think parents need to have more conversations about what their children are actually watching.
- Social media is definitely not helping social morale. It is impacting the way my friends talk, interact and confess feelings, if they do at all. Social media increases suicide rates, encourages vaping and other unhealthy things.

Dr Seton also explained the phenomenon known as 'infomania', which is causing problems for teens who have devices in the bedroom at night. If a teen has sent a message or posted something that they want to monitor the responses on and they have their phone in their bedroom, they will tend to be in a state of excited expectation which also makes it difficult to fall asleep. Neuroscientists have been able to demonstrate that access to the prefrontal lobe diminishes greatly at night-time. This means that the ability to make wise decisions, avoid being overreactive, and keep healthy boundaries becomes even more difficult at night, especially in a bedroom away from the parental gaze.

This is why so many teens can be easily led to take photos and videos of their private parts and share them with others. It's also a prime time for the worst trolling and cyberbullying. If we can help protect our teens by limiting their access to technology in the privacy of their bedrooms, we could make an enormous difference to the damage that can happen. Positive connectedness definitely can happen in the digital space for many of our teens. However, any one of them can make poor choices, especially late at night when they are tired.

- Getting angry at most times in the day where I can feel my mental health taking a slow turn in the wrong direction. Not sleeping enough during the night because I spend too much time overthinking many things that have or have not happened. Getting really really anxious and worried that something is going to happen if I do or don't do something.
- I was struggling to eat, sleep and talk to my friends. At one point I was even going off at my mum for no reason.
- Trouble sleeping – I was prescribed melatonin, feelings of nausea, strong anxiety.
- Trouble sleeping. Getting sad to the point of crying into my pillow and feeling anxious.

Another potential problem with having devices in bedrooms is that prior to these digital inventions, the only reason you were in bed was to rest or to sleep. The brain is a prediction machine and so now, if a teen has been using a device while in bed, the brain anticipates more device activity than sleep activity.

The use of phones and technology in the bedroom is one of the biggest conflicts between parents and teens. More and more parents are setting a clear night-time *curfew for everyone in the home*. This can mean that all devices are being charged in the kitchen or the lounge room and that all Wi-Fi accessibility is shut down. There are lots of clever devices and apps out there to help parents manage this. It can be really hard to sell the importance of sleep to 21st-century teenagers; however, removing some of the most powerful distractions from the bedroom at a reasonable hour makes perfect sense. I have had some parents reach out and tell me that they have appreciated the curfew for themselves because it can be difficult to hold healthy boundaries around smartphones and devices.

The sleep deficit

Most adolescents run on a 'sleep deficit'. This has significant negative effects on their wellbeing and can include:

- Missed school
- Sleepiness – including micro-sleeps
- Negative synergy with alcohol
- Decreased creativity
- Tiredness (decreased motivation)
- Lower school grades
- Irritability, low-frustration tolerance and emotional dysregulation
- Higher risk of car accidents
- Increased anxiety and stress symptoms
- Overeating and yearning for high-fat foods
- Unhealthy dietary choices including high-energy drinks and junk food
- Difficulties with self-control of attention and positive behaviour choices
- Difficulties with focused attention, emotional stability
- Direct effects on learning and memory consolidation, and memory deficits
- Health consequences: more illness, poor skin, delayed growth and development.

The extent of a teen's sleep deficit can often be disguised, even from parents. On the other hand, we see the signs of this deficit emerge in many young people, with each vulnerable in different ways. We see the teenager who falls asleep driving home late at night; another teen has a titanic struggle to wake up in the morning, often failing and resulting in late or missed school; another simply feels sad and moody and blue, lacking initiative or motivation; in another, grades begin to suffer as the teen struggles to keep awake during class and while doing homework; another may turn to heavier drugs to get some positive and arousing sensations; many just struggle along in a kind of haze, never knowing how to feel or do their best.

The sleep list

When I was working with teens, I worked through the following list of the possible effects of poor sleep:

1. *Poor sleep can make you sick.*
2. *Poor sleep can make you dumb.*
3. *Poor sleep can make you grumpy.*
4. *Poor sleep can make you negative.*
5. *Poor sleep can contribute to weight gain.*
6. *Poor sleep can make you become depressed.*

Poor sleep can make you sick

Tell teens that their immune system is compromised when they have interrupted or poor sleep. The cell renewal and revitalisation that takes place when we sleep also requires deep sleep – Rapid Eye Movement (REM) sleep. While we sleep, the brain uses the extra energy that the body is not expending to maintain all the cells in the body. With a compromised immune system, teens tend to get sick more often, take longer to recover and function on a much lower energy level. If they have skin issues like acne or they get cold sores, they will get them more often and more significantly. On my podcast, Dr Seton explained that new research shows that chronic lack of sleep is increasing the chance of more serious illnesses such as diabetes, cardiac heart function problems and high blood pressure.

Poor sleep can make you dumb

The more we learn during the day, the more sleep is required at night. Technically the brain uses sleep to process, sort and consolidate our memories from the day. Whenever a student is learning new concepts, new information, or exploring important processes like formulae, that means the brain has a lot to do and it needs to wait till you're asleep before it can do it. Not only is it storing and processing new information and learning, but vital gene activities need to occur during REM sleep to ensure synaptic plasticity or the strengthening of neural connections. Remember the chapter with all the brain pruning and the massive growth of dendrites and the myelination that's occurring? Well, it happens when the body is in the resting state of sleep, especially deep sleep. Without deep sleep, not only will a teen miss out on having that vital information stored well, their brain is unable to create new spaces for more learning the next day. So, your teen's brain would be like a motel with no vacancies about to receive 50 new people looking for a room. There is nowhere for them to go. Similarly, any learning that takes place after a poor night's sleep will be unable to be stored, remembered and processed into long-term memory the following night. The teen would need to review the learning on another day after a good night's sleep, or that learning will be missed.

How exciting it is to know that new spaces for learning grow every night after the existing spaces for learning have been filled! This information is critical for teens to know because they often think they are dumb when they don't retain information or fail tests when they have simply not given their brain a fair go.

Poor sleep can make you grumpy

We all become more irritable when we are sleep-deprived. This is of more concern for teens because they do not yet have a mature prefrontal lobe to deal with the emotional volatility and unpredictability that is developmentally occurring and is made much worse by sleep deprivation. The ability to manage the chaos of this bumpy ride is seriously impaired, and often, violence and aggression increase with the lack of sleep. I recommend parents allow sleepy teens to sleep in on the weekend if they can because you will have a calmer and more agreeable son or daughter for the next day or two.

Poor sleep can make you negative

The connection between sleep and negative thinking is supported by sleep research that shows sleep deprivation makes people recall unhappy memories rather than pleasant ones. This finding is vital in relation to troubled teens, as well as many people who struggle with depression and despair. It adds an additional layer of negativity that teens have to fight through to recognise their worth and value in our shallow world.

Poor sleep can contribute to weight gain

This point certainly makes teens take note! There is research that shows a powerful link between obesity and sleeplessness. The brain-body connection can interpret chronic lack of sleep as a significant threat to survival. And much like in times of famine, the body starts laying down extra fat cells to help it survive, even without overeating. It is a self-preservation process, and it impacts so many other things, especially hormone levels and the immune system. Sleep loss elevates the stress hormone cortisol. Too much cortisol can cause you to gain weight and human growth hormone is also disrupted. Normally secreted as a pulse at the beginning of sleep, growth hormone is essential for the breakdown of fat.

Poor sleep can make you become depressed

The final negative impact of sleep deprivation for our teens during this incredibly important time of growth and development is that it can contribute to depression, especially among our girls. Some studies suggest that chronic lack of sleep can contribute significantly towards anxiety disorders and clinical depression.

Switching on to sleep

Hopefully, by now, I have convinced you of the incredible importance of sleep for our teens. Unfortunately, convincing your son or daughter about the importance is another thing. Dr Seton explains that it can be difficult to work out if your often moody, grumpy teen is struggling with significant sleep deprivation or just being a normal, developing, emerging adult. He gives two significant red flags that can be helpful for parents and teens. If your teen is very difficult to get out of bed in the morning and really hard to wake up, that's the first flag because it shows that the brain and the body are fighting to return to full consciousness. The second red flag is those big, long sleep-ins they have on the weekend, often beyond lunchtime. He says they could be helpful for them, but when combined with the difficulty getting out of bed, they may suggest chronic sleep deprivation has kicked in and he encourages you to seek help.

Too many survive the crippling effects of sleepiness by consuming high-caffeine energy drinks, eating high-sugar and high-fat foods, disappearing down digital rabbit holes and playing loud music. Most teens think this is normal behaviour, but they are quite ignorant of the effects these stimulating forces have on their sleep-deprived bodies. What can you do to help your teen get a better night's sleep? It can be helpful to have a warm, curious conversation about what you've explored in this chapter. Remember, don't come with a lecturing voice as they just simply will turn off. If they know that getting a good night's sleep will improve their physical health, how they cope with school work, how they see themselves, have better moods and make better choices – they may explore the topic with you.

Tips for better sleep

- Avoid stimulating substances with caffeine, especially energy drinks.
- Create clear sleep boundaries before your child reaches puberty.
- Take a warm bath with Epsom salts.
- Get plenty of sunlight and fresh air.
- Avoid alcohol – especially at night.

- Create a predictable pattern of sleep preparation such as: shower, teeth, toilet.
- Avoid TV and all screens (especially phones) at least an hour before bed.
- Remove phones and devices from the bedroom and silence them.
- Use calming music or relaxation audios – ideally, the same one every night.
- Nature sounds can be helpful – lots of free ones are available online.
- Experiment with ASMR sounds.
- Read something that is difficult to read and boring.
- Try to be in bed at the same time each night.
- Aim for eight to nine hours of sleep each night.
- Try tapping on acupressure points like the K 27. These are acupressure points which are found on either side of the chest mid-way below the clavicle. They are tender spots and tapping them for up to one to two minutes can relieve emotional tension.
- Take some calming drops from Australian Bush Flower Essences or Bach flower remedies (you can get these at many chemists or health food stores).
- Create a calm bedroom by removing chaos or clutter.
- Drink calming teas (there are lots of them available) or warm milk-based drinks.
- Spend time in bed breathing deeply and relaxing the body.

Creating positive neurochemicals by having routines and predictability can be helpful. If your teen has something worrying them, encourage them to write it down before bed as this can stop worries rolling through their brain overnight. It's important to find what works for each individual because they can take it forward in life. Habits that help rather than harm are what everyone is looking for.

> Listen to music, read a book, draw down thoughts, write down some things that are troubling you, talk to a close friend or relative you feel comfortable sharing your mental-health problems with . . .

5

What is a lighthouse and why do they matter?

In traditional kinship communities the responsibility of adults to prepare adolescents for adulthood is taken very seriously. Boys are mentored or guided by men, and girls are prepared by women. The tasks and life skills that young people need in order to be capable adults are taught until an adolescent has mastered the required skill and maturity level required by the tribe. Without these skills, they're not initiated into adulthood. Initiations often take place through ceremony, after which adolescents (usually teens) are formally recognised as adults. This rite of passage sometimes requires physical challenge and pain, ensuring this step is not taken lightly.

In our modern world, we have lost most of the formal rites of passage that acknowledge that an adolescent is now an adult, and many of our young people no longer get the guidance required to grow into responsible adults. They can learn almost everything they need to know in the digital world rather than from safe grown-ups. The digital age has dissolved many traditional family and community structures that provided teaching and guidance for teens, especially on the bumpy road to adulthood. This weakening of social capital has come at a high price, as can be seen by the statistics in the opening chapter. Our emerging adults-to-be still need grown-ups to help them build their life skills, resilience and competence at a time when they're pulling away from their primary guiding source: their parents.

In these traditional communities, parents were not necessarily the main influences on children. The role of watching out for, supporting and guiding kids and adolescents fell to all the adults in the community. I call these adult allies or mentors lighthouses. While we don't tend to live like this anymore, we still need extended family and other people around our teens to care enough to be there for them.

A lighthouse stands solid and steadfast, unchanged no matter the weather. It does one thing: it shines a light to guide safe passage for travellers. When a teen's mentor or ally embodies the qualities of a lighthouse, it means they are effectively saying 'Here are the rocks you need to watch out for. I won't stop you from crashing into them, that's your choice, but I will show you a better way. I am here to help.'

Here's what the data said about lighthouses

One of the most disappointing results from the teen survey I conducted for this book was the large number of teens who had no lighthouse figure at all in their life. Almost one third had no one they could turn to when they were struggling. On the other hand, I was pretty chuffed to see that the leading lighthouse figures were grandparents and teachers! The extremely low percentage who saw their lighthouse figure as a psychologist or therapist shows why we must empower parents and lighthouse figures to be the supportive, guiding presence that our teens need.

Figures for lighthouses in our teens' lives:

- Grandparent 15.1 per cent
- Teacher 10.9 per cent
- Aunt 9.8 per cent
- A friend's parent 9.4 per cent

- Coach 4.3 per cent
- Uncle 2.1 per cent
- Psychologist/therapist 0.5 per cent and 0.3 per cent respectively

In the survey of teen boys that I conducted for my book *From Boys to Men* back in 2019, the statistics around lighthouses were similarly dispersed but the overall percentages differed.

- Grandparent 26.2 per cent
- Teacher 19.6 per cent
- A friend's parent 9.5 per cent
- Aunt 6.9 per cent
- Uncle 6.9 per cent
- Counsellor 0.3 per cent

Significantly, the number of teen boys who responded they did not have a lighthouse figure in their lives was only 2.3 per cent, compared to the current survey's 29.6 per cent, which includes girls and boys.

Human connectedness is a profound influence in all our lives and it's even more important during the turbulent teen years. Our individualistic material world has made it very difficult for adolescents to find their true selves or their authentic identity because they have so many distractions overloading them. Having stable, charismatic adult mentors can make the difference between thriving and flourishing, or struggling and failing.

- My mum and dad are really helpful and they always talk to me to make sure I am not putting too much pressure on myself. They remind me that no one is going to be angry if I don't do really well and, in the end, make me realise I am getting worried over nothing.
- Reassured me that I have their love and support.
- Only my favourite teacher was able to alleviate some of my concerns, encouraging me to focus on myself.

- My mum was great. She stayed with me in my bed, got me medicine for my aches, made sure I was comfortable, and made a really nice dinner with my dad. He helped too, but by buying donuts and ice cream ♥ they understand that I'm trying so they support me as much as they can, and they do a great job at it.
- They reinforced that I am a good-hearted person that will go out of their way to help others and they explained that reaching out and going as far as I possibly can for some people is a waste of my energy because I will never have it reciprocated back from these people. I need to choose my people and surround myself with givers not takers.

Qualities of a lighthouse figure

1. Have knowledge and understanding of the true nature of the child to adult journey

It is important to be able to share with teens some of the possible reasons for their moments of angst, confusion and emotional turmoil. It is important to reassure them that their brain is 'under construction' and that there are many other invisible changes happening that can impact their stress levels. It is important to tell them that their past is just a story, and it doesn't have to be the story for the rest of their life. Be careful not to stay too attached to sharing your story, because that, too, is over.

2. Have the courage to care

Sometimes standing beside a troubled teen can be hard work – it may test you, and what you believe. Being able to care when they are walking on the dark side of life is challenging, and yet it's often the only reason they find their way back into the light. One of the most common things I used to hear in my counselling room from teens who were struggling was 'no one really cares about me'.

This is a story I've told before in *From Boys to Men*, but it's so powerful I want to tell it again. A farmer approached me after a seminar one night and thanked me for helping him realise something important. He told me that many years ago a neighbouring father died suddenly, leaving behind a wife and three children – two girls and a 10-year-old boy. At times he would take the boy on long truck trips to Perth where they listened to whatever sport was on – cricket or football. They would eat junk food and chocolate, drink soft drink, and fart and burp like young boys. The farmer would also take him to local sporting events, and sometimes just take him for a ride on the quad bikes. He never mentioned the boy's dad or asked how he was coping, and for years, he said, he felt he had not done enough. When the boy left went to university he would still call occasionally and visit. He would throw a swag on the floor, stay a few days and ride the quad bikes or drive the trucks. Then he would leave again. After the seminar, the farmer finally realised he had been a lighthouse in this boy's life, and the fact the young man came 'home' occasionally just to spend time with someone who had cared meant the world to him. How important was that relationship in that boy's life? I'd say lifesaving! It's often not the big stuff, but the small stuff that can make a difference.

3. Be trustworthy and respectful

We must never lie, deceive or pretend to the adolescents in our lives. They need a safe adult ally, not a best friend. Teens can and will break trust – sometimes more than once – and until they understand the value of trust, they will test it and seek it out because, deep down, they know it's worth having. A 13-year-old boy was transferred into my class once because his relationship with his teacher had become destructive. I was warned about how terrible he was. On his second day in my class, I asked him to take a plastic bag of excursion money to the front office. Remember the days when we had real cash money for excursions? He looked at me a bit strangely as he left the room. When the bell went for recess, he stayed behind and shuffled to my desk and asked, 'Hey Miss, how come you asked me to take that money to the office?' I replied that I thought he had the face of a person whom I could trust. He mused for a moment and murmured, 'Trust. Is that what trust means? Hey, it feels good, doesn't it?' And with that, he left the room. I never had any problems with that student, and he began looking for other ways to be valued and trusted. This is an example of realising that until we can embody values and virtues, we really are just talking words.

Trust is important in adolescent–adult relationships because a high level of trust tends to bring out the best in adolescents. When they feel they have the trust of significant adults like parents and their lighthouses, teens are more likely to communicate openly and honestly, as well as to stick to rules and parental expectations. Research has shown that teenagers who feel they are trusted are less likely to engage in high-risk or delinquent behaviours.

Ways to develop trust with teens

- Share – share personal events and interests
- Be available to listen – keep in touch
- Vulnerability – acknowledge that to err is human
- Loyalty – stay committed to goals and visions
- Accepting others – accept the unique qualities and behaviours of others
- Involving others – ask others for input or decision-making
- Valuing – be willing to exchange ideas and ideals with others
- Awareness – be sensitive to the needs of others
- Communicating – be clear in your communication, both oral and written
- Openness – be willing to explore new experiences
- Honesty – be willing to share the truth
- Shared positive vision – be willing to dream
- Be accepting and non-judgemental – be aware that adolescents can be sensitive to criticism
- Only give advice when asked – show respect for the young person's ability to make good decisions.

4. Give hope and encouragement

These are much more powerful tools than giving endless praise. It is very helpful if lighthouses and parents help teens imagine a preferred way of being or doing, because they often get stuck in negative patterns of self-fulfilling prophecies. If we keep telling ourselves that we are dumb and useless, or ugly and no one likes us, we are certainly creating a reality that supports that. Negative mindsets are difficult for everyone, however, they are especially difficult for teens. Directing adolescents, both consciously and unconsciously, towards a more positive, solution-focused way of seeing themselves can have a dramatic impact on them. The simple act of telling them that in their twenties their brain will function so much better and the fogginess will lift gives them hope to know that the path ahead will be easier.

Also, we can educate them that failure and setbacks are a normal part of life and that once something is learned from the experience, we can move on. Rather than seeing such moments as signs they are incapable, we can help them realise that they are actually significant opportunities for growth. No, really, we can.

5. Build connectedness through genuine acceptance

This requirement is essential in being a lighthouse. It is especially important when we are working with teens from a culture different to our own, or those with additional challenges, especially those who have experienced trauma or our neurodivergent teens. It's even more important when you're supporting a teen who's committed a crime, is homeless, is in the juvenile justice system, or is experiencing problems with addictive patterns of behaviour. Being non-judgemental and accepting helps teens feel safe, and it can help them embrace diversity rather than feel threatened by it. When we withhold love and affection because they are not meeting our expectations of how we think they should be, we invalidate them on a deep level.

When we can accept them in their darkness, they often feel safer because they tend to hate themselves and believe there is no hope left for them.

If we still like them at their worst, then they often start liking themselves, and the pattern of negative thought can be broken.

WHAT HAVE YOU FOUND MOST CHALLENGING AS A TEEN?

That adults (parents) have forgotten what it's like to be a teenager and also that they think they understand everything you are going through. It's so different being a teenager now than it was 20–30 years ago, especially with things like COVID and social media, and a lot of adults (not all but a lot of them) have forgotten what it was like to be teenagers and therefore judge or punish you for just being a young person. We need to learn to make mistakes and if we aren't given the space to do that we will never learn.

6. Encourage mastery and teach life skills

Every adult on our planet should, in some way, mentor or guide teens to develop life skills and competencies that teach them to manage independently. Whether it's understanding simple protocols like not using someone else's towel or more complex tasks like checking your car's tyre pressure or knowing what to expect at a rental inspection, they need guidance. I know a lot of teens assume they can learn everything from YouTube these days, but there are so many skills that we can teach them incidentally, and there's nothing like learning face to face. On my website, I have a long list of recommended life skills I believe adolescents need before they leave home, so check it out if you need some inspiration.

7. Help adolescents manage big, ugly emotional states

There will be times when lighthouses have to help angry, frightened teens calm down because they cannot do it themselves. If we help them understand where some of their emotional intensity is coming from, it can help them develop emotional maturity and life-long coping skills. Most of all, they need human connectedness and to know that people care. Supporting adolescents through their emotional upheavals can prevent further adversity. Being an emotional coach is part of a lighthouse's invisible role and can help a young person navigate the myriad emotional challenges they face. Loving, caring relationships have a huge impact on the emotional stability of adolescents at home, school, and in sport and social activities. A sense of belonging feeds positive brain chemicals that help keep adolescents feeling optimistic and emotionally stable. Activities within the home, school or community that build inclusivity will support calmer, more compassionate and happier environments for young people. This is why connectedness is a vital protective factor in resilience regardless of a person's age.

When connectedness is combined with genuine compassion, concern, kindness, acceptance and understanding, there is a much higher possibility of an individual healing from adolescent patterns of aggressive or angry behaviour. Lighthouses help this healing process for young people.

Anything that can help teens diffuse or reduce their big, ugly emotional states may help prevent them from getting into serious problems – such as alcohol or drug abuse, aggressive behaviour, self-harm and patterns of self-destructive choices. Remember the prefrontal lobe supporting this emotional maturity does not generally develop until the mid to late twenties, so keep this in mind and act accordingly.

8. Practise caring, empowering communication

Being able to communicate in a caring way that builds a teen's sense of personal empowerment is a key aspect of lighthouses. *Never shame, blame, criticise, belittle or crush adolescents.* Lighthouses have a gift of communicating that builds connectedness and trust. There is more information on how to communicate effectively in the next chapter.

9. Give guidance when asked

Lighthouses may want to give advice or tell teens what they should be doing, however, it's best to wait until asked. Unsolicited advice is seldom effective. Lighthouses listen, reassure and give seeds of potential solutions through telling stories and asking great questions that make a teen think and ponder. It is always more respectful to ask, 'Are you open to having me give you some feedback?' than give unsolicited advice. If they say no, respect that and say no more, no matter how tempting it may be.

10. Strengthen the spirit

We can build a teen's connection to their inner world and their inner compass, as well as a deep connectedness beyond their physical self, by helping to strengthen their spirit.

In my book, *Nurturing Kids' Hearts and Souls*, I wrote about a 15-year-old who shared a story in one of my classes about an intriguing sense of 'knowing'. One day, while she was at home in her room, her father was on his tractor down in the paddock. She became aware of feeling uncomfortable and uneasy. When she went out into the garden, her unease became stronger. She clearly remembered thinking, *Something's happened to Dad*, and headed off down the paddock as quickly as she could. She soon discovered that her dad was injured and ran back home to arrange help. She returned to her dad's side and waited until help arrived. Uncanny, yet true. From that point on in her life, she would believe that she had a guardian who kept watch over her.

> 'Each of us has a wise part within, an intuitive part that knows what is best for us. Contacting, listening to, and trusting that inner authority are important skills. They are invaluable when life presents us with problems whose answers are not found in the back of the book.'
>
> Chick Moorman, *The Parent Talk System*

. . . or I would add on TikTok or YouTube! I have been wondering if the increased levels of poor mental health we're seeing are linked to significant social changes. The focus on 'me' rather than 'we', the influence of technology, the absence of time in nature, the shortening and stealing of childhood in the name of education and the massive global uncertainties from the pandemic, wars and natural disasters. All of this impacts the growth and nurturing of the inner world for everyone – the human spirit, often called the soul. In his book, *Care of the Soul,* Thomas Moore describes the symptoms of loss of soul as:

- emptiness
- meaninglessness
- vague depression
- disillusionment about marriage, family and relationships, and life in general
- a loss of values
- yearning for personal fulfillment
- a hunger for spirituality.

This sounds very familiar to those who work with teens who have lost their spark. The 21st-century world is driven enormously by egocentricity, consumerism, competition and a hardening of the human heart. It can be hard to nurture the human spirit among such pressures and many teens are disillusioned and feeling helpless as they face an uncertain future. They are deeply concerned about climate change, war and increasing cruelty and violence.

Author, teacher and founder of the Passageworks Institute Rachael Kessler shared seven gateways that can enable our teens (in fact, all grown-ups) to grow whole and healthy.

1. The yearning for deep connection
2. The longing for silence and solitude
3. The search for meaning and purpose
4. The hunger for joy and delight
5. The creative drive
6. The urge for transcendence
7. The need for initiation.

Rachael Kessler, *The Soul of Education*

My concern is that many teens are feeling profoundly lost as these gateways become harder to find our world. There is a serious hunger for the substance of each gateway, but without the adult world providing these opportunities with consistency, teens are seeking it for themselves. Many seek rituals or rites of passage, and when they are unavailable, teens will take to body piercings, tattoos and other forms of markings.

Deep connection is one of the best ways to strengthen the spirit, whether it's connecting to ourselves, others, community, family history, nature or a greater spiritual power.

Strengthening the spirit is an important role of lighthouses. Teens who have strong spirits have a protective mechanism that is difficult to measure, yet very clear when absent. Spiritual intelligence that parents and lighthouses can develop with children and adolescents includes:

- Wonder
- Respect and reverence
- Awe
- Relational spirituality
- Lightness and laughter
- Contemplation
- Calmness, stillness and quiet
- Tenderness and gratitude
- Simplicity
- Listening with the heart.

The positive impact of a lighthouse

It is important to keep in mind that the major role of a lighthouse figure is to walk beside our teens, with no need to rescue them or become responsible for them. Being heard and being seen are two fundamental needs of every human, however, these are particularly powerful in this confusing window of life. If they are unable to talk to their parents and do not have access to a counsellor, a lighthouse figure can be incredibly, deceptively powerful.

Advice from the voices in the survey . . .

- If you or anyone you know is struggling, give them space and time but also be there to talk and distract their minds off the bad things.
- It's incredibly important to find someone who you're comfortable with seeing you in any state, even if that means they might see you cry.
- It's so important to be open and honest about how you're feeling, and not just have a surface-level conversation. Find yourself a good GP who you trust and share with them how you're feeling. They generally have a network of local & preferred contacts in mental health that they can refer you to if needed. ALWAYS have at least one person you can confide in. There's nothing 'brave' about doing things by yourself and it is completely encouraged to seek help if you are struggling.
- If you're feeling low, please talk to someone. I know it's extremely difficult and you probably struggle like me but take each day at a time. Baby steps that's all that matters. If you try, then you can say you've tried your best. If you know someone else who is feeling low, don't overcrowd them with questions, just assure them that you're there for them if needed and that they'll be okay in time.

Lighthouses have to be able to develop a trusting, safe relationship that allows them to sow seeds of potential and shine a light on the invisible sign that hangs around every teen's neck:

When someone shines a light on that invisible sign of 'make me feel I matter' that hangs around every teen's neck, we recognise the goodness hiding within them just waiting to be found and shared.

Because so many of our teens struggle with self-worth and self-esteem and they feel invisible, unheard or that they just don't matter, having someone make them feel they matter can have a deceptively profound impact on them. This started to dawn on me when I noticed that some mornings as I headed from the staff car park to the English office, a student or two would be leaning on the brick wall that was on my route, seeking connection with me as I wandered by. These were students I had approached separately the previous day at lunch. They were not in any of my classes, but I had noticed how lonely they looked eating lunch by themselves. Recognising the impact of these little interactions, I started seeking out the students who sat alone, who had obvious physical challenges or who appeared to be avoiding their mainstream peer groups. I learned their names and made sure I smiled when I saw them, and I even acknowledged them in the street. It didn't take long before the row of students who greeted me every morning grew. The simple act of being noticed made these students feel better. It may not have seemed like a big thing in the scheme of the curriculum, but it was huge for the students. This is an example of how we can all pause and offer such a small gesture of connection to our teens, even if they don't respond initially.

Here is a beautiful letter that shows the importance of these small gestures.

Hiya

You might not remember me, but I certainly remember you. I was a student of yours some decades ago.

I have for many years, wanted to thank you for making my final few months of high school bearable. I don't know what would have become of me if you hadn't stuck up for me one day in class. I was the one who used to have a chorus of barking dogs whenever I entered the room, was constantly teased, and basically, had my self-esteem crushed at quite an early age.

I endured years of bullying from those in my school, and in my class especially. I still remember their names, all of them, and to this day am still haunted by the years of humiliation.

I wanted to let you know how much I appreciated what you did for me all those years ago. It was probably something quite insignificant to you in the scheme of things, but to me, it was like a life raft.

I think I probably would have taken my life at the tender age of 15 if it hadn't been for you Maggie.

I've wanted to thank you for many, many years, and now I have. Thank you!!

During my years of teaching, I realised there was more being learned in my classroom than the English lesson I was giving. I decided early in my career to make it easy for those who struggled with school, especially those who came to class without their files, paper or pencil cases because their home lives were difficult. Instead of beginning the class with negativity and a punitive focus, I created spare files, paper and a huge pencil case full of pens and pencils that students could use if they came to class unprepared. They didn't need to ask to borrow them, though most did. Creating a relationship based on safety rather than inviting conflict makes such a huge difference to all students, not just those who are struggling with being a teen.

> My thoughts circulating in my head. Just wanting to cry, wanting something to come along and cheer me up. Feeling sad and helpless. When I felt this way, I used to talk to my favourite teacher who really helped me.

Start being a lighthouse

My challenge to you is to step forward and be there as a guiding force of light in the lives of today's teens. Just choose one – a niece, a nephew, a neighbour or a teen you coach. The impact you can have on that one individual can be the difference between them thriving and just surviving. Sowing seeds of hope with a good dose of compassion and kindness can literally save a life.

One way to start is by giving a teen in your life a version of the letter on the next page, which I've used before with success. Of course, you can't force a teen to start seeing you as a lighthouse, but even reaching out to let them know you're available can make a difference.

Dear teen

I can remember being your age and finding life a bit tricky at times. Our world has become a little less kind, more unpredictable, more chaotic and in many ways less caring. To be honest, it must seem a lot darker for many young people.

I want to offer myself as a safe base should you ever need one. I will lean in for you when you need some support and that support will be non-judgemental and full of compassion with no lectures or unheeded advice. I will be a lighthouse for you, shining a light into the darkness and I will be a positive, reliable presence for you.

Side by side we can find a way to overcome obstacles and challenges. In good times, we can do fun stuff together that may include ice cream or chocolate – or both.

From your lighthouse

PS My contact details are attached.

6

The secrets of effective communication with teens

Let's start with the obvious; these are ineffective ways of communicating with anyone, especially teens:

- Lecturing
- Nagging
- Poor timing
- Arguing
- Unkindness
- Disrespect
- Shouting
- Sarcasm
- Criticism
- Guilt games
- Any physical abuse and shaming
- Ignoring them or freezing them out
- Using 'always', 'never', 'it's easy!', or 'it's going to be hard,' as a predictor.

All these forms of communication do is damage the relationship and create tension and resentment, which simply increase a teen's need to ignore you and rebel against you. The more connected any child is to their significant caregiver, the more likely they will respond to your guidance. Teens can be incredibly sensitive to negativity, especially from their parents. I will never forget a 14-year-old boy I was teaching who looked quite distressed one afternoon. I chatted to him after class, and he admitted that he was planning to end his life that day. He said his mum had been disappointed with his school report that went home the previous week. She had been freezing him out ever since, and he thought she had completely stopped loving him. He told me he would prefer to die than live without his mum's love. What a poignant reminder of the impact we have on our teens.

How teens can interpret an adult's communication style

Adult communication	Teen interpretation
Threaten	I don't matter
Command	I'm inadequate
Preach	You don't like me
Advice	You invalidate me
Lecture	I can't do anything right
Shout	I am frightened
Criticism	I am useless and incapable
Shame	I am bad and hopeless
Nag	You disrespect me
Smother	I am trapped
Withhold love	You make my world unsafe
Disconnect	There's no one I can trust
You solve my problems	You crush my search for solutions
You tell me what I am feeling	You invalidate me and my feelings
Be unavailable	I am invisible and unlovable

If there is one thing I have learned in all my experience, it is that communication that is respectful and effective impacts every area of a human's life. Not only have I completed a diploma in counselling, studied psychology at university, and trained in bereavement support, I've also studied many different modalities of education to improve my capacity to communicate. Often, people think communication is just about what comes out of our mouths. We could not be more wrong.

Good communication can lead to warm relationships, emotional and relational safety, cooperation and feelings of self-worth. Poor communication can do the opposite and cause kids and teens to turn off and away from adults. Poor communication can cause constant conflict and bickering, a profound sense of disconnectedness and make kids feel they don't matter and even lead to feelings of deep worthlessness.

Communication often seems to be done without thinking. It often happens spontaneously and is largely an unconscious act driven by a need for connection with others. It's mainly driven by the experiences we have had early in life and the narrative we have made up about that. Often, we assume that the words that come out our mouths will obviously be understood by the person we're speaking to and the meaning we had behind the words will be clear! Again, we could not be more wrong. Spoken words and the meaning of spoken words are two very different things, and then the interpretation by others is another thing again, and that's with mature grown-ups. Communicating with the teen who has a cracked-windscreen view of the world means things can get confusing.

Next time you're having a conversation with a really good friend or a respected workmate, I want you to take notice of the way that you speak to them. Then next time you're speaking to your teen, observe and reflect on the way you communicate with them. Following my training in communication, I chose to speak the same way to everyone I came in contact with in my life – the students I taught, the couples whose weddings I was going to officiate, my neighbours, my good bloke, my adult sons, strangers on the train and to people I have just met. I chose to speak with children the same way and when I was blessed with grandchildren, I chose to speak to them the same way once they became toddlers. I realised many years ago that every single human, regardless of age, culture, or perceived difference, should be spoken to respectfully, even if they don't deserve it. I have worked in maximum-security prisons and when I communicated that way with the men I met there, some mentioned they had never been spoken to that way before. I may be a little weird, but I do believe there is essential goodness hiding deep inside every human. Sometimes it gets crushed by life, by cruelty, by abuse or by manipulation.

Back to the art of communication, we can assume that the only way we communicate is through words. Again, we could not be more wrong. Neurolinguistic programming (NLP) is a modality aimed at improving the way we communicate and respond to others. NLP suggests that the art of communication is around:

7 per cent words
55 per cent physiology
38 per cent tonality.

Physiology matters

We are constantly communicating with or without words. If you either have an innate or learned ability to create a warm, safe physical presence, others notice. This is extremely important for those who live or work with tweens and teens. Physiology is how we stand, how we move, and how we project ourselves in the company of others. If a parent has their hands on the hips while standing upright and straight, that is a warning sign that things could be difficult. If, instead, they are leaning on a kitchen bench over a cuppa or sitting comfortably on a couch, they are sending signals that things are okay. I learned early on in my teaching career that a smile costs nothing from me, however, it can be a powerful connector for kids and teens, especially those who come from difficult homes where there are few smiles. Say hello, wish people a good day, and check in with a quick 'How are you doing today?' Even if it is a rhetorical question, it is a bid for positive connection.

I would argue that our digital natives are starving for real connection with real humans, in real time. If you want to improve your communication skills, start here first. Individuals who are non-verbal still communicate with those around them. Many of their loved ones and carers have told me they have become intuitive communicators with those who are unable to use words. How beautiful is that?

Eye contact is another form of physiological connection. Having eye contact with someone we are communicating with can be a positive thing if they are comfortable with it. Many boys and some cultures find eye contact can be threatening. I learned in my classrooms that sometimes students were paying attention and listening to me, even if they were doodling on a piece of paper while looking out the window. Be mindful to respect your teen's preference around eye contact.

Tonality matters

According to NLP, the second biggest influence on effective communication is tonality. I would argue that parents, educators and lighthouses who are able to maintain a non-threatening tone and respectfully communicate in quiet tones will tend to have less serious conflict with their teens. Then, when something very serious comes along, a loud voice is really taken notice of and the teen realises they may have stepped over some line in the sand. If there are a lot of raised voices or harsh tones, teens will learn to zone out in order to reduce the stress that it is causing them, and any serious message may be lost. When parents are stressed, the tone of voice will display a very different tone to when they are feeling more grounded and calmer. Volume of voice also matters, obviously.

Intention matters

When we communicate with people, we do have an intention in that act. Sometimes we are having a conversation to build meaningful connection and we might be sharing what has happened in our day. Other times, we communicate because we are seeking to have a need met – like we need to have the dishwasher unpacked, or we are seeking to have something clarified, like what our teen might prefer for dinner. Other times we are seeking information. Many parents, possibly due to their own childhoods, have intentions of wanting their kids and teens to do as they are told without question.

> To be an effective communicator, it can be really helpful to reflect on what your real intention is, in any conversation you have with your teen.

Essentially, it is like they are tuned into a different radio channel to you and to be able to understand each other, you need to be on the same channel. If you need to have a conversation with your teen that's going to be potentially awkward or difficult, *plan the what, the when and the how.*

Presence matters

Given the busyness of life and the many things that parents have to focus on and remember, it can be difficult to remember to be present when having an opportunity to communicate with your teen. A good habit to develop is to ensure that your phone is out of sight when you want to be present to your child of any age. Having alerts turned off on your phone is also really helpful, because as soon as a sound is heard from a phone, a teen will know that you are distracted and not fully present. Before the arrival of smartphones, an easy time for parents to connect was when a child got home from school. Making a snack in the kitchen, chatting casually about their day without anyone focused on the phone is probably something the previous generation didn't appreciate until it was gone. Having said that, being overly enthusiastic and overly attentive should be avoided as well, because your teen will smell a rat and know that there's something going on!

Matching your teen's physiology can be a helpful way of connecting. If they are leaning over the kitchen bench or sitting on the couch, doing the same is apparently a quick way of establishing rapport. Side-by-side is considered non-confronting and having a relaxed posture can also send silent signals that things are okay. This is why I often say chatting in the car or while walking the dog together can be especially effective.

Conversation starters matter – see them as door-openers

- 'Now that's interesting.'
- 'I see.'
- 'Tell me more.'
- 'Oh' or 'Ah' (Be careful on tone!!)
- 'Say that again. I want to be sure I understand you.'
- 'No kidding!'
- 'How about that!'
- 'Really?'
- 'WTH?'
- 'Aha . . .'
- 'I am a bit curious . . .'

Using 'I' statements matters

An important shift in our communication is so simple, and it is the shifting of using 'you' statements, to 'I' statements. Imagine your teen has left their backpack in the hallway, half unpacked with football boots strewn across the entrance.

You can say: 'You always leave your mess lying everywhere instead of packing it away. Someone could easily fall over it and get hurt.'

Or you could say: 'I feel so frustrated when I see that mess lying everywhere instead of you packing it away because I worry that somebody could easily fall over it and get hurt.'

'You' statements tend to trigger blame, which tends to make our teens become defensive and that will decrease the chances that they may hear what your message was in the first place.

Keep in mind this sentence structure:

I feel . . . . when . . . . because . . .

It is quite a simple strategy, and yet deceptively effective when communicating with anyone. Go on and give it a go!

Another simple tip that can help us address our concerns can be to ask fewer direct questions aimed at them. For example, if you are worried that your teen is stressing about upcoming exams – rather than ask them directly, start by asking if any of their friends are stressing about the exams. In my experience, teens are more concerned about their friends' wellbeing than their own. When they are asked to reflect on their friends' stress levels, it often opens their own mind to considering their own stress levels, however, without being asked directly.

Being trustworthy matters

Healthy, supportive relationships are built on trust. Trust is the belief in someone or something's ability, strength, truth or reliability. As a parent, your teen needs to know that you will always have their back – that they can trust that you can still love them even when they muck up and make big mistakes.

One of the biggest areas that breaks teens' ability to trust their parents is when the parents break the teen's confidence and share personal information or stories with others without their permission. This can even be stories of success – when they have won an award. There are many teens who have felt betrayed by their parents when they discovered how much of their personal childhood experiences have been shared online. Please check before you share anything to ensure you don't break the bond of trust that you have with your teen. Consent is a simple and very important thing, and asking permission from teens about things like using their photos models to them that they should also seek consent from others. The only time adults can break confidence is when a teen expresses suicidal ideation or an intention to hurt themselves or someone else, at which point duty of care must override confidentiality, and a professional must be informed immediately.

Building trust with us is also good for our teen's relationships with others. A *Growing Up in Australia* research snapshot into intimate partner violence between 18–19-year-olds showed that 'high trust and good communication with parents during adolescence reduce the risk of later emotional abuse victimisation by 39 per cent and sexual abuse victimisation by 77 per cent'.

Many of our teens can be quite trustworthy. However, there can be times when they make choices that will break the trust their parents have in them, which is developmentally understandable. One example might be, if you have vodka in a cupboard in your home that you have told your teen never to touch, they will most likely be able to do that when they are just with family. But imagine if a group of their friends are in the home, and the parents are not. One of the friends suggests that they drink the vodka in the vodka bottle and replace it with water and all the friends agree; it will be extremely difficult for your teen to say no. I have suggested putting a lock on the alcoholic-beverage cupboard until your teens are much older and can be relied on to make better decisions. The hunger to belong with their own age group is extremely powerful and the ability to make great decisions in the heat of the moments is questionable. There is also the factor of risk, which they are also wired to challenge themselves with.

> 'Trust is one of the most powerful forms of motivation and inspiration. People want to be trusted. They respond to trust. They thrive on trust. Whatever our situation, we need to get good at establishing, extending, and restoring trust – not as a manipulative technique, but as the most effective way of relating to and working with others and the most effective way of getting results.'
>
> Stephen Covey, *The Speed of Trust*

Being empathetic matters

Hopefully by now you would have come to understand that it is way more difficult to be a teen today than when you were one. Life is more turbulent and uncertain, and there are even more pressures on our emerging adults that cause anxiety and stress. To have genuine empathy, imagine putting yourself in your teen's position – navigating a world with an uncertain future, with all the developmental challenges, especially with an immature brain.

You can say helpful things like:

- 'Gee I think things are tougher for you than they were for me.'
- 'I can see why you're so angry; I would be too if that happened to me.'
- 'How did you feel about that? Yeah, I think I would have felt like that too.'
- 'The lead up to big exams can be really stressful – I remember that. Tell me how I can help?'

The feedback sandwich matters, and it can help

A classroom experiment showed that when giving feedback regarding a class assessment, if the teacher just began with what was wrong with the task, and then provided three key points to improve, the results on a repeated similar assessment did not change.

However, if the teacher began with a positive comment such as 'Everyone did really well and I'm really happy,' and then proceeded to give the three key points to improve, the results from the repeated assessment were significantly improved.

Essentially, when we start our communication with a negative, especially a criticism, our brain fixates on that thing to protect us and we don't hear the suggestions for improvement. The same goes for our kids. They are so wired to avoid negative communication from their parents, especially if it's been happening frequently, that they miss our wonderful constructive suggestions for improvement. So, the simple rule is to pretend the communication exchange is a sandwich. The top of the sandwich is something positive and affirming, such as 'You know I love your strong spirit and your cheeky grin'. The filling of the sandwich is where we give them the concern or the worry that we have: 'I am concerned with how you've been treating your sister as it's unkind and unfair and I would like you to try to be more respectful.' And then, we create the bottom of the sandwich with another positive message, 'Remember, I love you to the moon and back!' As your teen gets older, they will know exactly what you are doing – however, they still know why you are doing it, and that is for a good reason!

Life-affirming language matters

Teens tend to use life-negating language partly because it's cool to speak negatively or monosyllabically. We can help upgrade the language by offering reminders as lovingly and as gently as possible. It was something I needed to do in my classrooms, and I was pretty surprised at how their language change lifted their moods as well as their grades. It makes perfect sense that if they keep repeating the terms – 'I can't, I dunno, nup, whatever, it doesn't matter, who cares?' – then their unconscious mind is hearing clear directions to sabotage effort and success. Remember, the unconscious is constantly listening for clues as to what an individual wants, and if all it hears is negativity, then that's what it delivers. My students made large posters to have up in the classroom to remind them of how to upgrade their language and there were times I would ask if they wanted to upgrade their language.

Examples of life-affirming language:

- I choose – Expression of our will and identity moving towards our outcome.
- I can – Expression of our identity, will and potential in choosing our outcome.

- I have – Bring our desired state to now; collapses time from the future to the present.
- I am – Expression of identity, claiming the emotional state of our desire fulfilled.
- I create – Expression of identity, claiming our divine right as co-creators.
- I will – Expression of intention for the future.
- My highest choice – Leaves our highest possibility as a high priority.

I created a mantra for a group of students who were struggling with feeling confident and doing a performance in front of parents. The mantra was – **I am, I can, I will.** I gathered the students together before they went out on stage, and we repeated the mantra over and over again, gradually louder and louder, and it shifted their state from nervous sabotage to absolute confidence. They did a brilliant job and were really proud of themselves. This same mantra can work for grown-ups as well when we are struggling with our confidence.

Requesting rather than commanding or demanding matters

Absolutely no one likes being told what to do by anyone, not even toddlers! Obviously, parents have to ask their teens to do things and sometimes these are things that they would prefer not to do, such as chores. When we request, while also paying respect to their need for autonomy, we may be surprised by the response.

'David, you need to unpack the dishwasher now.'

Compared to:

'David, it is your turn to unpack the dishwasher. Would you like to do it now or just before dinner?'

The key difference is the second request is a request, not a command, and it respects David's need for autonomy. He can choose when to follow the request that has been asked of him. If David forgets, a gentle reminder will tend to be successful, because his unconscious mind is already aware that he has chosen to do the dishwasher closer to dinner.

Another example could be:

'Amy, you need to put your school clothes in the wash if you want them clean by tomorrow.'

Compared to:

'Amy, I just noticed that your dirty school clothes that you will need tomorrow are not in the laundry yet. Would you like to put them there now or after you finish your homework?'

Positive noticing with acknowledgement and validation matters

Even though we live in a culture of overpraising and over-rewarding, and it can be so easy to do that ad nauseam, moments of positive noticing with acknowledgement and validation are important. It can be so easy with teens to just notice everything they're doing wrong, or what they are forgetting rather than what they're doing right. So, it's important to spend some time positively noticing such as:

- 'Thanks, David, for putting your dishes in the dishwasher after dinner.'
- 'Amy, I noticed your clothes were in the laundry ready to be washed without me needing to ask you – thanks.'
- 'I really appreciated that you put the cereal back into the pantry after you had breakfast this morning.'
- 'Hey guys, I know it can be hard getting out of the house in the mornings, but I reckon we did a great job this morning.'
- 'I'm not sure which one of you fed the dog this morning, but thanks as I got a little bit sidetracked getting ready to leave.'
- 'David, I heard you encouraging your mate Steve on the phone and reassuring him that you would help him with his history revision. Well done you.'

Reflect back something positive that they say or, very importantly, validate their feelings by saying things like:

- 'Well done for being so honest.'
- 'That must have made you feel great!'
- 'That must have been challenging and yet you kept going!'
- 'Heck, that must have surprised you?'
- 'End of term can be pretty tiring for everyone, and I reckon you guys are doing okay this term – not long now till the holidays!'

Avoiding blame matters, as does encouraging cooperation

Teens are especially susceptible to feeling criticised or blamed and so upgrading our adult language to avoid triggering them and to avoid the instant push back or defensive attitude can really make a difference.

- 'Someone has left a wet towel on the bathroom floor. Please make sure you hang it up in future.' (Avoid any blame games because this message reinforces to everyone to hang up their towel – including parents.)
- 'Who left the milk out on the bench all day?' could be 'Whoever left the milk out on the bench accidentally today, can they check they don't do it again? Please?'
- 'You two seem to have a conflict going on today. Are you able to sort it out okay, or do you need my help?'
- 'We seem to be disagreeing about this and I wonder how might we resolve this?'
- 'What do you think needs to happen now?'
- 'Sounds like you have a problem.'
- 'How can we work together to get the best outcome here?'
- 'Dad needs someone to help with mowing the lawn this weekend. He will leave it until after he has done the sports run on Saturday morning. Any takers?'

- 'If you are unable to do one of your chores, and you can't swap it, let us know so we can sort it.'
- 'Remember, everyone is responsible for changing the toilet roll when it is finished.'
- 'If you drink the last of the milk after school, please let Mum or Dad know before we get ready for bed or even better, text us to pick it up on our way home from work.'
- 'We are all part of a team around here and each of us helps this home run smoothly.'
- 'May I offer a suggestion that may help?'
- 'I am thinking we need to have a chat about what holiday choices we have for the coming holidays. Let's do that this week sometime.'
- 'Steve, while I'm making your toasted sandwich, will you please take the bin out for me?'
- 'Pip, when you've finished feeding the dog, will you come over here for a minute and help me get dessert ready, please?'
- Say, 'What works for you after school tomorrow?' rather than, 'What are you doing tomorrow?' (This shows there needs to be a cooperative approach to family dynamics – some give and take.)

Avoiding arguments matters

Remember that being able to argue respectfully requires a mature prefrontal cortex to be able to weigh up different opinions and hear and comprehend each other's point of view. Teens are not very good at arguing in this way, however, they are really good at winding you up in an argument. They are often primed for a fiery debate when they first get home from school or after they have spoken to one of their friends about something they really want to do.

Let's pretend your teen has come home and asked, 'Can I go to the party with 200 teens in a paddock?' They are so ready to argue why they need to be there. My suggestion is to pause, listen carefully and then say either 'I will chat to Mum' or 'I will give it some thought and get back to you after dinner'. Then about 9 pm knock quietly on their door, pause (always pause for around 20 seconds after knocking on teen's door!), open the door a little and say gently, 'Love, [or any term of endearment that works] – the answer to the question about the party – the answer is no.' Quietly close the door and leave.

Another possible strategy around being asked about a party request that worries you for lots of reasons is to suggest an alternative. 'I am a bit uncomfortable about this party – how about you choose 10 friends and have a sleepover with Netflix and pizzas here, or let's go camping instead?'

Arguments can get hot quite quickly. It is okay to put your hand up and suggest, 'I can see you're really fired up about this/you're upset about this/you are really angry about this . . . Can we pause now and chat about it later when we both feel calmer?'

Today's teens are getting quite sophisticated in their arguments. A friend of mine had a teenage daughter who did a PowerPoint on the reasons why she should be able to choose her own make-up and hairstyle despite the school rules!

In her excellent book, *Untangled: guiding teenage girls through the seven transitions into adulthood*, Dr Lisa Damour suggests that parents of girls would have discovered at some point that their teenage daughter has developed an allergy to being asked questions. I think the same can be said for many teen boys as well. Despite this tendency, parents can refine their questioning technique to be less 'annoying' to their teen. Dr Damour recommends reminding teen girls to communicate politely rather than respectfully, and she does suggest that you call your daughter on her impolite way of responding. There is no question that teen girls can be surprisingly mean especially towards their mothers.

If your teen needs to vent or express big feelings, I suggest you pause and say, 'Are you just wanting to vent, or are you hoping I can help you with this?' Then pause afterwards, offer them a gesture of care – a Milo, cup of tea, a hug, a tissue – and stay present without contributing anything unless requested.

Allowing for autonomous problem-solving

The more opportunities that our teens have to solve their own problems, the better they get at problem-solving. I encourage all parents of teens to stop doing their homework, or to stop helping them with major projects because you are not helping them grow and mature. You will not be in the classroom the day they do their final exams.

When they come up against conflict or challenge, there are some excellent ways to communicate that encourage them to work their own way through. Remind them again, over and over, gently and respectfully, that when we make any decision – it will have a consequence. Sometimes, these consequences are exactly what we were hoping for, and sometimes, they are not. When we don't get the outcome we were hoping for, we often have to make another decision. *There is not always just one solution to a challenge.* Being able to assess the decision we made without beating ourselves up if it didn't work is a sign of maturity.

Remember if they share a dilemma that they are having with you, stay present, acknowledge and validate the challenge they have, and then try saying:

- That sounds a bit tricky – have you given it much thought?
- Can you help me understand why this is important to you?
- Maybe check out your choice on the inside – does it feel right?
- What do you think needs to happen now?
- I am curious as to how you are gonna tackle this?
- What's your plan? (Then ask what their plan B is if their original plan does not work out.)
- Why don't you sleep on it, and we can revisit it tomorrow?
- You don't seem to be enjoying that new app on the phone – how is it working for you?
- I believe there is a part of you that knows the answer – just check it out within yourself over the next few days.
- May I offer a suggestion?
- Tell me how I can support you as you work this out.

Let's be honest, even the best parent can't resist the temptation to jump in quick to solve their teen's problem! But one of the reasons why it's important for lighthouses or counsellors to be able to communicate effectively is that it gives teens a better chance at learning to solve problem for themselves in the long run.

Timing matters

As a sweeping generalisation (but one I have found many people agree with), girls tend to be much more efficient communicators from childhood. Not only can they remember much more effectively what has happened during the school day, they are often more likely to want to chat to decompress their day. Yes, there are some boys who do this as well, however, a statistically significant number dislike being interrogated after school even from a loving parent. Given that my lived experience was with four sons, I learned how important timing was when I wanted to have a conversation that mattered. Consider the following points when choosing to have a conversation with your teen.

Times to avoid important parent conversations with tweens/teens:

- When you're upset, especially angry
- In the heat of the moment (when that glitter jar I wrote about in Chapter 3 is all shook up!)
- Before you have all the information or the full story
- At breakfast when kids are often still half asleep
- Right after school
- While they are watching a TV show
- If they are busy on a device, gaming or watching other people gaming on YouTube
- When anyone else is in earshot
- When they are hungry or while they are eating
- When they are tired
- When they are having a growth spurt

- Within hours of a significant misdemeanour
- Within 24 hours of a public misdemeanour
- Within a day of having returned home from a sleepover or a school camp
- On their birthday/special family day
- Just before visitors arrive.

Top tips for good timing and inviting a chat for teens

- Approach them when none of the above is happening.
- Building rapport – a bridge of connection – is incredibly helpful when having conversations with tween and teens. Use terms of endearment, soft physiology, a gentle tone, possibly a gentle ruffle of the hair or stroke on the back. Each teen will have a different way of responding to your bid for connection.
- If it is a serious conversation and not just checking in about what they want for lunch, ask them when a good time for you would be to have a chat – most teens are very sensitive to feeling ambushed.
- Remind them gently just before it is chat time, and possibly check if they want a hot drink or a snack.
- Have a private space around your home to have these serious conversations so that they remain private and no one else can hear what is being said.
- Your opening statement is incredibly important. Remember the power of being curious and not furious, regardless of how serious the conversation may need to be. Beginning sentences with indirect observations can be helpful:
    - o *I was wondering what your thoughts are around preparing for the upcoming exams.*
    - o *I'm a bit curious as to know how your study plans are going for the upcoming exams?*
    - o *I am curious about how your friends are preparing for the upcoming exams?*

The power of the 'what if' conversations

One of the most common mistakes that parents make, especially as their teens head to the 16 plus years, is to keep on lecturing them about what not to do. Take, for example, when your teens are heading out for a night with their friends. So often, we tell them not to drink, smoke or take drugs, and I tend to remind parents what happens when we tell you not to think of a blue elephant!

Our teens are learning all the time, especially as digital teens. A much more effective way of communicating with them is to ask them what they would do in certain scenarios.

For example:

- What would you do if some older gate-crashers turn up at the party you're going to tonight?
- What would you do if you went to text me to come and collect you – as we have arranged – only to find you had lost your phone?
- What would you do if you saw someone leading an inebriated girl into a bedroom or outside?
- What would you do if a fight broke out at the party?
- What would you do if someone collapsed at the party into an alcoholic coma?
- What would you do if one of the boys at the party has decided to do burnouts around the campground where you are all going to be camping?
- What would you do if someone had a serious laceration and was bleeding heavily?
- What would you do if you were offered free pills or tablets that you are told are fun and safe?

What tends to happen is that most teens have got quite good ideas already on what they would do. They are also more open to an adult offering an additional idea.

The power of shared thinking tools

We can help our teens learn how to improve how they think, especially around big topics. We all have different views and opinions and when we can listen or read different perspectives, we can reconsider and review and possibly change our views. When teens get told their views are invalid or, worse still, stupid, they will defend them at all costs! If we allow them to explain their reasons for having those views, we can explore them with respect.

In my endeavours to reconnect students to their authentic sense of self, I was very grateful for Edward De Bono's work. I often used the Plus/Minus/Interesting (PMI) decision-making and critical-thinking tool. This is where, when you are trying to make a difficult decision, you do up a table/list with those three words as headings. You consider the positive, negative and interesting aspects of a situation/scenario in order to make a balanced decision.

A practical example of this could be deciding whether a teen should work longer hours outside of school while doing upper school.

Plus	Minus	Interesting
• They will earn more money and have more financial freedom	• They won't be able to play their favourite sport or they will have to drop a dance class they enjoy • They will drop some study time that may create more stress especially around exams	• They are attracted to one of the permanent workers and want to see what may happen

Another De Bono tool I used a lot was called Other People's View (OPV) thinking strategies. This is where, in assessing a situation, you look at not only your own view but other people's views. Why might they think that? Are they seeing things you're not or different consequences? Who's right if you don't agree? Why do we need to see each other's points of view? Should your decision be based on your own view, or is it important to consider others? It's a great exercise to build empathy and understanding, especially during a time when teen brains are undergoing such massive changes.

In my last years of teaching, I began to weave mindfulness activities as well as thinking and memory strategies into my classrooms. What I discovered was that a calm mind can be a much more effective platform from which to explore interesting topics, form convictions, express oneself and genuinely feel safer within oneself. I used calming visualisations that I created myself (all on my website now) to help students see themselves as they really wanted to be. Every single student was running a video in their mind of who they thought they were in that mindset that had been created earlier in their life.

If elite athletes at the Australian Institute of Sport were using visualisations to become more successful, then I wanted my students to be able to free themselves from negative thought processes and perceptions, and to imagine themselves being happy, confident and capable instead of the opposite.

When you use tools like these in problem-solving at home, they can also help you and your teen to better understand each other.

The power of the parent letter

Given that our boys are often not as competent as our girls at listening to things that may be uncomfortable or being able to remember the whole conversation, I sometimes used the 'mum letter' approach with my boys. If it is a long message with many key points, I found that writing a well-thought-out, longer letter around a serious concern was really beneficial for my sons. I have had many parents tell me they have had the same success and, often, the boys keep the letter and sometimes revisit it.

The parent letter can work for any teen, and it can, of course, be written by Mum or Dad. It's helpful to have a similar structure to the feedback sandwich and it needs to be well thought out without any criticism, accusation or blame. *The intention behind the letter is to help your teen see and reflect on an opportunity for growth, which could help them be a better human.*

In the Appendix, I have included a couple of letters that you can modify, which may be helpful. I have also included two other resources. The first is an outline for a letter to someone special in my life. I have used this several times with families, with incredible success. So often, a teen will think their mum or dad just doesn't love them, doesn't care and that they don't matter at all. When a parent takes the time to write the letter to their teen, it can build a beautiful bridge of reconnection.

The other resource at the back of the book is called the truth letter and it is one that I have had for over 25 years, thanks to Jack Canfield, who was the co-creator of the *Chicken Soup for the Soul* series of books. This process is excellent for anyone who is struggling with a relationship anywhere in their life, as a way of understanding the emotions around a conflict. It is deceptively powerful and often brings a sense of resolution.

Little written or digital messages matter too

Sometimes a teen who finds an unexpected message of love and connection on the pillow, in the lunchbox or on the mirror in their bathroom can be given a big dose of positive neurochemicals, especially when they are struggling or feel they least deserve it. Obviously, getting a message of love via a text or a DM can work as well. Sometimes just sharing a funny meme or reel on socials can do the same. Connecting in a digital world also needs to have restraint, though. I've had a number of teens tell me that their mum texts or reaches out far too many times in a given day, and they wished she would stop. Not completely, just wind it back a bit. The best way to know if you've got it right is to be curious and ask them.

Communication maps

When we can find effective and respectful ways to communicate with our teens, we can bridge the chasm of difference. I have already used the metaphor of having a map that we navigate our lives with. Mature adults have a very different map to their teens.

Anyone who lives or works with adolescents, from tweens to young adults in their twenties, needs to fully grasp that they have a unique map of the world with which they are navigating their choices. Our job is to help them to create more helpful maps, or to allow them to see the map of the adult world. Remember, our behaviour is the result of choices we make based on our beliefs and past experiences, and we make assumptions and expectations automatically. Our reality is our reality, though – no one else can share our view of reality. Effective, respectful communication is the best way to bridge the differences in our world maps.

Here is an example of a mother–son conflict (also shared in *From Boys to Men*) that shows how different maps can cause angst:

> The son was having difficulty engaging at school and had been wagging occasionally. Mum gets a call to say he has not arrived at school and she was pretty angry because she had dropped him off at school before it started.
>
> She frantically phones his mobile and it's turned off. She goes home to check and then starts to get really worried. Then the school calls to say he has shown up.
>
> She quickly goes to the school and finds her son and confronts him in front of other staff and students. After she has yelled at him and told him how stupid he has been, he then loses the plot and in front of the same group of people tells her to get #&%$#@!
>
> Mum's map of the world told her that he had intentionally and deliberately wagged after she had dropped him off and she was worried the school would expel him because he was on a final warning. The son's map of the world was very different.
>
> When he had arrived at school, he was told there was a seminar for his year group that cost $20. He didn't have the money, plus he didn't want to go, so he went downtown until the seminar was over. He had left his phone in his bag back at school.
>
> Once they were able to have their different maps decoded, they had understanding and were able to appreciate how the conflict had erupted out of misunderstanding – not malicious intent.

Totally different maps and different worlds, and neither side could see the other side. Ineffective communication at its best. A supportive lighthouse or adult ally can help decode the parent's and the teen's map to the other so they can both understand each other's behaviour. The mother in this example had done something very dangerous in teen land: publicly shame a teen on their own territory. Social inclusion and the biological need to belong is profoundly strong, and she had – unintentionally – made him 'look stupid' (his interpretation) in front of his social group. The son had reached a tipping point and exploded; partly to defend his sense of identity and also to retain his place socially.

The teen years, especially those under 18, are a time of incredibly intense emotions and feeling criticised, excluded, unacceptable, dumb, not good enough and unloved are valid reasons to feel awful, frightened, unwanted and out of control. Home needs to be a safe base where they can find refuge. Being able to develop effective communication strategies and skills will help you navigate the different maps that are playing out in your home. Just choose one or two simple different sentences or strategies, and practise those until they become automatic and then adopt some more. Sometimes, the wisest thing you can do with some of the things that will come out of your teen's mouth is to let them float off into the ether or like water off a duck's back. *Not everything needs to be commented on, assessed or reviewed.* They are just spontaneous words being said, without great thought, from an individual who is still maturing and growing into being an adult.

If we keep in mind that every human, especially our emerging adults who are going through a confusing time of transformation, want to be seen, heard, accepted, valued and loved exactly as they are – not for who they could be – then the power of effective, respectful communication can be truly appreciated.

WHAT I WISH MY PARENTS HAD DONE BETTER:

- To have been loving and warm. Just accepted what I was feeling and stay with me in it.
- I would have liked them to let me talk rather than assume things or try to argue.
- To just stop yelling and find a way to de-escalate situations.
- I think if they could have just kept things running at home and done the work on themselves to improve THEIR mental health, and parent my sibling a little more, that would have been a great example for me to follow, and it would have really helped me find the strength to pull myself out of my head.
- To trust me and believe me.
- Not ask questions and instead just understood that I was struggling and unable to cope.
- Listened to me instead of assuming they are always right and [that] if I disagree with what they are saying, I am wrong.
- Just vocalising words of encouragement and love. Validating my feelings and helping me to work through them empathetically but logically.

7

Cultivating character and building resilience

Character is shaped by life experience and cannot be seen from the outside or from physical appearances. Character cannot be judged by prizes and accolades and nor can it be judged by age or culture. Character can only be ascertained from the personal values and virtues that shape the words and actions that show how an individual lives, navigates the experiences they have and how they interact with others.

It seems that in this chaotic, modern world we seem to have lost sight of what is important in raising our children. We focus so much on the grades our children achieve and their physical, musical, artistic and mental abilities that we seldom recognise or celebrate their humanity and the depth of their unique character. It is only when we see an absence of this dimension that we bemoan the fact and complain about our young people.

I have long rallied against the push down of formalised learning and the over-testing of children because I think it makes our children look like brains on seats and sources of data. There is a whole child there with a mind, a body, a heart and a spirit. So maybe we have come to neglect the growth and development of character – the ability to be a valuable member of a social group and to support the growth and development of everyone within a group. Our consumer-driven world holds sporting heroes, actors and influencers in places of high status and value regardless of their true character. Questionable 'news' sites and magazines that often have appallingly poor journalism and a lack of truth, and online apps keep the world informed of infidelities, and alcohol- and other drug-fuelled excesses as though that is something to aspire towards!

Someone with a depth of character acts with honour, respect, concern, unconditional regard and the courage to hold their ground when confronted with choices that compromise being their true self. Sadly, we have to look really hard to see these decent humans.

Historically, Indigenous tribes focused on the development of the of the whole child, including the character within their children as well as their physical growth. Responsibility for the development of a child was shared by everyone in the tribe. Physical growth was important, and children were taught new skills when they were ready. They were also taught the gifts of the spirit and the heart. These are what we loosely term values, virtues, social manners and etiquette. They were taught these skills through stories, songs, the arts and through ceremony. Without these templates, young people are often unaware of how to behave and what to value; they basically live a life that is code-less. Without these skills and without the guidance and mentorship of safe grown-ups, teens can become 'untethered' and the journey to adulthood can cause far deeper scars that can last a lifetime.

In my third year of teaching, after only ever working in country schools, I spent a year teaching in a metropolitan high school that was considered to be rough and tough. I was given a class of Year 10 students who were listed as 'at risk'; they were the biggest challenge I had encountered in my short time teaching. These 'difficult' students had a range of cultural differences, coming from Greek, Italian, Macedonian and Indigenous backgrounds. They also had low literacy skills, and many were enmeshed in a strong gang culture and hated school.

I was very unfamiliar with city life, especially when surrounded by a marginalised group of first-generation migrant children. My 12 months with this class showed me that we held completely different values and beliefs.

We saw the world very differently and had very different interpretations of life experiences. I felt that my best option was to develop an authentic relationship with them and to give them an understanding of the values and life skills that could help them make better choices in their lives. Over time we came to trust each other and we explored and challenged many of the perceptions they had about life and living.

We detached many layers of victim mentality. We built a new understanding of cultural acceptance and learned about socially acceptable ways of communicating, using manners, positive language and positive assertive behaviour. The end of the year culminated in dinner at a French restaurant. We had spent many weeks exploring French words, dining etiquette and manners. I still have a clear picture of those neatly dressed young adults, excited and enthusiastic about showing off their new skills. It was a fun night and I saw first-hand that, with more information and knowledge, all young people can make better choices: socially, personally and interpersonally. On the last day of the school year this class of 'animals', as the principal had called them, presented me with a huge bouquet and a silver platter. It had engraved on it:

'Thanks for everything.

From your favourite class of stirrers.'

What this group of 15-year-olds did not know was that they had been *my teacher.* I had come with many stereotypical beliefs about kids who belonged to gangs, were sexually active before fifteen and who abused alcohol and drugs. They taught me to see within, to avoid judgements and to look for the good within all of us. I was and still am deeply grateful to them.

An understanding of values and virtues is important for children and teens to develop the qualities that build character and provide a sense of humanity that will bring out the best in themselves, others and our world. If their parents haven't guided them to have values and virtues, then lighthouse figures and often teachers can help them cultivate them.

What is character?

Character can be seen by how a person lives and interacts with others. It is shown in a person's capacity to be themselves and not an imitation of others. It is a quality that is felt and experienced through the human body, mind and heart and it creates a 'knowing'. My best understanding of a positive human character that is worthy of respect and honour is a person who uses their unique gifts to make the world a better place, while holding a place of unconditional regard for all. Having a good character does not depend on privilege.

In his excellent book *Brainstorm*, Dr Dan Siegel reminds us that despite the threat of potential harm:

> '. . . the 'work' of adolescence – the testing of boundaries, the passion to explore what is unknown and exciting – can set the stage for the development of core character traits that will enable adolescents to go on to lead great lives of adventure and purpose.'

I found that Siegel's description of emotionally mature behaviour was helpful in understanding how people with a good character tend to behave. In his 2010 book, *Mindsight*, he says broadly that they have the skills to:

- Regulate their own body
- Be attuned to others
- Find balance in their emotions
- Be flexible in how they respond
- Soothe fear
- Be empathetic
- Have insight

- Have moral awareness
- Draw on their intuition.

I think there is one thing missing off this list and that is the ability to be assertive. If you can be assertive, you can set and maintain your own healthy boundaries, and you can speak up for yourself and for what feels right for you. Being assertive can sometimes create conflict between parents and teens, however, effective communication can help reduce that drastically.

Literature and books can build a deep sense of character. I grew up in a home without TV, which meant that I was deeply affected by the books around me. The digital world has definitely displaced a lot of the time that previous teens spent reading. One study showed that in 1980, 60 per cent of senior students reported that they read a book, newspaper or magazine for pleasure (not assigned for school) every day. Sadly, by 2016, this figure had dropped to only 16 per cent, even though they may still be doing some reading on digital devices (the survey question didn't ask which format the reading material was in). Either way, our teens are reading fewer long-form texts, and that can definitely impact the shaping of the character and their own unique identity. I have been saddened to see the incredible focus on STEM in our schools, which diminishes the importance of the arts, shaping the inner world of our kids and teens.

Another great way to help build messages about character is to watch movies with your teens, especially the uplifting ones. Chat with them about it afterwards, about what happened and the choices the characters made. Here are some golden oldies.

- *Dead Poets Society*
- *Good Will Hunting*
- *Alaska*
- *Life is a House*
- *The NeverEnding story*
- *Forrest Gump*

- *Moneyball*
- *The Fault in Our Stars*
- *I Am Sam*
- *Pay It Forward*
- *Braveheart*
- *The Lion King*
- *Shrek*

Don't just think that age is the only factor that can shape the emotional competence of our teens. I have met incredibly emotionally mature teens aged 14 and 15. Many of them came from challenging home environments or had experienced incredible adversity like recovering from cancer, surviving a natural disaster or having a parent die suddenly, and they stepped up to meet the situation. *Life experiences, when coupled with at least one safe, caring human in their corner, can be a fast way for teens to develop a strong sense of positive character.*

Values and virtues matter

From infancy, we learn what is valued, especially by our significant carers and educators, and from these interactions we develop our own invisible value system, which shapes who we decide we are. Values are a very significant determiner of behaviour as well. As children, we need to know the value of the word 'no' and that there are rules and guidelines that create a template for us in our society. Even though there are different versions of right or wrong, children need consistent guidance around these expectations. I have had many concerned teachers telling me they are meeting more children in primary school who have not had consistent boundaries. These kids struggle in class, especially in terms of following directions and being respectful of other students.

Values give us a guiding framework by which to live our lives; they are ideals that guide our behaviour and decisions and help us distinguish between right and wrong. They also allow us to live in communities with a degree of civility if they are based on positive values, however, the reverse can occur as well. The way we are parented shapes our values and beliefs significantly, however, there are other influences. Modelling is the most powerful way that our children and our teens can learn from someone with a good character.

These are some of the things you can be modelling for your children and your teens.

- Model fierce, unconditional love and care
- Allow your children space to 'be'
- Be truthful and honest
- Create a safe place for them to share their emotions
- Be a positive dreamer and goal-setter yourself
- Be real, not perfect or a know-it-all
- Be joyful and laugh often
- Have clear, firm boundaries
- Model personal health and wellbeing
- Be connected to your own spirit
- Have relationships that you value and nurture
- Surround yourself with the tribe of good humans who genuinely care for your kids.

> The best way to inspire your children to develop into the kind of adults you dream of them becoming is to become the kind of adult you want them to be.
>
> – Robin Sharma, *The Greatness Guide*

There are many ways that we can build values and guiding expectations in our families. Having simple rules such as:

1. Try not to hurt yourself
2. Try not to hurt anyone else – physically or verbally
3. Try not to damage the world around you.

Having clear expectations around appropriate language, sibling behaviour, personal hygiene and chores around the home does matter. There are lots of suggestions on how to create these in the chapter about communication. Having family meetings where our teens have input into the family guidelines can be incredibly helpful and shows that their input and views deserve to be heard.

Kindness matters

Kindness is the capacity of an individual to act from a place of genuine concern for oneself and others, and includes the qualities of empathy, compassion, generosity and consideration with the intention of making a positive difference in our world. Being kind is a choice made from the belief that every action influences others, and it honours our deepest, invisible motivation to have value and worthiness in our lives.

The effects of being treated fairly and with kindness have been shown in studies in neuroscience to make a significant difference to the way the brain integrates and, subsequently, to how individuals feel and behave. When we are treated with kindness, it allows our nervous system to relax and sensations from endorphins, often serotonin and sometimes oxytocin, to flood our body. It makes us feel safe, valued and connected.

There are a number of ways children and teens can learn and practise the gift of concern for others and to discover the benefits of loving service. Here are some ideas for modelling service and community spirit, and things to encourage your teens to do:

- Collect papers or mail for a neighbour when they are away
- Care for friends' pets when they are away
- Take soup to sick family, friends or neighbours
- Help elderly people with tasks like shopping and gardening
- Make cookies, scones or muffins for people in need, or for birthdays
- Take small gifts of gratitude to teachers and carers
- Phone, text, or message and send cards or letters to thank people for kindnesses
- Practise random acts of kindness to others
- Make a family member a cuppa without being asked

- Help with family chores without being asked
- Smile lots
- Offer to help a friend with their homework
- Say hello to people at school or in the community, especially those who seem sad or lonely
- Help fundraise for important charities
- With permission, gather blankets for a blanket drive
- Pick up broken glass on the road or path.

One of the most interesting things I discovered in working with or living with teens was how they were often quite quick to offer kindness to their friends rather than family members.

If you want to develop a stronger relationship with your teen, start with small gestures of kindness, especially when they are struggling with being their best selves, and then notice the difference. To be honest I found that kindness was my most powerful discipline tool to help facilitate connection and correction in my home, my classrooms, my counselling room and in the wider community. It is difficult to be unkind and mean to someone who has been kind to you!

Fairness matters

Social psychologists and researchers Dr Matthew Lieberman and Dr Naomi Eisenberger discovered that being treated fairly activates the same parts of the brain as having our basic needs met like, coming in from the cold, having a cold drink on a very hot day or eating chocolate. It triggers the pleasure response.

> Being treated unfairly activates the social pain and disgust circuitry. In our evolutionary past being accepted and valued by one's group is important because it means access to critical resources for survival and thriving.
>
> – Lieberman and Eisenberger, 'The pains and pleasures of social life', *Neuroleadership Journal*

Having conversations about the importance of fairness can help build that awareness deep inside your teen. They may not be capable of always choosing to be fair, but, as they mature, the chances are it can become a part of their life. However, if they've never experienced it, or have never had it explained to them, they can maintain an immature, often selfish attitude to their behaviour towards others.

> I am lucky to have very supportive parents and feel comfortable telling them my feelings. My mum does this thing where she will ask me, 'Do you want me to just listen, give advice, give reassurance, or something else.' This lets me be able to speak and know that she won't just interrupt with useless ideas for my situation. She will usually ask this beforehand if I've asked to talk or after I've vented to her and it's her turn to try to help me.

What happens when teens get their values from the Internet

Your teen has been raised in a rapidly evolving digital environment. Fake news abounds on the web and even well-educated adults can struggle to find authentic, evidence-based information.

> I feel like being a teen now is in some ways worse than it was before. Social media has impacted us so much because if you want to be 'cool', you need to look a certain way, have follows, be popular, be this and that and a lot of people lose track of who they really are. This can impact relationships with your family because it's no longer 'cool' to be nice to them so you start being disrespectful and pushing them away so you can maintain your status of being 'cool'. Also this can lead to mistreatment of women in general because you see them as an object for you to use as pleasure not as a real loving human being.

I have become increasingly concerned for today's digital natives, especially those under 18. How can today's teens truly discover themselves in among the noise, the 24/7 negative news cycles, the insidious pressure from idealised and often sexualised images and videos, the plastic search for notoriety and fame – at any cost? How can they do this amidst the selfies, the filters and the unquenchable thirst for endless connectivity, regardless of whether it is positive, negative, painful or destructive? On top of that our kids who have phones are being marinated in age-inappropriate content from violent videos, endless gaming that often involves killing, the dark side of social media and disgusting pornography, often stumbled on accidentally. What a depressing background for raising our kids to have a healthy sense of self with good character.

Indeed, another issue that the digital world brings is lower levels of focus, slow reflection and deep thinking. The research is very strong that the human brain is much better at focusing on one thing at a time, even though we are subtly conditioned by technology to believe *we can do* many things at once and have many windows open on our computers. Switch tasking, where we go from one task to another and back again – like we do online – diminishes our capacity to effectively complete tasks. Given that most of our teens will be doing homework while getting regular updates from WhatsApp, TikTok and Snapchat, is it any wonder that our educational standards are dropping? They are biologically wired for connectedness with their peers and being online feeds that need, often at the expense of deep pondering and schoolwork.

Another downside of the digital world has been the increase in social anxiety for many teens and their lack of confidence in verbal communication, quite simply because they do less of it. Again, the best way that we learn life skills is through experience – by doing it. I had a mum talk to me recently about the reluctance of her 16-year-old daughter to go into the local bakery and order bread and a cup of coffee. She just hasn't had enough practice to feel confident doing this. How can teenagers develop their authentic selves and individual character if they aren't getting the chance to build their social skills and understanding?

Given that adolescence can be a time of struggling confidence, increased stress and often an increase in the influence of the negative inner voice, disappearing down the rabbit hole of the digital world to find ways to trigger dopamine – the feel-good neurotransmitter – makes perfect sense. Of course, that means sharing endless highly filtered images on Insta/Snapchat, gaming and scrolling through celebrities' and bloggers' posts.

If we want to encourage our children to be independent thinkers, problem solvers and highly creative humans, they need to be practising freedom and autonomy as often as possible within their childhoods – not spending hours in a highly orchestrated and curated environment that is shaping the way they think and experience life.

As I have already mentioned in Chapter 1, it's important for parents to provide real opportunities for children to contribute in the home, whether that's being part of family decisions and conversations or having the chance to solve problems on their own. The chance to share their opinions and explain their beliefs, without judgement from adults, can make a huge difference to the growth and development of a child's authentic sense of self.

In our digital world it is harder for our kids to become unique, authentic individuals rather than 'anybodies' or 'nobodies' who are unknowingly conforming to norms created by their digital influences.

The ego is feasting on the selfie/social media/fake news world while the higher self quietly starves.

It's a little like putting children in a lolly shop that has one small basket of fruit and saying, 'Go for it!' Their choices are often driven by a child's sense of uncontrolled desire and instant gratification. Our teens are being driven by similar urges!

Teens need to be guided and taught how to manage themselves, interact with others positively and accept responsibility for their place in the world. This has always been seen as the responsibility of parents, extended family, schools and other significant members of the community in which the adolescent lives. The angry and defensive teen who always tends to blame others is displaying an immaturity in the social and emotional domains of development.

How the Internet shapes teen values

1. **The developmental hunger to be accepted** used to take place within the family and community – it now needs to take place in the public eye (even better, to receive exposure across the world). Sadly, parental acceptance and love has lost some of its potential to fill the hearts of our teens. Now they need the adulation of those in the ether – the more likes, follows, shares, comments and positive emojis they get, the better they feel! To be honest it can be difficult to have a conversation with a teen about being careful not to become too egocentric in a world that celebrates exactly that.
2. **Privacy is no longer respected or valued** as it was when parents were teens. The days when it was accepted to value modesty or to be a little discreet (especially around our private parts, both in our homes or in public), has almost disappeared. Things have changed drastically in the last 30 years, and we need to be mindful to see these changes as different, rather than wrong or inappropriate. Having said that, in a non-sexualised context, we too need to watch what we model in this space and value our teen's privacy online – once again, always check with them before posting images of them or sharing details of their lives online (even if you're just being proud of them!).
3. **Sexting images** of breasts, penises and vaginas is seen by some – however, thankfully not the majority of teens – as fun and a part of courtship. Teens are particularly susceptible, emotionally and mentally, to being crushed and destroyed by such behaviour. Often our teens won't come to their parents when these things occur, due to their incredible embarrassment and fear of getting into trouble.
4. **Children are being exposed to sexualised images** from the minute they are born, from so many different places – billboards, advertising, online, TV shows and films. I have heard of four-year-old girls asking their mummy if they are 'sexy' and eight-year-old

girls refusing to eat because they are fat! Body-image pressures are impacting both our boys and girls in such unhealthy ways and it is so much worse than in the previous generation. Again, social media comes into it . . . there are 10-year-old girls using filters to make themselves look thinner and more beautiful. WTH? Teens can spend hours hating themselves for not fitting the images being portrayed. So many of our teens are struggling with significant body image challenges and that will be explored further on in the book – so you will know how to help.

5. **For many teens, sex has become just something physical** – not something to be savoured with someone you have feelings for. It is just something you can do if you want – to have fun, to fit in and to hopefully have someone notice you. Both boys and girls have been watching pornography – and by the mid-teens they have been conditioned by it in ways that would horrify most parents. Many girls are engaging in sexual behaviour that sees them physically injured and scarred – and many boys think that hitting, slapping and choking is a part of having sex. Anal sex is very common among teens – often it is the first sexual experience that a teen girl experiences, thanks to the porn-saturated world that our teens live in.
6. **Violence is now so prevalent** in so many forms from our 24/7 news channels, to videos of beheadings on YouTube, violence in online games, the sharing of fight videos from school grounds, and the endless senseless violence of films that (despite adult ratings) are viewed so easily by teens on pretty much any of the major streaming services. As I write this, there has been a lot of concern around a sharp increase in knife crime in parts of Australia and overseas, and sadly young people are represented highly in the statistics around this. Common sense would suggest that if you marinate kids and teens in violence they will become desensitised to it, and violence can become normalised.
7. **The Internet has become like the proverbial rabbit hole** that most of our teens have disappeared into. Technology actually addresses

the three core psychological needs of our teens – connection, competence and control or autonomy. They are being defined by their relationship with their online world – it is irreparably connected to who they are. It is *so much more than FOMO* – the constant need to be connected in their many spaces online. It is a strong biological drive to be connected to friends and peers, and a normal part of the shift from being more connected to parents. Sadly, the more they are connected to the digital world, the more disconnected they are to those closest to them, especially caring family and friends. We cannot cut them off from this world because that is how they stay connected. Yet this is also where teens connect with sexual predators, bullies and trolls who cause so much suffering. Helping them to navigate this world safely is a huge responsibility for parents.

Ongoing education is incredibly important in our homes and our schools to teach our kids and teens how to be responsible, respectful digital citizens.

8. **A generation of digital natives is less prepared for the schooling system.** Challenges in schooling and education are seeing more students than ever before not attending school. School reluctance and school refusal would only impact a very small number of students in years gone by, but children raised online are often harder to engage in traditional classrooms and less resilient to the difficulties of school. COVID-19 certainly created enormous challenges for many students and transitioning back into mainstream school for some simply became too difficult. I will explore more on that later on about what you as a parent can do if you're facing this dilemma in your home because it can be an enormous source of stress for the whole family.

There has always been a generation gap between parents and teens. In our global, fast-paced digital world the generation gap can feel more like a chasm – and one which seems to keep widening almost day-by-day!

But things change from one generation to the next and this is perfectly normal.

For teens, developing a strong character and a deep sense of personal values can help them navigate the challenges of being an adolescent. They can't develop that without the guidance of wise, caring adults, especially in their homes – so it's important to bridge that gap through communication and care.

Resilience matters

> Mum said it's okay to not know what to do, and that all I need to do is take one small step in a forward direction, make one little change or take a risk by trying something new.

It's important to understand that developing a good, well-rounded character is not always enough to protect teens from the difficulties of life. They also need to develop resilience.

Our children are less resilient than those of previous generations. Many parents, teachers and allied health professionals are deeply concerned about how our children, tweens and teenagers are coping with the pressures of modern living in a digital age, especially.

In the wake of the global pandemic, some might argue that the shift in the way we parent our children is contributing to lower resilience as we seem to be focused on keeping them happy rather than walking through the ups and downs of life. Even though we know that many of our choices to protect our children come from a place of great love, we can simply do too much for them and not give them the opportunity to develop some of their capacity to manage their own lives. Sadly, the parenting landscape has many very judgemental voices that have made it more difficult to let your child stretch and grow.

Julie Lythcott-Haims was Dean of Freshmen at Stanford University for a decade, so she was used to dealing with young adults in their first year away from home. She noticed that regardless of how academically excellent the new students were, far too many of them were overly reliant upon a parent or two to manage their day-to-day life for them. This was a sharp contrast to the students she'd worked with 10 years earlier.

Resilience refers to the ability of a person to successfully manage their life, and to successfully adapt to change and stressful events in healthy and constructive ways. It is about survivability and 'bounce-back-ability' to life experiences – both the really advantageous ones and the challenging, traumatic ones. To be fair, some of life's traumas can seem impossible to bounce back from, because they are so huge. When these involve challenges such as sudden unexpected death, major physical trauma or betrayal, individuals can take years to recover to a place of healthy functioning.

The digital world has stolen many hours of connection with our children who have now become teens. Many of those who work in allied health and education have been expressing the same concerns as Lythcott-Haims: that there is a lack of resilience with today's children, especially our teens and younger adults. I have explored many of these concerns earlier in the book, however, I feel it is important for us to explore how we nurture resilience and develop grit once adolescence arrives.

These words come from Melanie Woss, a Perth girl who struggled with depression before finally taking her own life when it got too hard:

> Why not be proactive instead of being reactive? Why not implement a program where school-aged kids learn skills to help them cope with stress? Decision-making skills. Problem-solving strategies. Relaxation activities. Communication skills. Why not address the issues that kids talk about today? Sex; drugs; politics both within the community and the school, family life, racism, etc. etc. etc. Why not give kids the skills that generate confidence, the ability to speak articulately, how to present oneself for different occasions, how not to put your foot in your mouth. Kids need to be taught that stress exists and it is very real, and most importantly, that they can cope with it.
>
> Melanie Woss, Aged 18, *Melanie*

So much insight in one so young. How incredibly sad that she found it too hard to stay in our world.

If you experience instances of significant imperfection, failure, disappointment and frustration as a parent, rather than beat yourself up, use these as 'teachable moments' for life. Resilience is not about you or your children toughening up; it is about helping them learn to be adaptable when adversity turns up uninvited. No one is 100 per cent resilient all the time. We're much more resilient when we've had eight hours sleep compared to two hours sleep. We are much more resilient when we are only dealing with one adverse experience rather than multiple experiences. The research is strong that modelling from parents (and other significant grown-ups in their life) is the most significant way our children learn how to be resilient and to have grit.

Father Chris Riley is now retired but created and worked with Youth Off the Streets in Sydney. He wrote the following:

> 'When we see troubled kids, we begin the journey to understand the quality of their early relationships, the psychological condition of their inner life and the development of their spirit. At the heart of the matter is whether the child is connected rather than abandoned, accepted rather than rejected, and nurtured rather than neglected and abused.'
>
> – Father Chris Riley, Towards a National Strategy for Young Australians

That last sentence is the key to building resilient capable young people. Many young people engaged in criminal activity are untethered and disconnected from safe grown-ups, and they feel rejected and neglected by their communities. We all need to do better as the grown-ups in our kids' lives.

Resilience is more about human connectedness, rather than individual strengths. Indeed, when hard times happen and trauma occurs, an individual's capacity to cope and recover is largely determined by the systems they exist within – such as families, school communities, neighbourhoods, sporting clubs, faith communities – and what resources are available within those systems. The final key to recovery is do we ask for help? Help-seeking behaviour is an important thing for our children and our teens to learn as they navigate our uncertain world.

Characteristics of a resilient person – sometimes, not necessarily all the time

- The ability to bounce back and recover from almost anything
- Optimistic and flexible thinking skills
- Have a 'Where there's a will, there's a way!' attitude
- Tend to see problems as opportunities to learn and grow
- The ability to hang in there, persevere and persist
- Have a healthy, authentic self-esteem
- Capacity to set clear, realistic and attainable goals
- Have a healthy social support network
- Practise assertiveness rather than aggression or passivity
- Seldom dwell on the past or the future
- Have well-developed emotional and spiritual competence
- Learn from previous challenges and mistakes
- Have a capacity for detachment
- Have a well-developed sense of humour
- Have meaningful involvement with others or their community
- Treat themselves and others with respect
- Have problem-solving and conflict-resolution skills.

From birth, we are building personal resilience through the acquisition of various life skills and understandings about how to be a human in social systems. The better the quality of parental care that children are exposed to, the stronger their resilience – provided the care has allowed for children to have opportunities to explore the world, make mistakes and learn how to overcome adversity.

Adversity is not all bad. Many of the most successful, competent and influential people in the world are that way *because* of adversity in childhood. This is where we can develop a social conscience and understanding of the need for change to existing cultural attitudes.

The ability to overcome setbacks, disappointments or failure can be determined by minimising risk, building protective factors and/or patterns of behaviour acquired by a person. Any teen can suffer from depression, even high achievers. Any teen can make a spur-of-the-moment decision that can be fatal regardless of school grades or prior patterns of behaviour. We must not assume that any teen will be reliably and consistently resilient and able to make decisions that guarantee their safety. Neither vulnerability nor resilience are fixed constructs.

Bonnie Benard is often considered the mother of the concept of building resilience. For many years she worked with children who were at risk, and rather than just looking at the factors that made them at risk, she shifted the lens and looked at their protective factors. By looking for things that were working positively for these children, she was able to identify how to put more of those protective factors into the lives of children and teens. This study led to her developing a list of protective factors that are needed in all communities to promote resilience.

Protective factors that enrich resilience in 12-year-olds and above:

- Increasing bondedness
- Learning life skills
- Establishing and maintaining clear boundaries
- Providing care and support
- Communicating high and positive expectations
- Creating opportunities for participation and involvement.

This was a significant shift in the studies and the application of resilience therapy and strategies. Helping families and those who were struggling to focus on strengths rather than deficits not only created better outcomes, it created more hope for those coming from seriously disadvantaged backgrounds, especially those who have experienced traumas.

Feeling the burden of making big decisions on my own constantly because there's no one to say, 'We're in this together. You don't have to do anything or decide on anything on your own.' When I express my worries, I need an ear and wisdom and I'm confident! Everything was always my siblings' business too apparently. Mum could never listen without blabbing to other family members.

How to build resilience

Back in 2004, I created a model of 10 essential building blocks from birth to 12 years of age that explore how the small things in childhood can become big things later in life. My book, *Real Kids in an Unreal World: Building Resilience and Self-esteem in Today's Children*, was based around this model. These essential building blocks in childhood were aimed at building strengths and capacity for children to better manage adolescence and adult life. This model can be equally as applicable for teens. The model was a combination of resilience research and also an overview of the ways that traditional kinship communities raised children. Interestingly, they meld perfectly together. The model draws from Maslow's hierarchy of needs as well.

This strength-based approach to building resilience is from clinical psychologist Lyn Worsley, who created a holistic model that can work for children and grown-ups called the Resilience Doughnut.

Her model has an inside circle and an outside circle. In the inside circle there are three things:

- I have
- I am
- I can.

Your teen might say about themselves: 'I am a nice person' or 'I can play saxophone well' or 'I have a great group of friends who help me cope'.

These realisations come through navigating seven different factors. These help them to identify what is working for them, instead of focusing entirely on what is not working for them. These factors are:

- The parent factor
- The skill factor
- The family and identity factor
- The education factor
- The peer factor
- The community factor
- The money factor.

When I was still counselling troubled teens full-time, I found that this Resilience Doughnut was really helpful. We all have a negative bias – an awareness of the risks and dangers in life so as to ensure our survival – but it is particularly strong in the adolescent mind. Negative self-talk, ruminating loops that catastrophise and high levels of self-loathing and self-hatred are so common in adolescents. Often tweens and teens are overly focused on everything that was going wrong in their world and they could find it hard to identify what is working for them. This gave them a new lens and a potential new map that they could use to consider.

> I felt like it was a totally different person in my body. This person was selfish, anxious and unreasonable. They said and did things that in my right mind I would never do but I was watching them through my own eyes. I didn't like who I was in the moment and it felt like it had been like this way forever and it would never get better. I hated myself and anyone who saw me like that.

One of the strategies that Lyn encourages that I found incredibly effective is for anyone helping a struggling teen to focus more on keeping their strengths strong and working for them, rather than just trying to fix the things that they are struggling with.

> My parents offer support, helping me by allowing me to take mental-health days, checking in on me to help regulate my emotions. My mum will break down my tasks into a checklist to help when I feel overwhelmed.

The below image shows you the balancing act that every human is navigating every day of their life. We all have to deal with stressors and working out how to build protective factors, coping skills and problem-solving strategies while holding a strong belief that we can overcome hardship can be helpful in building genuine resilience.

Resilience Model

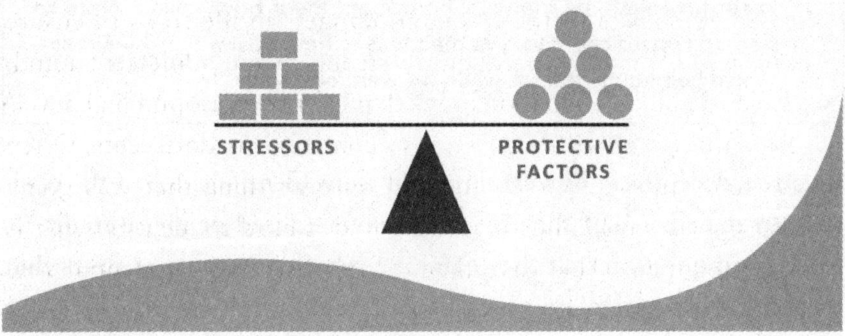

The more positive resilient protective factors or patterns of behaviour you have, then the better your chance of overcoming setback, disappointment or failure of any kind. The choice to fight everyone who may represent the perceived cause of your life challenge, such as authority figures, is simply that: a choice. The choice to make a positive difference by accepting your share of the responsibility (if there is any), and then finding ways to prevent that happening to another is a sign of high resilience with good character.

- My mum made me an assessment calendar which helped me manage my assessments so I knew what I needed to do.
- I remember that it got to a point where I knew I had to tell my parents and when I did they were just so supportive of me, they told me that it was okay to feel like this but if I wanted to go see someone about it to try and help me deal with it I could. Knowing that they were just there and that they would love and support me, really helped me deal with what was going on.
- Trying to help me cut back on the amount of weed I smoke.
- Helped me to zoom out and see the bigger picture (staying grateful) and reminded me of the magnitude of goodness in my life despite being in the bad. Specifically, to my situation, my mum told me to just come home if I was missing them which showed me how I had dramatised the situation in my spiral.
- Mum encouraged me to go to camp and told me I would have a great time with my friends. She bought me a book called 'Note to Self' to take to camp to give me ideas to help deal with my feelings – it also helped my friends while we were on camp.

It can be deceptively powerful to help teens identify some of the positives in their life that they may not have realised or given credit to. There's no question that they can take some convincing at times that something is positive, however, keep trying.

Resilience should be understood as a vital ingredient in the process of parenting all children. It is a process that directs our interactions as we strengthen our children's ability to meet life's challenges and pressures with confidence and perseverance. Parents need to keep in mind that early adolescence – under 15 – is the riskiest and potentially most dangerous time. Resilience can help lessen these risks.

Making resilience a life skill

These days, we almost expect teens to work out what they need to learn by accident, rather than through conscious education about life and teaching them the skills they need to master to be considered an adult. Schools have placed such a huge emphasis on learning that can be measured and assessed, and many people think this is where teens will magically learn everything they need to become a worthwhile member of society. This is a serious flaw in our modern world. Life skills and competencies that a young person should learn and master must be given a much higher priority. Many get to adulthood with few skills, especially social and emotional skills, and they struggle with relationships, managing money and coping positively with positions that require responsible choices and consideration for others. They may have all the modern gadgets and 24/7 access to the digital world – things they believe show they are part of the adult world – but they may lack the mature mind and ability to make sound decisions because they have not been given these skills by significant adults.

In their book, *The Millennial Adolescent,* Nan Bahr and Donna Pendergast outline that identifying resilience for adolescents as a competence is useful because it's something that can be *actively developed, taught, practised, demonstrated and deployed.* This means we can impact young people's lives by providing the right configuration of experiences and learning events. If we don't provide these experiences, then we are dooming people to suffer the nastiest consequences of adversity. It seems a callous approach to refuse to actively attempt to develop resilience attributes because it is assumed to be an immutable trait.

Every teen can grow in resilience and grit regardless of their situation. Self-efficacy essentially means being able to do things for ourselves, and with guidance and mentorship, especially from a warm, safe grown-up, to make a world of difference. I once met a lad in one of my classrooms who was quite bright academically, but who had no idea where a stamp went on an envelope. Given that so few letters are posted these days, I am sure we could meet a few more of them but, back then, that was pretty extraordinary.

One of the key research findings over the years in child development is something called emergent development. This means that as a baby grows through toddlerhood, if they have been able to be completely dependent on the safe grown-up, they will reach a point where they demand to do something for themselves! This window of an increasing hunger for independence is so similar to the teen years. Sadly, this emergent development can be delayed or impeded without a parent encouraging their tween or teen to grow in competence and capacity. So often, our teens want independence, and yet they still want you to keep doing things for them, especially the things that take time and energy and aren't much fun. This is a chance to talk about preparing them to leave home to go and live their own lives as capable humans.

Competence matters

The three keys to self-determination are connection, control and competence. For a teen who is struggling academically, or who is struggling with a neurodivergent brain in a neurotypical environment, who is coping with trauma or who is struggling with being excluded or bullied, their sense of competence is often diminished or shattered. This can feed into the negative mindset that I'm wrong, I'm bad, or I'm useless. One of the keys to turning this around is finding something that your teen can be competent at. You may remember that I explained the 14-year-old boy who loved to race motorbikes earlier in the book. Being so competent at that helped him feel okay at school despite struggling with the death of his father. Sometimes, a teen may find an option at school that they find not only pleasurable, but that they are quite good at, and it can lift their mood significantly. If this can't happen within the school environment, then it's important to find something outside of the school environment. I firmly believe that my sons' passion for surfing allowed them to cope with the academic pressures of high school. It can be quite a small skill like growing vegetables, cooking the best pancakes, making their own cards or small gifts, doing a triple flip on a skateboard. Whatever it is they will have needed to have practised in order to improve their performance!

A teen cannot tell themselves they are completely useless if they know they are competent at something. This leads me into the importance of teaching life skills to your teen. Yes, they do need to know how to do household chores efficiently. They do need to learn how to wash clothes and to return them to their bedrooms. My lads had to start doing their own bedding in Year 9 – well some of the time. Not only that, they needed to learn how to mow the lawn, wash windows, vacuum and take the bins down. I believe that boys and girls need the same competencies. Learning to do stuff on your own is an important competency and teens need to learn to do these to develop grit and persistence. When you teach household chore competencies, remind them that you are preparing them so they can go and live independently successfully with their friends or other housemates.

On my website, I have a comprehensive set of life skills lists that will be helpful for all teens to master by around the age of 18. So many of the life skills can seem incredibly obvious, especially around social etiquette, managing money, learning the basics of living out of home and big ones around consent. Some of the things seemed obvious to us, however, they are not necessarily obvious to a teen. Please make sure your son does not get away with not learning these skills and make sure that your daughter doesn't take too much responsibility for these things.

Learning to manage money matters

It can be tricky to help build an appreciation of financial responsibilities in our teens, especially as they have grown up in a largely cashless world. When money magically appears out of the wall, or when you tap a phone, or a watch or even a ring, it can be hard to learn to appreciate the value of it.

Every family has to work out their own model of financial distribution as their child gets gradually older. However, by the teen years, your son or daughter needs to navigate a way of funding their needs, whether that be a phone, travel costs, clothing costs, or even in-app purchases.

There are many ways that teens can become responsible to earn their pocket money. They can do chores around the home, get a part-time job or they create self-driven earning opportunities outside of the home, such as:

- Mowing the lawn for you, friends, family, or neighbours
- Looking after pets or taking neighbours' pets for a walk
- Cleaning cars
- Window cleaning
- Delivering pamphlets
- Babysitting
- Selling items they no longer want on eBay, or helping you sell items on eBay and earning a commission
- Doing odd jobs for people you trust
- Making stuff and selling it.

An important message is that if your teen wants a high-priced item or to pay for an expensive event, they need to take the initiative to earn the extra money required. This really helps to develop an appreciation of the value of things that they can take forward into adulthood.

On one of the episodes of my ABC podcast, *Parental As Anything*, I spoke with finance expert Effie Zahos. She explained that it is incredibly important to explain to children about the non-negotiable expenses that families have to contend with. It is important to introduce the word 'budget' – so that they can appreciate there will be times where financial freedom will not exist within the family, and that is not necessarily a bad thing, it is just a fact of life. The cost of utilities, rent or mortgage, travel costs and insurance are just some of the things that teens need to know about.

I think a key message to get through to our teens is that work is not just to achieve our purpose in life, it is to help us support ourselves to live in a way that we would like.

It can be helpful to engage your teens in planning family holidays, not just for the fun but from a budgeting point of view. This will give them a true appreciation that sometimes fun can cost money and that fun can sometimes happen for free.

In today's world, credit cards are seen as a little old-fashioned by young people. They are far more drawn to pay-later apps, and sadly many are being caught in the debt cycle even without credit cards. The temptation to have something you want immediately, especially with an underdeveloped brain and a desperate need to appear acceptable to friends and peers, means the temptation can be hard to resist. Be prepared for them to make mistakes, and then to work with them to correct them. Heck, we've all made financially poor decisions in our lives!

Because very few teens would have a piggy bank with real money these days, there are many online apps that can help kids and teens navigate their money and to help them budget. Scott Pape is well known for his books that have helped parents and kids navigate their financial competence. My own sons all bought his book *The Barefoot Investor* while they were at uni, without my knowledge. Pape has also written a book specifically for kids called *Barefoot Kids: Your Epic Money Adventure* that could be helpful.

Teens who are responsible for paying unexpected expenses themselves (rather than asking their parents for the money) are much more likely to keep track of their money. However, this needs to be a gradual transition, and your teens need to have some autonomy in making those decisions. Goalsetting and planning around money and needs in the teen years can really help set your teen up for a responsible financial future.

I thought I was a mean mum when my boys were teens. If they broke their surfboard, they would have to earn enough to pay for half of it and then they would get a new board at their next birthday or Christmas! However, as they became adults, they realised that this gave them a good appreciation of the value of things and they noticed that some of their mates did not have that value and did not look after their things as well as they did. I still think they thought I was mean at the time!

Connection is critical

Seriously, teens value having parents who care – and it's the best way to help teens develop character and resilience. Just a few responses from the teens in the survey as to what their parents did that did help:

- They said that it is okay to feel these emotions and that it is a part of puberty.
- Gave me space & were there when I was ready to talk.
- My dad bought me chocolate and my mom allowed me to work and recover rather than doing dishes.
- Mum trusted me in the fact I followed my own gut instinct.

If you can share an interest with your teen, this is an enormous help – walking the dog, watching nature programs, love of maths, stargazing, volunteering, playing a game online (or in real life), cooking or growing vegies – find something. Have some regular one-on-one dates doing stuff you both like. One parent told me she began taking her 15-year-old daughter for breakfast at Starbucks once a week, and she has been amazed at the difference in their ability to communicate. Sometimes taking a grumpy teen son for a walk to buy a bucket of chips – with no agenda – can shift lots of angst. Some parents have told me they have binged on the couch watching a series that they both love. Cooking pikelets or pancakes at random times with your teen can also shift the dynamics. If you start early in life, this will be something they will come back to.

Please avoid being the doomsayer who just brings the bad news and worst-case scenarios. They seriously need people to show them the good news – the hope-sowers who share inspiring and uplifting messages and lift their spirits. Share these stories with them! It's great to share funny and inspiring reels with your teens and they'll probably do the same with you, especially the ones that mock parents! Laughter and lightness are something everyone needs to counteract the stress and anxiety of life. It certainly helped me raise my four sons, and that lightness and laughter are still a huge part of our family.

Surround them with passionate, authentic people who share their interests – even if it is at dance, football, music, the pool, the beach, the dance academy or at the skate park or BMX pump track. Find the place in the real world where you can help your teens stoke their spark – and then help them find the positive places online! There are so many fabulous sites and social media pages that are a positive influence on our teens.

Remember to encourage your fledgling adult to find 'lighthouses' who can be guiding lights on the journey of massive growth and transformation – the more, the better. In the teen survey, many mentioned their lighthouse figures were grandparents, uncles and aunts, coaches, teachers, the parents of their friends and therapists. Sadly, many of the teens who responded had no one as a lighthouse figure.

May I also encourage you to please make some time to strive to care for all the young people around you – your kid's friends, nieces and nephews, the teens in your community, at school and beyond. If your teen is shutting you out, help someone else's teen.

I have a special memory when one of my boys came home from high school to tell me one of his mates had been injured in an accident. He asked me to take him up to the hospital and when we found the injured lad, he was surrounded by his tribe. Not just his mates, there were some of the parents and one of his teachers – armed with chocolate and lolly bags!

Without the light of an adult's open heart, our teens can enter a dark place from which some never return. It is always taken a village to raise healthy children. I recommend creating a tribe while you are parenting your teen – a circle of other teens and their parents, where everyone agrees to watch out for each other's kids. You can offer to pick them up after dance or sport, lend a school blazer if you have one spare for the teen who has lost theirs, and you hang out socially from time to time. Embrace and encourage their friends – give them a safe place to hang out, your garage, around a fire pit or in a caravan in your yard. It can be great if the tribe is keen to go on holidays together because teens just want to hang out with their friends, mostly on holidays.

Practise patience, curiosity and kindness, and create the safe base they need at home.

As parents, we hold the greatest responsibility for raising our children. Often today, parents are hoping that schools will take that responsibility, and many teachers feel they have become surrogate parents to the kids they teach. If parents are unable to do this and many teens make it difficult for them to do this – then this is when lighthouse figures are needed by every teen. The shaping of our teens' character is significant in the years of high school, just as in developing resilience.

We must collectively focus on building character and resilience in children and adolescents so they can better manage living in this chaotic, changing world. It is not just about being capable and having life skills, it is really determined by healthy human connectedness with as many safe, good humans as possible.

In some areas, many teens are better informed and more worldly than their parents – and many have developed strong social consciences as a consequence of being a part of a global community.

This can be a good thing, and we adults can sometimes empower them to be the teacher and not just the student. Heck, I have been turning to my sons for help in the digital world for years and will continue to do so. They are way smarter than me in this field and they've taught me how to check for spam very efficiently! If parents and teens can work together as a team in our homes – each seeking answers and solutions to challenges – everyone can learn and grow.

We grown-ups need to model good character and values, and provide unconditional positive regard to our teens, to weaken the toxic influences of the 24/7 digital media landscape. Collectively, we can turn the awful statistics around. The good news is that statistics show that the majority of our teens are still doing okay most of the time, despite all the unhelpful changes in the world since their parents' own adolescence.

With awareness, compassion and action, we can help teens navigate the hero's journey to adulthood. Please don't throw your arms up and give up. Capture their hearts and souls with enthusiasm and passion.

Trust me, teens can be easily influenced in a positive way despite what the world suggests.

PART 2

HOW CAN I HELP?

Now, we get to the nitty-gritty part of the book. I can imagine that some parents may have skipped to this section without reading Part 1, and I totally get that. The information in the first section helps to explain why it can be very different parenting a teen to how you parent a child, and may be helpful background for handling any specific concerns.

Hopefully, by now, you will appreciate that despite your biological drive as a loving parent or significant safe ally to rush in and rescue your teen when something goes wrong, it is not going to help them grow into the confident, mature adult you want them to be. Often parents get angry because they may feel they are responsible as the parent and want to fix things to end any discomfort. That is also a normal response to the fear of their child being harmed in any way. It was appropriate for younger childhood, however with tweens and teens that strategy needs to change. Some parents do the opposite of panicking and rushing to help, they just step into denial by minimising or trivialising something of great concern to a teen. Neither of these approaches are helpful in growing and empowering our young people in their maturity as emerging adults.

The main reason we shouldn't automatically do things for kids and especially our teens is that we need to gradually teach them to recognise and solve challenges using their own initiative. Teens need to learn about the various choices they have in responding to challenges, whether that challenge is an immovable lid on a jar, a disagreement with a friend, a lost tennis match, a nasty comment on socials, or a Minecraft fail. Remember our main job is to raise our children so that they can leave home to live their own lives competently and healthily.

It's easy for them to think they might be able to learn everything in life from YouTube, but learning from someone they love and respect makes the learning far more likely to become part of their life. Children who are surrounded by optimistic language that encourages thinking and decision-making are much less likely to succumb to 'learned helplessness', where they expect adults to always be there to do things for them. We have to find the balance between doing too much and expecting them to do things that they might not be ready for. It's a fine line.

One of the key reminders in this section is that you are wanting **to respond and not react** and until you have all the relevant information, neither you nor your teen are ready to collaborate your way through the experience. The moments of adversity can be excellent teachable moments about life, and gradually – because there are bound to be many moments of adversity – you will coach your teen to learn, explore the challenge, gain perspective, ponder and question possible solutions and to seek help if need be. The goal is to empower your teen to navigate life's bumpy moments and challenges, with more confidence and competence rather than always relying on you to be able to fix things, or rescue them or to ignore them and shut them down. Our fully developed adult brains are built for logic and reasoning, and your teens do not have that capacity – yet.

Next, when something really big and challenging happens, we are often triggered to panic. Remember the metaphor of the glitter jar. Until your glitter has settled, you will be unable to be the safe, reliable guide or mentor who can help your teen explore a challenge without judgement, with curiosity and compassion. In every concern covered in this section, I will be reminding you to go and find your calm and allow your glitter to settle.

You will also need to practise your unshockable face in a mirror – followed by 'now, that's interesting!' Every one of the dilemmas we share in Part 2 will need you to have the unshockable parent face.

Over the years I have had to reassure many parents that many teens do not necessarily make better choices after one challenging experience. Do your best to be patient, as you go through the same process when your son or daughter may have done exactly the thing that caused them great difficulty before, possibly even within the same week!

If you have not read the chapter on communication, please do that before you follow the suggestions that are coming in the rest of the book. Teens can shut you down very quickly if they feel there is a lecture coming, or that you are overtly disappointed in them, you haven't connected emotionally with them or that you are going to tell them what to do. Remember when we are told what to do, even as toddlers, we are wired for 'counter will'. We are wired to do the absolute opposite.

- My parents are good listeners. Sometimes, the most helpful thing to do is to listen intently without judgement. Advice is not always necessary.
- My parents are well connected with local mental-health resources and have undergone mental-health training/been to therapy themselves. This can be very helpful if I need to take the next step and find professional assistance.
- My mum often wrote me cards or letters to communicate because she knew I couldn't do it verbally. For me this was definitely a good way to avoid the conversation face to face. I don't have a problem with confrontation either; I'm probably one of the most confrontational people I know, in the sense that if you do something wrong or I don't agree with it, I'm not afraid to say something.
- Remind me to breathe. I find this the most useful coping strategy. This along with occupying my hands while breathing (holding a ball, pretend to play the piano) has help me recover from the emotional wreck.

For each of the dilemmas, there will be a brief outline of some of the key areas of concern that parents may need to be aware of.

At the back of the book in the Resources section, there are lists of websites, free resources, podcasts and books to help you explore the challenge with your teen, to explore more reputable and evidence-based or evidence-informed information together. There are also suggestions on some people to follow on socials who are wise, passionate and full of hope.

What your teen needs from you is the reassurance of fierce unconditional love as you both explore the challenge they are experiencing, while respecting their need for agency and autonomy. Exactly as we need to do with our toddlers, it is about connection and then correction, while feeling secure that they have a safe base.

FIVE BASIC TOOLS TO SUPPORT ADOLESCENTS

- Safe, loving human connectedness.
- Good nutrition.
- Plenty of sleep.
- Meaningful involvement and physical activity.
- Laughter and lightness.

Trust me, today's teens need more TLC than previous generations and you have the mature prefrontal cortex – so please use it to be the reliable, safe place to rest when things get tough. There will be times that will be very difficult, and if you really struggle, I recommend seeking some professional help for yourself with a psychologist, counsellor or therapist. Start with a chat with your GP. Many of the biggest challenges that happen between teens and their parents are triggered by the parent's own experiences when they were a teen. Our baggage can create more conflict, just as irrationally and unpredictably, as it did when we were teens.

But remember, even if your teen is one of the lucky ones who is able to find a mental-health professional to support them, your job is not done. They may see that person once a week or once a fortnight – but every day and every night in your home, you can be making a positive difference for a son or daughter who is finding the going really hard.

Please keep in mind what you would want to happen if your teen was involved in a car crash. Would you want them to think *OMG don't tell my parents*? Or would you want their first thought to be *OMG – please call my parents*.

When you are really angry or unhappy with your teenager, close your eyes, take three deep breaths and imagine how you would feel if suddenly you had been told that they had died in an accident – then bring your awareness back

into the present moment; now, how do you feel?
How serious was the issue, really?
What would you now like to do about resolving it?
At the end of the day, what really matters?'

Before you have the conversation

Firstly, reflect deeply and ask yourself – am I the right person to have this conversation? Even though you are the parent, consider whether another safe grown-up your child respects may be more effective.

Secondly, sow a seed of possibility with your teen around your concerns in a general way BEFORE you have the chat, so that the topic doesn't come out of the blue.

Next, be realistic about what can be achieved in this first conversation and reassure them that being a teen can be tricky and hard at times.

Finally, reassure your teen how much you love them and that there is nothing that could ever change the way that you love them.

Remember:

1. Try not to panic, or to deny or ignore your concerns.
2. Find your calm – let the glitter settle. Keep breathing.
3. Choose a time and location that works for you both.
4. Check your physiology and your tone.
5. Connect – term of endearment, a cuppa or a snack.
6. Sometimes it's better being beside rather than facing each other front on as it can be less threatening for big conversations.
7. Remember to be calm, curious and compassionate.
8. Listen. Listen. Listen.
9. Ask your teen how you can support and help them.

The next steps are:

- Keep listening, listening and listening.
- Validate and accept their feelings.

- Lean in with love. Be patient. Be reflective. Be kind.
- Reassure them that they have your 100 per cent support.
- Together, collaboratively, work out some possible steps to resolving the challenge.

Read on for information and advice on specific concerns, or refer to the Resources section starting page 373 for more.

8

When is a moody, grumpy teen a depressed teen?

Background

Hopefully, by now, you will have an understanding that teens can be unpredictable in their behaviour due to the internal stress caused by the massive changes happening in their bodies visibly and invisibly. Teens are enduring collisions of surging hormones, brain reconstructions, functioning from the amygdala rather than the prefrontal lobe and body changes. Remember, for a time, teens may misread physiology and facial expressions and their sensitivity to threat (mostly perceived and not real) and this means they are in defensive mode much of the time. The stress they feel because their world is out of control and so confusing translates into a chemical war in their brains and bodies. If you have jumped to this question without reading the first four chapters, it may be helpful to do so to gain a deeper understanding of the *what and why* around your teen and the fact that they may be experiencing a higher frequency of grumpy moods than they were before puberty.

The emotional world of most teens is like a rollercoaster ride. Most of the time teens see themselves through the 'cracked windscreen', where they struggle with self-acceptance and self-worth. Their inner critic has become extremely loud during this time, and when you combine these factors, plus being grumpy and having moods that can last for days, much of their behaviour needs to be seen as pretty normal.

In the past couple of decades, an abundance of research and work has been done in the area of mental health and wellbeing to raise awareness and to improve our ability to recognise when we are struggling with our mental health. And that's a fabulous thing. My only concern, however, is that after hearing many anecdotal stories and from what I've learned in my conversations with teen coaches and school psychologists, I believe many teens can see their normal moodiness or grumpiness as a sign of mental illness. They seem to have interpreted the awareness campaigns around mental health to mean that if they're not happy all the time, they must be mentally unwell. All emotions are valid for all humans, and the same goes for feeling a bit down in the dumps or a bit grumpy. When teens can come to understand that their emotional world is possibly more intense and unpredictable than before they became a teen, and that the impulsivity that sometimes leads to poor choices and the struggles to navigate all the pressures of living as a teen are all pretty normal, it can be helpful for not only them, but also for you as their parent.

When to really worry

A good place to start is to recognise that stress is pretty normal for everyone. Significant distress is when we start to worry.

> 'Stress is the body's response to a perception of a lack of control over an aversive situation. Distress is when there are chronic levels of elevated stress over a longer period of time.'
>
> Eric Jensen, *Enriching The Brain*

When an individual stays in their flight-fight-freeze state of stress without reaching the rest-digest state of recovery, it can impact not just their emotional world, but their brain development as well. Long-term distress, which is commonly known as chronic stress, affects the brain the following ways:

- Neuron development can be halved
- Reduces effectiveness of the dendrites
- Reduces the brain to survival mode rather than using upper cognitive processing
- Reduces blood supply to the brain
- Stimulates emotional meltdowns
- Impedes the immune system.

These impacts on a teen's developing brain can be profound. It means having only half as many spaces for new learning every morning when they get to school. This seriously impedes a teen's capacity to learn, and they can fail to absorb as much information as an unstressed teen. Over time, this leads to a massive cumulative effect of missed learning. Plus, the integration of the learning is negatively impacted, which also has a significant cumulative influence.

Within high schools, a toxic teacher in a threatening school environment can have a serious long-term debilitating effect on student learning on all levels – cognitive, social and emotional. Significant bullying from others has the same long-term impact as it is chronic distress, not just stress. Remember, teens can create more distress because of their inability to manage their negative self-talk, their immature cognitive capacities to manage challenging situations and by having ineffective life-management skills. The immune system can be compromised as well with chronic distress because the adrenal hormones tend to directly suppress the immune system to conserve energy supplies in order for the individual to survive their stressful experience.

When I have worked with teens who have experienced a significant trauma, especially a sudden death of someone they love, they can struggle with their former capacity for learning in the classroom.

Many of them explained that they just felt 'dumber'. It can take as long as up to 18 months to recover from these impacts, and imagine how long this may be for teens who constantly live with trauma or abuse, or who struggle in the school environment for other reasons. The same can happen to teens experiencing issues such as serious bullying, partner violence or significant parental abandonment.

The brain tends to adapt to chronic stressors with either of two extremes:

1. Numbness – listless, apathetic, unresponsive: disappearing
2. Hypervigilance – edgy, suspicious or overactive: acting out.

If you are worried about your teen, you might like to consider whether they are experiencing normal adolescent stress, or whether their level of stress has become distress.

Based on my experience, I would be concerned if a teen were experiencing one or more major challenging experience. An example of a challenging experience that might cause emotional overwhelm is any of the following:

- Car accidents
- Bullying and harassment
- Nasty, malicious gossip
- Failing at school
- Depression
- Other mental illness
- Death of a loved one
- Loss of job
- Abuse of any kind
- Teenage pregnancy
- Betrayal
- Criminal activity
- Global crisis/natural disaster
- Alcohol or drug abuse
- Gender confusion
- Discrimination
- Serious illness
- Personal injury
- Family disharmony/violence
- Divorce of parents
- Unresolved conflict
- Pressure of expectations
- Perceived failure
- Being late
- Living outside your honour code.

What to look for when you are worried about your teen

The following are some signs of mental-health problems in children, teens and young adults. **If these symptoms last for more than a few weeks, it may be time to seek professional help.**

- Depressed mood, feeling sad or low most of the time
- Social withdrawal and inability to get along with others
- Marked fall in school work, particularly grades
- Changes in usual sleeping or eating patterns
- Marked weight gain or loss of appetite
- Reluctance to go to school or take part in normal activities
- Fearfulness and heightened anxiety
- Restlessness, fidgeting and trouble concentrating
- Excessive disobedience or aggression
- Fatigue, lack of energy or motivation
- Irritability
- Withdrawal from previous activities they enjoyed
- Crying a lot
- Feeling hopeless or worthless
- Odd ideas or behaviours
- Suicidal thoughts/thoughts of death. (Please see Chapter 24 on suicide for more information.)

Another thing to consider is whether this anxiety or stress is rational and based on reality, or if it's irrational and based on what has or what may happen.

What to do when you are worried that your moody, grumpy teen is depressed

Firstly, take a look at 'Before you have the conversation' on page 171. Then, once you feel like you're ready, prepare your opening questions.

Possible opening questions

Please preface this conversation by reassuring your son or daughter how much you love them, no matter what.

- Bud, you seem to have been a bit down in the dumps lately. I feel I need to check in with how you are?
- Hey sweetheart, I know the last few months have been pretty hard for you and you seem to have been more tired and grumpy than normal – and I wonder if you have noticed? Has that been how you have seen it?
- Ava, my love, I have noticed you have been super tired and out of sorts over the last few weeks and I need to check in to see if we need to be worried?

Next steps

Depending on your teen's response you may explore the Brave program as it has a questionnaire that may be helpful and which can be done at home: see brave4you.psy.uq.edu.au/teen-program. The result will be helpful for both the parent and the teen as to what to do next and whether further intervention is needed.

If the same concerns continue, please encourage your teen to see either their family GP, school counsellor or a mental-health professional.

Learning to tune in to one's emotional state from time to time can be helpful in managing stress. Just by using a scale of 0 to 10 (see page 297), a teen can tune in to what their body is telling them. If 10 is when they are feeling calm, content or even happy, and zero is when they're feeling awful, then they can use this strategy to begin to recognise how they feel at different points on the scale. If they notice they are around five, they could make a choice from the list below, before they get to 0. The same goes for us grown-ups – keep tuning in and making choices. Even if it's just doing some deep breathing, or some tapping on an acupressure point, having a big drink of water or walking outside. Small gestures can impact the nervous system.

This list may be helpful for your teen to consider strategies or activities that may help them manage negative emotion or stress.

Safe, easy ways to create positive brain chemicals

- Get active – especially outside – doing something they enjoy like walking, riding, yoga or tai chi
- Call a friend, especially one they can trust
- Do a guided relaxation (I have several online and you can find plenty on apps like Smiling Mind, Headspace and more)
- Play uplifting music that your teen enjoys
- Play calming music
- Read a book that is pure escapism from life
- Drink some water
- Make a juice with fresh fruit
- Do something creative – paint, draw, play music, take photos
- Get out family albums with their baby photos
- Watch a positive film like *The Lion King*, *Shrek* or *Forrest Gump*
- Share their emotional state with a family member who loves them
- Cook something for the family like biscuits or melting moments
- Go to the park or beach
- Go to their special place in nature
- Read a great kids' picture book or cartoon book
- Read a joke book
- Write in a journal
- Do something for someone who needs help
- Arrange to speak with a school chaplain or counsellor
- Have a long bath or shower and wash everything clean
- Try some energy releasing techniques such as star jumps, 'tapping' (Google it), sit ups or tai chi
- Get as many hugs as they can
- Write a letter to someone special
- Watch ants

- Find a butterfly
- Look at the stars and count them all
- Pretend they have just fallen in love with their fantasy person
- Wash their sheets and clean the windows in their room
- Light a candle and pray for help
- When all else fails, walk at least three kilometres to buy a small bar of chocolate that has fruit and nuts in it – this is really a health food! Eat this very slowly and then walk home.

For more resources on this topic, such as books, podcasts, websites and helpline information, see the Resources section at the back of the book (page 375).

9

What to do when you find a vape in your teen's bag (or worse, that they are addicted to vaping)

Background

Yet another thing that today's parents of teens did not have to navigate when they were teens is vaping. 'Vape' is a slang term for electronic cigarettes or e-cigarettes. They look (and smell) harmless enough. They are bright, colourful little plastic devices with liquid in them which turns to vapour as you breathe it in. They come in hundreds of flavours, from lemonade to watermelon, custard donut to blueberry apple pie to name just a few. They were originally created by a Chinese pharmacist to help long-term smokers reduce their smoking intake. Technically they give you the nicotine without the smoke and this is where the 'safer than smoking' perception came from.

Sadly, vapes have become problematic because they are prime targets for children rather than grown-ups, and even primary school students are 'chuffing'. Of course, social media has helped to promote vaping to be cool, and yes, there are even vaping tricks videos on YouTube! Vapes are much easier to use and hide from parents than cigarettes ever were, because they can have a quick puff and pop them back into their pocket, and they won't smell of cigarette smoke.

When I wanted to learn more about vaping, I turned to my colleague Paul Dillon, director of Drug and Alcohol Research and Training Australia (DARTA). Paul is one of the world's leading alcohol and other drug educators and for the past 30 years he has been presenting in schools so he has spoken with hundreds of thousands of students and is across all the latest research and has his finger on the pulse. I've also mentioned him in the sections on alcohol and other drugs so please do check out his work.

In an episode for the ABC podcast *Parental as Anything*, Paul reported that while there are a substantial number of kids and teens who have experimented with vaping in Australia, a far smaller number are doing it regularly. It looks like around one in ten Year 11 and 12 students vape regularly, and about one in twenty Year 9s and 10s are vaping regularly. Since that chat, new figures have been released that show the number of 14–17-year-olds vaping rose from 1 per cent in 2018 to 14 per cent in 2023. It is definitely an area of concern for many parents, and some have had to withdraw their teens from school because they cannot cope with a whole school day without vaping.

In some countries, the stats are a bit higher. A 2022 US Centers for Disease Control and Prevention study found 14.1 per cent of high-school students had vaped recently. In the UK, the number has risen sharply in the last few years with over 20 per cent of kids aged 11 to 17 having tried vaping and the number of 16–17-year-olds who currently vape rose from 5 per cent in 2018 to 15 per cent in 2023. Countries like China, Italy, Germany and France have reported a two-fold or greater increase in youth vaping. While we can't say it's an epidemic, we can say it's a big worry.

So, what do we know about vaping?

Let's get the technical information out of the road so you understand the legality of vaping. Well, first of all, in Australia it is not illegal for kids under 18 to use a vape but it is illegal for them to purchase e-cigarettes and accessories for those devices. It's also illegal to sell e-cigarettes to juveniles. Large fines can apply. Most teens buy vapes from friends, online or from shops.

An Australian Institute of Family Studies report released in October 2023 on the mental-health impacts of vaping on adolescents said that existing research has found the main reasons adolescents identify for vaping are:

- To fit in with peers and social groups or because they enjoy the social element of vaping with friends
- To reduce or manage stress and anxiety, unwind or 'escape their problems'
- To experiment or rebel
- For the taste, fun and entertainment.

The same report also identified that 'vaping is associated with various mental-health related conditions including increased depressive symptoms, perceived stress, anxiety disorder symptoms and suicide-related behaviours'.

While there may be a strong link between vaping and mental health, the cause-effect relationship is unclear. Researchers do not know whether the mental-health symptoms come before the vaping behaviours or vice versa. What the research does tell us though is that regardless of the cause, we need to, as the AIFS report says, 'provide adolescents with alternative strategies to cope with stress and deal with negative moods, poor concentration and anger'.

The nicotine factor

A huge issue with vapes is that they generally contain nicotine even if they say they don't – in particular the little plastic, disposable vapes we most commonly see. In fact, according to Paul Dillon, a University of Wollongong study showed that all the vaping devices they'd tracked, even the ones mislabelled as 'nicotine-free', actually did contain nicotine. Some vapes also contain THC, the active ingredient in cannabis (see Chapter 12 if that's happening in your home).

The first and biggest concern with nicotine, though, is that it is a highly addictive substance, and secondly, it can make people sick. Paul said that, while it's not common, nicotine poisoning is on the rise. This can cause vomiting, stomach issues, and, in very rare cases, it can cause death. Certainly, you wouldn't want to leave these things lying around in a baby or toddler's reach! Research is continuing on the long-term risks of inhaling chemicals that get vaporised. There are obviously no positive benefits to vaping for teens!

In the chapter about the brain, I mentioned the potential to become addicted to anything is far higher in the early stages of adolescence, and vaping definitely can be problematic in this space. If you identify that your teen has become dependent on vaping, you need to remember that nicotine addiction can develop quickly. Your teen will need your help, as well as some professional support. A good place to start would be your family doctor and then possibly they may need help to access some sort of nicotine-replacement therapy.

Also, since my interview with Paul, in Australia at least, the government has very belatedly introduced legislation making it illegal to import non-prescription vapes into the country, as well as single-use disposable vapes, which will make them harder (but not impossible) for teens to access. The vapes will no longer be marketed to children so obviously; I applaud this move, and it may now be a real challenge for teens who've come to depend on vapes. Although as I write, we are hearing about new flavoured nicotine pouches called Zyns (among other things) that have nicotine absorbed through the gums. Some people are proposing these are potentially a good way to come off vapes. However, the World Health Organization cautions that many contain 'exceptionally high' levels of nicotine, and other experts are sceptical of their effectiveness as a quit smoking/vaping measure and concerned that they may become as addictive for kids and teens as vapes have.

So, what should you do if you find out your teen has been vaping, or you find a vape in their stuff?

Firstly, take a look at 'Before you have the conversation' on page 171. Try to gather as much information as you can from both sides before you begin the conversation and remember *aim for curiosity with compassion.* You will be curious because it's something that you did not experience as a teen and that's a great place to start. If you can, sow the seed of potential around the subject before you have the conversation. Possibly say something like 'have you noticed vaping at school or are any of your friends vaping?'

Remember a teen will be very defensive and less likely to open up to you if they feel they have been caught out – they will be like a deer in the headlights! Maybe disclose that information towards the end of the conversation rather than the beginning. You may like to preface this conversation by reassuring your son or daughter how much you love them, no matter what.

Possible opening questions

- They didn't have vapes when I was young, what are they like? Why do you reckon people like them so much?
- Do many of your friends vape?
- How often are they chuffing?
- Can you tell me how vaping makes you feel?
- Can you tell me how vaping tastes on your tongue?
- Have you heard that it is now illegal to buy vapes without a prescription?

Next steps

So, if they say, for example, 'but it's not as bad as smoking' you can talk about some of the things mentioned above about the lack of knowledge about long-term effects, levels of nicotine and, especially, that it's a kind of poison. You could also say that while vaping may be safer than smoking, it's not as safe as *not* vaping. In our podcast interview, Paul compared vaping vs smoking in terms of asking someone if they would rather be hit by a bus or a car. Having healthy lungs and brains matters!

You might like to remind your teen that you know taking risks is a part of being a teen, and that often we make choices that our friends are making. Explain that you get that, and that the family values in your home would prefer your teen say no to vaping. Remind them it may take courage in front of their friends, but you think they have the courage.

Creating adolescent outrage may be more powerful than telling your teen not to do something that they see as potentially cool. Maybe you could suggest that the vaping companies have been deliberately targeting children so they could make huge profits and they don't care at all about making kids sick or addicted. They just don't care. They just want kids' money!

The second angle is that many of our teens are concerned about the future of their world. Vape containers are plastic, and they are being found everywhere, including in our fish and dolphins, and in larger birds. There is an enormous environmental cost, and your teen could be part of the change. After all, it's their world they are creating!

Reassure your teen that you understand that it can be difficult to always make the right choices. It's important that they are making a choice based on good information, knowing what your family values are. In an excellent article she wrote in the *New York Times*, Lisa Damour pointed out that in regard to teens and vaping, research shows that just because we have strong information that doesn't mean we will necessarily make better choices. This is particularly true of our dopamine-seeking adolescents, whose executive function isn't fully formed yet.

What if my teen is clearly addicted to nicotine?

Any habitual behaviour is hard to change and being addicted to substances or alcohol or nicotine adds a whole extra layer of difficulty.

Nicotine withdrawal is no picnic. It can leave an individual feeling irritable, grumpy, upset, anxious, sad or depressed, restless, jumpy, hungrier than usual, unable to focus, and it can make sleeping difficult. Given this is how a lot of teens feel much of the time, adolescence is not a great time to withdraw from nicotine!

Once you've had the conversation (using the guidance above), there are a few things you can try:

- Support them to set a date and make a plan to quit (see the Resources section on page 376 for some apps/sites to help with that)
- Often plans follow the SMART method, so you aim to make your teen's goals Specific, Measurable, Achievable, Relevant, and give them a Timeframe
- Help your teen identify things they can do when they feel like vaping, such as going for a walk, having a glass of water, contacting a friend, drawing, putting on a song, or fiddling with a pencil. You will notice that many of these are similar to how to shift feeling anxious or really moody.
- ReachOut also suggests teaching them the 4D model for dealing with urges: Delay acting when you get the urge to vape, Deep breaths, Drink some water, and Do something to occupy you until the craving passes.
- I am also a big fan of role-playing a bit with teens. If they feel peer pressure is a factor in their vaping, help them come up with statements they can use to help them say 'no', such as: 'Actually, lately I'm finding when I vape it makes me nauseous' or 'No thanks, I'm doing a detox' or 'I've decided not to support companies that are getting rich off us kids' or 'I want to save the planet, so it's no more plastic vapes for me'.
- Your teen may benefit from counselling (some of the quit sites do offer online/phone support)
- If that isn't sufficient, nicotine replacement therapy may be helpful. Under 18s should see a GP to prescribe NRT and even over 18s should speak with a pharmacist to ensure it's being used correctly

and find the right treatment for them. It should be used for at least eight to 12 weeks.

For more resources on this topic, such as books, podcasts, websites and helpline information, see the Resources section at the back of the book (page 376).

10

What to do when you find out your teen is sexually active

'Sex at the right time with the right person is a great thing. Sex at the wrong time or with the wrong person can be the most damaging decision of your life. At some stage, you are going to choose to have sex. I'd like to help you make sure it is at the right time and with the right person so it doesn't cause you any damage.'

Michelle Mitchell, 'What to say if you think your teen daughter is having sex', *The Daily Dad*, dads4kids.org.au

Background

Let's be honest. The emerging sexual development of our teens is something we all wish wouldn't happen until they were much older! The concept that our precious sons and daughters are developing sexual desire as well as growing mature bodies, often while still in middle school, can be terrifying. For our teens, having conversations with your parents around sex is always awkward and yet incredibly important in our sexualised world. The world has come a long way from where sex was very taboo, and no one spoke about it – not parents or teachers. I'm pretty sure most parents today may have had a sex-education lesson where much of the lesson was putting a condom on a banana or a carrot! Thankfully, sex-education lessons have evolved with the times, and much of the focus is now on safe sexual behaviour that is respectful.

Yet again, the world for today's teens is very different to the world their parents experienced and definitely around sexuality, especially since the #metoo movement. For many in the Western world, in the 20th century, there were messages that shaped our attitudes to sex that were unhelpful and these can still play out today. One was that it was important for teen boys to have sex to prove they are a man, while the teen girls who participated were seen as sluts and morally at fault. Sex was seen as something naughty or bad, and many of those attitudes can trigger complete panic in a parent who's discovered that their teen has been sexually intimate. Obviously, the same physical and hormonal changes occur today as they did when we were young, and the same drives exist. However, today's teens have had access to digital information, including porn, from much earlier ages and that has been shaping some shifting attitudes and behaviours around sex. Regardless of this shift in awareness, in many conversations around sex, our role as parents is still to guide and reassure our kids that as they get older they will take a bigger interest in sex, they will experience desire and they will want to experience physical intimacy with another human. It is important that we give messages that sexual intimacy is so much more than sexual intercourse. Our key message all the way along is that we would like them to explore and experience their sexuality, without being harmed or doing harm.

We also need to keep affirming that any type of physical intimacy can have unwanted and possibly serious consequences. They may not realise that we care about them, and we want to help them make good decisions. Yes, we do have conversations about avoiding pregnancy and STDs or STIs, however, we need to reassure them that being sexually active is far more than a physical experience. The older they are, the more mature they are, the better they will be able to navigate the complexities of sharing their body with another – so rather than just about talking about sex, it's about physical *intimacy*. Yes, they will get sick of hearing you talk about respect and consent, however, they will have heard you affirm that sexual pleasure is a two-way street, not a one-way alley.

In the past, sex was mainly considered as intercourse between two heterosexual humans, in a committed relationship. Today, sex has expanded into many forms – including friends with benefits, faux lesbianism, hooking up, digital sex, sending nudes and phone sex.

In her book, *Parenting Teenage Girls in the Age of a New Normal*, Michelle Mitchell mentions that many girls are doing the pursuing – something that previously was seen stereotypically as a boy's role. Girls are pushing their own boundaries around their sexuality and some feel if they don't, they are missing out or they are 'out of it'. In some ways the new sexually active young lady can be pursuing just as much as the boys are pursuing them. This is obviously anecdotal, as there is no research to support this observation. Certainly, there is a lot more pressure on young women particularly to be sexual beings, and they are sexualised on social media from a very young age. This can be a positive and a negative thing. It's great if your daughter feels confident about her body and sexual identity, but not if she feels sex is something she needs to do in order to be accepted.

Going forward, it is important to keep in mind that today's teens have a very different attitude to sex to their parents. Obviously, this can also happen for teens whose parents have strong cultural and faith expectations, where sex before marriage is seen as unacceptable. I have worked with teens whose parents' expectations were very clear, and when the teen had a sexual experience that they knew broke their parents' rules, afterwards their shame often turned into a deep sense of unworthiness. We need to continually keep in mind that teens can make poor choices in the heat of the moment, but they still deserve to be loved and valued.

Some of today's teens see sex as a form of entertainment or a commodity that can be exchanged. The online world affirms that sex is purely a physical experience, and that oral sex and anal sex are often seen as the entry-level sex rather than intercourse. Thanks to their online experiences, many teens no longer see that sex needs to be something private and many teens think that it's okay to be shared on a public forum. Much of it is shared on social pages and sexting is very common. This does not mean that your teen lacks moral fibre. It just simply means that they are desensitised to the seriousness and impact of sexual activity and nudity. They are growing up in a very different world.

An Australian survey of 600 girls aged 15–19 found 51 per cent believed that girls were pressured into sending sexy images. Former detective in the child exploitation area Brett Lee travels around the country speaking about the implications and dark side of sexting. He discusses the legal issues that come into play and also people having their images used against them in incidences of bullying, exploitation and in some cases blackmail. Sextortion has become very problematic, and the main target is teen boys. The latest figures in Australia have shown that over 90 per cent of the victims of sextortion are boys aged 15 to 17 and there have been some as young as 10. This can create profound shame and distress in our boys and many find it difficult to disclose what has happened to their parents. We need to have these awkward conversations well before they become a teenager to reassure them that they are not the problem. Sexual predators pretending to be teens are grooming others to send photographs of their private parts. They then threaten to share these photographs with the world if they don't pay money. How things have changed! Sad but true. The massive influence of AI is also creating opportunities to reproduce people's photographs, or to create deep fakes that pretend to be other people for the purpose of embarrassment and shaming.

Half of all Australian children aged 9–16 experience regular exposure to sexual images, and 93 per cent of boys and over 60 per cent of girls have viewed pornography by age 18 (mostly between the ages of 14 and 17). Porn is not always something our kids seek out either – often, it comes looking for them in innocent places like Minecraft, in hashtags or embedded into YouTube videos. Even

Snapchat thought it was okay to add a site featuring pornography to their 'Discover' feature – thankfully, our guardians and advocates have had that stopped.

The ease of access to hard core porn that is often degrading for women is distressing. It is sad that porn that objectifies women and has no respect, consent or mutual pleasure is influencing so many of our young people as they develop their sexuality. Sexual exploration and intimacy for teens should not see girls being slapped or choked or ending up in an ED department because of anal tears. Education around respectful relationships and consent needs to happen at home, as well as in our schools.

This message could be helpful: in our family, we believe this type of intimacy isn't something to be taken lightly even if you do have strong feelings or you feel pressured because your friends may have taken that step already. These choices can have serious consequences. We care about you and want to be sure you make decisions that work out well for you. We hope that your first sexual experiences are pleasant and do not scar you for life.

What to do when you find your teen is sexually active

One of the reasons this could be so confronting for parents is that your child, your beautiful innocent child whom you have loved since birth, is evolving into an adult, far faster than you are ready for. *It is really one of the biggest freak-out moments of parenting!* Make sure your teen does not see your freak out and know that it might take longer to calm your glitter before you can have the conversation about your concerns. I can remember this moment clearly with my oldest son!

Hopefully, you have already had conversations with your son or daughter about protective behaviours. This means that they have learned about consent, and that no one has the right to touch them without their consent. You need to affirm that **no means no**, and pestering another person until they say yes is not enthusiastic consent.

Also, a person can withdraw consent partway through a sexual experience. Respectful relationships mean that we respect the needs and wants of both people engaging in the activity.

It can be helpful if you have sown the seeds of possibility through having a conversation around the sexual behaviour of teens generally, *before you have the big conversation* with your son or daughter. You might also drop the message that when you were a teen, sex was seen as something naughty or wrong, and no one really educated you completely about how to be intimate with another human. Yes, you can ask them to educate you and that is the power of being curious rather than furious if you discover your teen has become sexually active.

Maybe try some conversation openers such as:

- Do you know what? One day I hope you grow up to have fabulous sex because it's one of the best things you can experience – unfortunately porn is not teaching you how to get that . . . [mic drop and walk away].
- Having sex with another human can be really awkward when you're a teen (even when you're an adult) and that's pretty normal because you are learning how to do something new.
- I reckon the media paints teens in an unfavourable light, especially around sex – what do you reckon?
- I just read an article about how common sexting is – are any of your friends sexting?
- I know talking with parents about sex can be so cringeworthy or awkward but we need to chat – shall we do it in the dark while eating ice-cream?

Having the conversation

Firstly, take a look at 'Before you have the conversation' on page 171. Start by reassuring your teen how much you love them and that there is nothing that could ever change the way that you love them.

Maybe mention this might be one of those really awkward conversations that a parent needs to have with their kid and try it in the car as it often works best!

Possible opening questions

Do not bring up that you know that they've already had sex. When the teen feels caught out, they tend to become defensive, and they will not be open to any conversation. Pretend they have not had sex yet, no matter how difficult that may be in the moment. They may share that information with you, however, your main purpose is ensuring that the choices they make going forward regarding their sexual choices mean they'll avoid harm, whether physical, emotional or psychological. You also want them to come to you if they experience sexual violence and not be too scared of your reaction and keep it a dark, troubling secret. Most teens are really concerned about disappointing their parents, letting them down or having them feel ashamed of them.

- Bud, I know you've done a sex-ed program at school and so I know you know some stuff about being sexually active but being sexually intimate with another human is very different than being sexually intimate with yourself. Are any of your mates having sex yet?
- Hey sweetheart, I've noticed that you and your boyfriend have been getting especially cuddly lately and I wonder if you've given thought to taking your relationship to the next step and being sexually intimate with him yet? I trust that you have given this thought and consideration, and let's look at how you can ensure your own safety when you make that choice.
- Ava, my love, even though I'm finding it hard to accept that you are almost an adult, and that means that you'll be making choices about sharing your body with someone at some point – can we have a chat around ways of taking that step that are safe?
- You know, I heard this podcast the other day about how watching porn has changed the way kids are having sex. So it's common for

them to choke each other and stuff. Have your friends talked to you about that?

- It can be tricky for a parent to talk to their teen about sex. Even though it feels awkward, I want us to explore how sexual intimacy, in whatever form, in whatever place and with whoever, needs to be safe so that you are not harmed in any way . . . Are you okay with that?

Next steps

We must keep affirming that as parents, we cannot control all of the choices our teens make, however, we can help them be informed around possible consequences, so that they may make better choices, some of the time, if not all of the time.

Encouraging your teen to have a conversation with the family GP or a trained social worker who specialises in this area is a good idea so that they can explore options around keeping sexually safe as well as to avoid unwanted pregnancy. Give your teen the option of choosing who they would like to speak to, and whether they do it independently of you.

One of the most informative, up-to-date websites that gives teens accurate and balanced information is sexedrescue.com with sex education expert Cath Hakanson. One of the short videos found on her website is called 'Your Body During Sex', which explores exactly what happens for both males and females during intercourse. There are some other short videos that come from European countries, especially Norway, that explore puberty in a much more open and nuanced way. Given that teens are much more disinhibited nowadays, these videos are a much better alternative to porn for education purposes.

Another excellent video series is 'About Sex', which was commissioned by Canada's national public broadcaster, CBC. It is a funny and frank exploration for teens of 'what goes on inside their head, their hearts and between their legs as they navigate life and love as an emerging adult'.

If your teen is preparing themselves to become sexually intimate, or if they already are, they may gain some excellent insights from the TV comedy *Sex Education*, a UK series that explores the sexual awakening of an insecure teen boy, Otis, who is full of advice thanks to his sex-therapist mum.

Heartbreak High is a series created in Australia that explores the awakening and maturity of teens in a high school. Some parents may find these entertaining series difficult to watch because they are exploring sexuality in a much more uninhibited and open way for 21st-century teens. Again, even watching one episode with your teen will give you so much to reflect upon and to have a conversation about. In these series, there are teens who are sexually active, there are teens who are not and there are teens who are confused and wondering what comes next. These shows also cover a wide gamut of sexuality and gender identity so they can help with having conversations about that. And often, they pepper the serious side of things with humour. After all, sex is supposed to be a wonderful, joyful experience so it helps to keep a sense of humour about it.

For more resources on this topic, such as books, podcasts, websites and helpline information, see the Resources section at the back of the book (page 377).

11

What to do when your teen 'comes out' or is confused while exploring their sexuality or gender

WHAT HAVE YOU FOUND MOST DIFFICULT AS A TEEN?

- Feeling shame for my emotions – having attraction towards other boys and sexual feelings.
- I wasn't sleeping very well. I was hurting myself and having suicidal thoughts. I was feeling very hopeless, because of climate change but also because I'm gender fluid and it's hard to transition when your gender changes all the time. I was doubting myself a lot.
- The most challenging experience of my teenage years was realising I was physically and emotionally attracted to my best (guy) friend in a world that doesn't accept gay people and knowing that I was different from everyone else in my world. Wearing a mask and lying to my friends and family about who I truly was is the most difficult part of my teenage years. Constantly wondering if they would truly accept me if I revealed my true self.
- Dealing with my sexuality in a small country town. The fear was almost unbearable but once I accepted it myself so much of that fear dissipated. It definitely gets a lot better and a lot easier when you're not constantly hiding your true self.

Background

The awakening of one's sexuality in the teen years can be confusing for both teens and parents. It must be more confusing than ever to go from being a child to suddenly being someone who has urges and arousals they've never had before and a drive to have sex in today's digital world. Many of today's teens are embracing diversity around sexuality and gender, so much more freely and openly than their parents' generation. Exploring and questioning their gender identity and sexuality is a natural part of that. However, some teens experience gender dysphoria, which is a feeling of distress, either emotionally, physiologically or both, as a result of feeling a mismatch between their gender and the sex they were assigned at birth.

Let's begin by clarifying something important. You are assigned a gender at birth, you come to identify with a gender, usually based on social or cultural norms, and then you may develop attraction to a gender or genders. Through the traditional lens, there was an expectation that a biological male and female would identify as such and be attracted to the opposite gender. But as we've learned more and more, these characteristics can be expressed and experienced in different ways – there is no rule. When we talk about someone's sexuality or sexual orientation – whether they identify as gay, straight, lesbian, bisexual, asexual, pansexual or otherwise – we're talking about their emotional and sexual attraction to other people.

Commonly, gender and sexual identity are included together under the LGBTQIA+ label and they both form part of an emerging adolescent's identity, which is why I am covering them together.

Gender diversity

Firstly, I'd like to acknowledge that I am not an expert on gender diversity, and it's a very hot button issue for many. My aim in this chapter is not to do a deep dive into all matters gender diversity nor to argue the legal, medical and ethical perspectives surrounding this issue. That is a whole book in itself and, to be honest, not one I am qualified to write.

However, I want to identify some of the things you may want to consider if your tween or teen is questioning their gender – and where you and they can turn for support and further information.

This can be such a difficult thing to talk about. It's such a nuanced, complex and emerging area and a lot of people don't talk about it for fear of being cancelled if they say the wrong thing or hurting their loved ones. So, the first thing I'll say to you is it's okay to feel awkward and uncomfortable and full of hesitation about approaching the subject with your teen. Be reassured that, as with many difficult conversations that may come up when you are parenting your teen, you will probably muck up and get it wrong from time to time. Just ask their forgiveness and tell them that you are really doing your best to understand more and with their help, together you can become better informed and educated.

As I often say, we can't do better until we know better.

Before moving on let's clarify some terms that can be helpful to avoid confusion. These will cover both gender and sexuality. Remember, many of these terms were not even around when you were a teen, and they continue to evolve!

Terminology

LGBTQIA+ – this is an evolving acronym, which means lesbian, gay, bisexual, transgender, queer/questioning, intersex and asexual.

Cisgender – when someone's gender identity matches the sex they were assigned at birth.

Gender dysphoria – this is a form of distress that someone feels when their gender identity doesn't match their sex assigned at birth.

Gender diverse – this is an overarching term that encompasses all kinds of gender identity other than cisgender. So when I talk about gender diverse people in this chapter, I mean trans or transgender, gender fluid, gender questioning, non-binary and any other term that may be used to describe someone who expresses a gender identity different from their sex assigned at birth.

Gender identity – your gender identity describes the way in which you experience your gender. It's entirely personal and this identity may be expressed through how you act and dress, through your body and in the labels and pronouns you choose to use (i.e. he/him, they/them, she/her).

Trans/transgender – generally (a bit like gender diverse) this is a term that broadly describes when someone's gender identity differs from the sex they were assigned at birth. Even though transgender appears in the LGBTQIA+ acronym, it's important to note it is an experience of gender, not a type of sexuality. A transgender person can be asexual, bisexual, gay, heterosexual or any sexual orientation.

Non-binary – describes someone who doesn't identify as a man or woman exclusively. They may be fluid (i.e. their gender changes over time) or be somewhere in between or choose to express no gender.

Bisexual – means you are attracted to more than one gender, while **pansexual** means you are sexually attracted to someone regardless of gender.

Asexual – is when someone experiences little or no sexual attraction to others.

Transition/transitioning – some trans people will choose to transition in order to affirm the gender they identify with. Some will not pursue any of these processes. Transition can be social, which involves things like changing pronouns and possibly their name, the way they dress, etc. Medical transition may involve receiving treatment such as puberty blockers, hormone therapy or gender-affirming surgery. There is also legal transition, which involves changing one's name and sex/gender on official documents.

These are just some terms. I'd encourage you to seek out the Australian Institute of Family Studies 'LGBTIQA+ glossary of common terms' online for a more comprehensive list.

However, regardless of having the right understanding of terminology, things are not that simple and so we need to be prepared to be more open and compassionate as today's teens discover their own identity and how they want to play that in the world. Sadly, and unfortunately, there's a lot of ignorance and judgement out there in our world. Even more sadly, the statistics around mental health, bullying, self-harm and suicidal ideation among gender-diverse and LGBTQIA+

individuals are absolutely compelling – we need to do better to understand and support our gender and sexually diverse kids.

To illustrate why it's important for us to take our teen's gender and sexual identity seriously, here's what we know about what's going on for our LGBTQIA+ young people right now.

LGBTQIA+ people have the highest rates of both suicidal thoughts and suicide attempts in Australia: 15 per cent of lesbian, gay and bisexual people report current suicidal thoughts, and same-sex attracted Australians have up to 14 times higher rates of suicide attempts.

The Telethon Kids Institute's excellent research study Trans Pathways is the largest study to be conducted into the mental health of trans people (aged 14–25), and it also surveyed parents of young trans people. The findings are sobering:

- Almost three-quarters (74.6 per cent) of Trans Pathways participants have at some time been diagnosed with depression.
- 72.2 per cent have been diagnosed with an anxiety disorder – 10–13 times more frequent than we see in the general adolescent population in Australia.
- Self-harm and suicidality are also very high, with 79.7 per cent of Trans Pathways participants ever having self-harmed, and 48.1 per cent having attempted suicide at some point in their life.
- Further, the study found trans adolescents who were experiencing mental ill-health 'faced problems with accommodation, abuse, educational environments that were not safe and inclusive, and a lack of family support. Family support is key to a trans young person having good mental health and wellbeing.'

The study's authors pointed out that while we do not know specifically what factors contribute to poor mental health within Australia's trans populations, 'previous studies suggest that external factors such as abuse and discrimination are major contributors, in addition to internalised factors such as body dysphoria and distress related to their assigned sex'.

Around the world, mental-health statistics around LGBTQIA+ youth are equally grim.

In the UK, research from charity Just Like Us showed that 46 per cent of LGBTQIA+ 11–18-year-olds surveyed have had or currently have depression (compared to 20 per cent of the general youth population surveyed) and half reported having anxiety (compared to a quarter of non-LGBTQIA+ participants). Young lesbians and trans young people were three times more likely to experience depression than non-LGBTQIA+ students surveyed.

In the US, CDC research from 2021 showed that 69 per cent of LGBTQIA+ young people struggled with persistent sadness or hopelessness and 27 per cent experienced online bullying. This group commonly has experiences of bullying, physical assault, discrimination and social exclusion.

Statistics from US non-profit organisation The Trevor Project are similar around self-harm, suicidal ideology, anxiety and eating disorders.

In terms of young trans people, there are some other interesting correlations. Some clinicians and researchers have suggested there is a significant link between eating disorders and gender dysphoria. Also, research shows a high representation of autistic people in the trans population, with some research suggesting up to 35 per cent of trans adolescents are autistic (compared to, for example, between 1.0–2.5 per cent of the general Australian population).

The good news

According to research from The Trevor Project, the good news is that LGBTQIA+ youth reported lower rates of attempting suicide (often by up to 40 per cent) when:

- They had at least one accepting adult on their side
- They had high social support from their family
- Adults and peers around them accepted their identity
- They lived in an accepting community

- They found that home and school were LGBTQIA+-affirming spaces
- The majority of people in their lives respect the pronouns they chose to use.

Obviously, there is much we can do to support our teens in their search for their authentic identity. Let's start with gender. What do you need to know as a parent if your child tells you (or you suspect) that they do not identify as the sex they were labelled with at birth?

How do I know if my child is questioning their gender?

When I was young, I would've considered myself a 'tomboy', which is what we used to call girls like me who got on better with boys than other girls, and maybe who dressed and played in ways that we'd stereotypically expect boys to. I seriously disliked dresses and frilly things even in my teens. Even though I had that preference very clearly, I never considered that I was meant to be a boy.

The University of Sydney's Dr Victoria Rawlings researches the intersections between gender, sexuality, youth and social structures. She says most trans kids would 'persistently, consistently and insistently' say that they don't identify with the sex assigned to them at birth. This is something to keep in mind if your teen comes to you with questions about their gender identity. Technically, what I was experiencing was more gender nonconforming than gender dysphoria.

The advice is fairly consistent regardless of whether your teen is coming out as gay, bi, queer, or as trans or gender diverse.

Many parents and close friends are not surprised when a teen comes out as gay. Thankfully there has been a significant cultural shift around the acceptance of being gay and with same-sex marriage legalised in many countries now, this is no longer the enormous challenge it would have been last century. Sadly, that does not mean queer kids are still not bullied, often in our school grounds, nor that they do not encounter parents who react with fear, shame or disbelief. And you only have to read the comments from the teen survey which appear at the beginning of this chapter to realise that homophobia is still a deep concern for many young people.

Unfortunately, gender diversity and gender dysphoria can be more confusing and complex for both you and your teen due to the lack of social and cultural acceptance of gender diversity. You may be surprised by your teen's initial questioning, however, this may be something they've been grappling with for a long time and the onset of puberty and adolescence has brought it to the surface of their awareness. Content that is available exploring these topics through the lens of teens and their stories, especially on TikTok and other apps, may have helped an uncertain teen identify some of their concerns. If your teen is coming to you distressed or curious about their gender identity, it's important to hear them, keep the conversation going and get some support and advice for both of you.

If your teen is displaying any of these significant signs of heightened anxiety around their gender confusion, please be concerned and suggest a visit to the family doctor/GP.

- Withdrawing socially or social isolation
- Lack of interest in previously enjoyed activities
- Increased irritability or other mood changes
- Changes in eating and/or sleeping patterns
- Expressing ongoing lethargy or exhaustion
- Increased restlessness and/or anxiety
- Expressing hopeless or suicidal thoughts or self-harm
- Ongoing physical symptoms such as a headaches or stomach aches.

Having the conversation

Firstly, take a look at 'Before you have the conversation' on page 171.

Start by reassuring your teen how much you love them and that there is nothing that could ever change the way that you love them.

This is incredibly important for gender or sexually diverse teens to hear, and having a supportive parent has been identified as an incredibly significant protective factor.

Possible opening questions

- 'Darling, I've noticed that you have been spending a lot of time online searching trans stuff and I wonder if we can have a chat to see if I can support whatever you are questioning or to help you understand what might be happening in your world?'
- 'Hey, working out who we really are as a teen can be pretty tricky and even I remember that. I wonder if we can have an honest conversation about some of the worry you may have around your sexuality?'
- 'Ava, my love, I have noticed you've been wearing more rainbow colours lately and I am wondering if that means you are identifying yourself with the queer community and if we could have a chat around what you've been discovering and what your thoughts might be?'
- 'Did you see that G-Flip video the other day? Do you like their music? I reckon they're showing how you can create your own sense of self today as a non-binary individual – you reckon?'

Your most important job is to allow your teen to be heard – without judgement and with compassion – while owning your own concerns about being confused and needing more information. The media and the entertainment world have not made it easy for parents and teens to navigate the journey of discovery if the teen believes they are trans. Other than remaining unshockable and being prepared to really listen and be your teen's safe base, the research also suggests you don't be too enthusiastic. This is a long journey, and it can go in all sorts of directions. The more measured and informed the journey, the better. Thankfully there are well-qualified organisations with allied health professionals and support services that are becoming better and better informed all the time.

How to support your teen who is exploring gender or sexual diversity

- Please thank them for trusting you and for sharing their biggest concerns with you and maybe even suggest that you are proud that they were brave enough to do so.
- Try to be as inclusive and respectful in your language as possible.
- Every journey is different and be careful not to assume that a particular pathway lies ahead for your teen.
- Please don't ignore their concerns by saying nothing because it can agonise them about whether you are okay with it, or even whether you were listening in the first place.
- Please don't assume it's just a phase because they need to know you are walking beside them on the gender-questioning journey, or as they explore their sexuality.
- Keep asking how you can support them because the way they need your support may change, in the moment or over a specific incident.
- Educate yourself about gender issues from reliable sources.
- Be prepared to advocate for your child and educate the people around them, from family and teachers to doctors and allied health professionals, so that they don't have to.
- Avoid saying that you already knew because that tends to minimalise how big and important this issue is for them.
- Check in with your teen about who else can know the information they have shared and please respect their wishes. As time goes by, they may feel more comfortable with sharing the information with more people, however, they choose when that is, not you. For some individuals, rather than 'coming out', they prefer to 'invite people in' to their circle. Sometimes writing a letter to close friends and family explaining what's happening with your teen (when they are ready) can be more effective than just a conversation.
- Have conversations with your teen about how to be an ally or a supporter for others on the same journey.
- Support your teen to look the way they feel most comfortable with – either their hair or with their clothes – and also recognise that they may want to change that look over time.

- If they are transgender, please use their chosen name or gender pronouns straight away and encourage those in your family and circle of friends to do the same. Sometimes you will muck up, and that's okay – don't make a big deal, just apologise and keep trying.
- Get support for yourself through this challenging time. Join parent support groups or seek counselling. You can better support your child when you feel supported yourself.
- Not all teens experiencing gender dysphoria will or should undergo medical transition. It is worth reading the Standards of Care developed by the World Professional Association for Transgender Health (WPATH) to educate yourself about considerations in this area. They recommend a comprehensive process of biopsychosocial evaluation before considering any physical interventions for an adolescent. This evaluation should take into account psychological issues, social issues, family dynamics and more for each individual adolescent.
- Something that can happen that is a little unexpected for parents of trans kids is that they can feel like they're losing their son or daughter and they can feel a sense of grief or mourning. Your teen may not really understand this, so it can be helpful to reach out to other parents of trans teens and talk to them. Online support forums can also be helpful as you transition into this new reality.

I was chatting to a mum the other day of a trans boy who is 23. He has just announced that he is transitioning back to being a woman, and he wanted his mum's advice about whether he should use his old name or choose a new name. I reassured her that her unconditional and fierce love for her son during these confusing years of adolescence was something to be incredibly proud of. The fact that he comes to her for advice after being on a journey that was confusing for them both was quite special.

Protective factors

The Trans Pathways study had some interesting insights into ways that young trans people coped with adversity and living in a discriminatory environment. If you are a parent or lighthouse who's trying to support a gender-diverse teen, this can give you some useful clues and it can be helpful to share with the teens themselves.

Young trans people listed a wide range of activities/factors that helped them 'feel better about their lives and themselves'. These came under several themes, including 'distraction, escape, feeling "normal", being around like-minded people, expressing their gender, calming themselves, and finding acceptance and support'.

Some of the main activities listed, which actually could benefit any teen, I reckon, were:

- Music or art (83.4 per cent)
- Peers and friends (83.3 per cent)
- Social media (74.7 per cent)
- Spending time with pets (65.5 per cent)
- Books (65 per cent)
- Movies (60.1 per cent)
- Mental-health support and/or counselling (54 per cent)
- Computer games (57.7 per cent)
- Activism or volunteering (41.8 per cent).

One of the biggest protective factors for any young gender diverse person is parental support. The Trans Pathways study reports that 65.8 per cent of trans young people have at some point experienced a lack of family support. And all of those negative mental-health statistics I mentioned earlier in the chapter are worse in trans teens who have experienced a lack of family support.

So, you can have a big positive impact.

For more resources on this topic, such as books, podcasts, websites and helpline information, see the Resources section at the back of the book (page 378).

12

What to do when you find a bong, some weed or a small plastic bag with random pills in it

Background

In Australia, cannabis has many names, including weed, pot, grass, marijuana, dope, mull, hydro, yarndi, ganja, bud and green. Research shows that most teens are not regular cannabis users, but of course it is part of the drug landscape our teens may find themselves in.

I remember an evening around 30 years ago when, at age 16, one of my sons was quite obviously under the influence of cannabis. His eyes were glazed, and he was acting very 'goofy'. It was the first time that I had realised he was experimenting with smoking weed. I am really glad I handled it the way I did. I made no comment about his state and gave him the usual warm hug and wished him a good night. However, I didn't sleep a wink as I was catastrophising and awfulising all night wondering, what the heck do I do now?

The next day, once I had calmed my panicking parent brain, I went online to make sure that the information I knew about cannabis and the developing teen brain was accurate. I printed off some information and waited until I found a good time for us to have the chat that needed to happen. He read the printed information on his own, and then we checked in about what we had both learned. I then left him to make his own choices. He knew about the cumulative effect of using weed and the side effects and I hope it helped him navigate that journey. He was very careful not to be seen with those glassy, red-tinged eyes in our home again even though I knew it was a thing in his circle of friends.

Risk-taking and experimentation are a normal part of adolescent development, **even though no parent wants their teen to do any of that.** No matter whether it is with alcohol or any other form of drugs, legal or illicit, our key focus needs to be on the prevention of addiction.

Paul Dillon, director of Drug and Alcohol Research and Training Australia (DARTA), knows teens very well. In all his face-to-face drug and alcohol education programs in high schools right across Australia, he is very respectful in not telling teens what to do, but rather giving the information to help them make better choices. This same approach is recommended for parents and lighthouses. Apparently, cannabis is no longer the cool thing to do and even among some people it seems it's considered the 'loser's' drug and there are pretty negative connotations about someone being considered a 'stoner'.

In his excellent book, *Teenagers, Alcohol and Drugs*, Paul Dillon writes reassuringly that 90 per cent of experimental use with cannabis will be problem-free. He also reassures parents that there is no black or white. When you have conversations with your teen, there are a lot of grey areas. Your job is to make sure that they are getting accurate information given non-judgementally while still loving them.

In the chapter on the brain, I wrote that early adolescence, particularly under 16, is a window of sensitivity where massive brain reconstruction is happening. Among all the pruning and overproduction, there are rapid changes in the levels of neurotransmitter chemicals such as serotonin and dopamine, which control and regulate the pleasure response in the brain. Unfortunately, alcohol, nicotine and many other drugs appear to trigger the same responses in the brain as serotonin and dopamine. This window of sensitivity means that a teen can become addicted far faster than before or after this window. These addictions can be much more difficult to cure later in life as well, and this is a really important message that our teens need to hear.

Often teens will use alcohol, nicotine, especially in vaping, and other drugs to help numb deep emotional suffering and pain – just the same way many adults do. They are really seeking to feel 'better' or 'more' and that makes sense, on some level. Unfortunately, the negative impact on the developing teen brain can be very problematic. Sadly, there are many who simply stumble into an addiction because of what their friends and peers are doing.

Cannabis

Cannabis is a fat-loving substance that is very damaging to the developing brain. It eats up the myelin that the brain is trying to cover the axons with in order to prepare it to be more mature. A dependency on cannabis can delay key brain development and the growth of the prefrontal lobe. Cannabis is particularly toxic to young adults because it can de-motivate. Combined with the lack of motivation already present in many teens, marijuana can put a huge obstacle in the middle of their already unpredictable and confusing journey to adulthood. There are enough potential blockages without adding any more.

Problematic drug use and alcohol misuse is linked to educational failure, impulsive violence, eating disorders and self-harm. The links to mental illness are now overwhelming. Cannabis has been shown to be particularly dangerous because of its impairment of myelination in the developing brain. More use means more myelin is lost, and the final stages of brain development will be much more impaired. Cannabis slows down the brain's processing and strips motivation – which is already in short supply during adolescence!

Cannabis can be smoked, vaped or eaten. The effects of edible cannabis generally last longer and can be more intense. Cannabis use has been legalised in many countries around the world. However, it is still illegal in Australia – although it is decriminalised in many states.

Medicinal cannabis can be somewhat different to the cannabis most teens will be accessing, but there are still side effects and if it contains THC, it can impair your capacity to drive. Medical marijuana is mostly prescribed for pain management and helping with anxiety, insomnia and epilepsy, and that is a wonderful thing. However, some teens believe that it makes cannabis safer in some way. It's a bit like folks say vaping is safer than smoking, or being hit by a car versus being hit by a bus, as Paul Dillon explains. We don't want either for our teens.

Another piece of information to keep in mind is to ensure our teens know about synthetic cannabis, which is a psychoactive chemical substance often mixed with solvents and sprayed onto herbs. The chemicals are supposed to mimic the effects of the active ingredient in cannabis, THC, but according to the Alcohol and Drug Foundation (ADF) website, they produce many effects that cannabis doesn't and can actually be more harmful than cannabis. The effect can be more like that of methamphetamine. Side effects can include chest pain, breathing difficulties, irregular heartbeat, delusional behaviour and high body temperature. Synthetic cannabis is sometimes marketed under names like Spice, Kronic, Northern Lights, Mojo, Lightning Gold, Blue Lotus and Godfather. Some teens can access synthetic cannabis via websites, and it can be delivered directly to them. That also needs to be an alarm bell of concern.

A study led by the National Drug and Alcohol Research Centre (NDARC) at The University of New South Wales reviewed all recorded cases of synthetic cannabinoid-related sudden or unnatural death in Australia between 2000 and 2017. They identified that in 55 cases synthetic cannabinoid use did contribute to death. The most common cause of death was accidental drug toxicity. The message our teens need to receive is to avoid synthetic cannabis completely.

When to worry

Many of the symptoms around anxiety and moodiness can also apply to the experimentation of cannabis and other drugs.

Frequent cannabis use in teens can, but will not necessarily, lead to:

- Memory impairment
- Depression
- Slower reflexes
- Bloodshot eyes
- Increased heart rate
- Mild or significant anxiety and paranoia
- Significant school disengagement
- Drop in general life motivation
- Psychotic symptoms.

Other drug use and misuse

Any drug can have lethal or dangerous consequences, whether it's taken at dangerous levels or quite innocently. The nature of the risk is partly what drives an adolescent's need to take drugs, illegal or otherwise.

Although the available evidence clearly shows that **the vast majority of school-based young people do not do illicit drugs,** some teens will experiment and will suffer the consequences if they get caught up or they can be impacted in a bad way.

One thing I didn't know was that teens can purchase drugs via social-media apps. This comes from a blog on Paul Dillon's website:

> Some of these deals involved meeting strangers at train stations, shopping centres and fast-food outlets, but most involved home delivery. Snapchat was the platform that parents were most likely to identify as the one used by their child. Its appeal seems to be that not only can it connect buyers with a seller, the self-deleting feature of 'snaps' is particularly attractive to them as it also seemingly removes evidence of transactions.
>
> Parents were totally floored by how easy it was for their teens, some as young as 13, to access such a wide range of substances.

> Of course, there were the usual ones – cannabis, ecstasy (MDMA) and cocaine, but in some cases very young people were purchasing drugs like ketamine and DMT,
>
> – Paul Dillon, 'Buying drugs via social media apps: They're all just a click away!', Doing Drugs with Paul Dillon Blog, darta.net.au

Illicit drugs, such as methamphetamine, ecstasy (MDMA), speed, LSD, ice or cocaine are often stimulants that speed up the central nervous system.

Something that definitely wasn't in the mix when I was teaching or counselling was 'Special K', 'ket' or 'K' which are street terms for ketamine, a powerful anaesthetic used in both human and veterinary surgery. It is a dissociative drug, which means that when used, the mind leaves the body causing the user to experience quite intense hallucinations. There are reports that some teens and young adults are adding ketamine to ecstasy or MDMA. Obviously, you need to discourage your teen from using any of the above.

Prescription drugs that are also stimulants include amphetamines [Adderall® and Dexedrine®], methylphenidate [Concerta® and Ritalin®] and diet aids [such as Didrex®, Bontril®, Preludin®, Fastin®, Adipex P®, Ionamin® and Meridia®].

Here are some other signs that could indicate that your teen is experimenting with drugs other than cannabis. Parents need to monitor teen behaviour and be mindful of any changes, because they can be an indicator of drug or alcohol misuse – but not always.

- Decline in school work or after school sporting activities
- Changes in attendance and being unwilling to participate in group or school activities that they use to participate in
- Unusual outbreaks of temper, mood swings, restlessness, or irritability
- Excessive spending or borrowing of money
- More time spent away from home, possibly with new friends or friends in older age groups

- Excessive thirst
- Stealing money or goods
- Sores or rashes, especially on the mouth or the nose
- Stomach issues, changes to eating patterns
- Paranoia
- Trembling or twitching
- Aggression
- Use of drug-taker's slang
- Being the subject of rumours about drug taking
- Changing physical appearance or personal hygiene.

What to do when you find a bong or weed under your teen's bed or what to do when you find a small plastic bag with random pills in it?

Firstly, take a look at 'Before you have the conversation' on page 171.

Be careful to avoid accusing teens – even if you have clear evidence, like a bong or a bag of pills – because you may not have all the facts. Obviously if you find a bag in your son or daughter's room that has strange-looking pills in it, you will need to work out exactly what they are, where they came from and what possible harm they could do to your teen. Even if the facts show that what you found doesn't belong to your teen, the way to navigate going forward is about responding, guiding and being curious. Remember that overt punishment and messages of profound disappointment do not change behaviour. They often create more rebellion, and the behaviour will go underground and probably worsen your relationship. Your connection is one of the most powerful protective factors for your teen. Boundaries and consequences definitely matter, and they can be done firmly and with compassion. As my sons grew into adults, we were able to look back on some of the tricky conversations and moments they experienced as teens and appreciate when we were able to find the balance between connection and boundaries.

Possible opening questions

It can be helpful if you have sown the seed of possibility for your conversation a day or two before. Maybe you've seen something in the news or social media and make a casual comment about it. I know it can be really hard not to tackle the problem head-on and immediately. However, the better prepared you are the more success you will have going forward. Also it's important to NOT have this conversation when your teen is under the influence of drugs.

- Bud, on Saturday night I noticed that your eyes were glazed over and you were behaving a little differently so I am curious if you and your friends have been using weed?
- Hey sweetheart, can we have a chat about taking risks as a teen, especially around using drugs – what have you noticed happening with your friends?
- Ava, some of my parent friends have been talking about how they are worried about their kids using weed – have you noticed anything?
- Hey, a teacher at the high school found a small bag with pills in it in the science class – have you heard anything about pills being sold or used?

Next steps

A key message to affirm to your teen is that:

> 'All drugs are risky and although the harms are different for different drugs and different people, they are real and young people need to be aware of them.'
>
> – Paul Dillon, *Teenagers, Alcohol and Drugs*

It can be helpful using the 'what if' strategy around potentially harmful and dangerous experiences of teens using drugs. For example, what if a friend takes ecstasy at a music festival and starts expressing intense thirst and gets overheated – what do you do then? Or what if someone passes out or has a seizure after taking unknown drugs, what you do then?

Encourage your teen to be an outlier – one who simply declines to participate in taking drugs while watching out for their friends in social situations. This is definitely something that is happening more and more. The statistics are showing that our teens are drinking less and taking fewer risks and we need to affirm how fabulous that is. Being the guardian of your friends, while still being connected and having fun, needs to be something to aspire to. I have had messages from teens who have chosen this path who have saved lives.

It's important to understand why your adolescent is using drugs, if you are going to support them to meet those needs in other, healthier ways. The Positive Choices website (developed by the Australian Government) suggests exploring what they like about the drug before asking if there's anything they don't like about it. The site has a series of videos for parents called 'Making the Link' which show some examples of motivating conversations with young people.

Many parents mistakenly believe that by the time their children reach 20 years of age they are safe from illicit drug use. This is a common mistake because of the illusion that parents only have to worry during the teenage years. Research shows that your son or daughter will struggle more with problems with alcohol and drugs after they leave high school and in their early twenties.

Parent tips

- Avoid using shock tactics to scare adolescents about the effects of alcohol and drugs – it simply does not work and is not necessary
- Never use shame if there is an incident about inappropriate use of alcohol or drugs
- Remind them to watch out for their friends
- Caution them to be careful of drink spiking – never leave a glass unattended, taste anyone else's drink or accept a drink from anyone
- Reassure your adolescent that you can be called if ever they are worried, frightened, stoned, drunk or hurt – no matter what
- Reassure them that having them alive and safe is your number one priority – no matter what

- Dillon recommends you encourage your adolescents (if they're in Australia) to download the Emergency Plus app. This helps emergency services find them using GPS functionality.

Adolescents are more receptive to important information if it's given in the context of respect and caring, and usually when it's more about their friends than themselves.

When your teen is not willing to stop/change their drug use

If your adolescent indicates that they're not planning to stop using drugs (i.e. they may feel their use is at a safe level), then Positive Choices recommends a few steps:

- Let them know you're there for them and ready to talk when they are – keep the door open
- If they get angry with you, try to keep the conversation related to their drug use and related behaviours, rather than bring up other aspects of their character or any disagreements you may have had in the past
- Encourage them to reduce their risk of harm until they do feel ready to stop
- Let them know that help is available, and you are happy to support them to find the right help for them
- Be aware that recovery can be a long process. You may need some support yourself in supporting your adolescent.

Remember, being a safe base for your teen means that you will have many conversations around alcohol, drugs, sex and vaping. Your job is to keep on providing sound information and support so that, hopefully, they can make better choices.

For more resources on this topic, such as books, podcasts, websites and helpline information, see the Resources section at the back of the book (page 379).

13

What to do when your teen comes home seriously drunk

Background

As a parent of teen boys, I made it as difficult as possible for them to access alcohol and our family rule was that there were no parties until Year 11 when they turned 16. Of course, there was the occasional party that they attended 'without my knowledge' before they were 16, and that risky behaviour was accepted as a part of their development. My other rules were that I would never provide them with alcohol and that they were never to get in a car with anybody who had been consuming alcohol. They could call me, call a taxi (it was a time well before ride sharing was a reality) or they could walk.

When they were over 18, if I was nearby, they could call me at any time of the night, and I would come and collect them to ensure they got home safely. If they vomited in my car or any one of the friends vomited in my car, I would ensure that they were safe after arriving home but it was their responsibility to clean my car the next morning. There would not be any lecture or admonishment because they needed to learn how to navigate the party scene, and experience is a great teacher. My main concern **was to ensure they were home safely.**

At the time of writing this book, we don't yet have the statistics around alcohol use post-COVID, but we do know that the use of alcohol among young people aged 12–17 has been declining over recent years. In 2017 only 27 per cent of young people used alcohol in the past month. Additionally, more young people in Australia are choosing not to drink. The number of young people who never consumed alcohol has increased from one in four (26 per cent) in 2011 to one in three (34 per cent) in 2017.

Among young people who drink, one in four report drinking five or more alcoholic drinks in a single session in the past month (23 per cent). While any alcohol consumption is risky for teenagers, high-risk drinking is defined as drinking an amount that increases the risk of accident or injury.

Recommended alcohol guidelines in Australia

It is important to start this chapter with the recommended alcohol guidelines for mature, healthy adults:

- No more than 10 standard drinks per week
- No more than 4 standard drinks on any one day.

An additional recommendation for women is no more than one standard drink a day or seven in a week. And it goes without saying that people under the age of 18, and women who are pregnant or breastfeeding, should not drink alcohol.

Research in recent years has shown very clearly the damage that long-term, excessive alcohol consumption has on men and women, physically with alcohol-related diseases, mentally including a significant link to increase the possibility of suicide, and emotionally, especially the impact on family relationships, particularly domestic violence.

Long-term effects

According to the Australian Department of Health Care and Ageing, 'for both men and women, the risk of dying from alcohol-related disease and injury remains below 1 in 100 if *no more than 10 standard drinks are consumed each week and no more than four standard drinks are consumed on any one day*. The less you drink, the lower your risk of harm from alcohol'. Please check their website (healthy.gov.au/topics/alcohol) for more sobering statistics.

Australia is known internationally as having a problematic relationship with alcohol, especially in our social settings. Parental modelling around alcohol consumption can impact children and teens and can shape attitudes and expectations either positively or negatively. There is an enormous difference in the impact of alcohol on the developing teenage brain and on the mature adult brain. **The first key bit of advice for any parent of a teen, though, is to make it as difficult as possible for your teen to drink alcohol.** Lock up your spirits cupboard, have many conversations around alcohol and parties, have clear expectations about drinking alcohol and model healthy, responsible alcohol use as their parents. Maybe you can trust your teen around your drinks cabinet but you can't if they have friends who want to drink your vodka and you are not home!

Several years ago, research showed that the earlier adolescents use alcohol or other drugs, the more chance there is that they will have problems with binge drinking and future health and addiction problems later in life. It has taken quite some time for this information to filter down into homes, schools and sporting clubs.

> 'Research shows that parental provision of alcohol to underage teens does not protect against increased alcohol consumption later in life. In fact, there has been evidence to show following serves of alcohol, teenagers are more likely to report binge drinking . . . [and] be involved in fights or problematic drinking in their future adolescent years.'
>
> – www.drinkwise.org.au

In Australia, the provision of alcohol to teenagers is now seen as a cultural problem. Giving them small taste of alcohol as children and tweens needs to be avoided at all costs. It does not encourage healthy attitudes to drinking alcohol. The secondary provision of alcohol to minors other than your own teens is a criminal offence in many parts of Australia and significant fines apply so it's worth familiarising yourself with the laws (adf.org.au has a good breakdown). Either way, it's not a good idea.

When making decisions, teens have a tendency to exaggerate the good (i.e. the rewards) and positives and to diminish the possible risks or negatives and they have a tendency to think 'that won't happen to me!'

> No amount of reasoning, logic or lecturing from well-meaning parents can change that tendency.

So, adolescents, especially teens under 16, need strong parental guidance and expectations. They will break boundaries – this is also a part of claiming their autonomy and there needs to be some serious conversations about consequences if they do it more than once.

As you prepare your teen to navigate the world where alcohol is often freely available, especially at social events, another thing to consider is the influence of siblings, especially older siblings. And in many ways it's a little bit similar to the influence of friends. If they have siblings who have chosen to be mindful and to monitor their experiences with alcohol, this can influence the younger sibling in a similar way. If they have an older sibling who is staggering home drunk quite often, especially one who has left school and is in the workplace, this can definitely influence your younger child to behave in a similar way. Sometimes a sibling who has had a very negative experience with alcohol can be a very helpful influence in teaching a sibling not to do the same if they are prepared to share the story in all its glory. However, a recent Dutch longitudinal study found adolescents who were exposed to more sibling drinking were 'more likely to have drunk alcohol during the past six months and past four weeks and also to binge drink'.

Teens don't want to die or hurt themselves. They simply want to have fun and enjoy life. Sadly making poor choices can mean terrible things can happen. Affirm often that you will love them no matter what happens on this bumpy ride to adulthood – even when they muck up.

Education is the best pathway to the prevention of harm around alcohol and most schools across the country now provide great education in this area, and some bring in external speakers too. Parents are also important and should not just rely on what happens at school though – you need to play your part as well.

The first time you witness your teen very drunk can be frightening and upsetting. I have spoken to many parents who have had this experience who wanted to ground their teen for the rest of their life! Risk-taking behaviour is a normal part of adolescent maturity, and when in the company of friends and peers, it can go one of two ways. It can become dangerous and lead to potentially fatal choices. Alternatively, the sensible behaviour of friends can save lives when a teen becomes very drunk.

It is important in the conversations, the many conversations, you have around alcohol that you explain how it can deeply impact the developing brain. It is also important to explain the difference between the impact of alcohol on girls and boys. When I was still working with teens in high schools, I was staggered how few girls knew that alcohol has a very different impact on them than it does on boys. Not only do girls not process alcohol as quickly due to having higher body fat compared to muscle mass, alcohol stays in their system longer and will often affect them in greater ways. They need to drink less than their male counterparts to get the same effect.

And there's more for girls to be concerned about. It seems that changes in hormones during the menstrual cycle may also affect how alcohol is metabolised. Research indicates that changing hormonal levels slow down alcohol metabolism and this can mean in the week leading up to their period, girls experience higher levels of intoxication. Oral contraceptives and other medications containing estrogen can reduce the rate at which alcohol is processed too.

Another part of the conversation needs to be around how alcohol impacts individuals differently. If a teen is on other medications or struggling with other medical conditions, alcohol can impact them very differently.

It's important your teen knows that alcohol will impact them much faster under the following conditions:

- If they drink on an empty stomach
- If they have a naturally lower tolerance to alcohol
- If they weigh less and have less muscle
- If they don't usually drink alcohol
- If they don't drink any water between alcoholic drinks
- If they drink too fast.

I've heard teens express concerns about going to parties and feeling the pressure to drink because their friends were drinking. I've suggested to them that they sit on one drink and to pretend they are under the influence of alcohol. I've added that they could become the secret guardian of their friends, keeping an eye on them to ensure that they were not making unsafe decisions. Many teens felt really empowered by this and found that they could help their friends when they became really drunk and yet still felt they were belonging in their social group.

Paul Dillon is one of the most respected drug and alcohol educators and researchers in Australia and speaks to young people all year. If young people are going out to parties and social events, Paul suggests they eat a palm-sized amount of carbohydrates before leaving home and to 'always start the night with a drink of water to prepare for the potential dehydrating effect of alcohol, and then continue to hydrate throughout the evening'. Paul emphasises to young people to keep drinking water throughout the evening but cautions that too much water is potentially dangerous as well. It's the first drink that he says is the most important. Paul's message cuts through. His Instagram account (@dillonpauldarta) has some fantastic information for young people and it's full of photos sent in from young people on nights out enjoying #watertime. I thoroughly recommend you explore his website and follow him on socials.

Before your teen goes to their first party where there may be alcohol, hopefully you have had many conversations over many years about your expectations around alcohol. One conversation you definitely need to have is about the potential for alcoholic poisoning.

Know the symptoms:

- Confusion
- Irregular breathing (a gap of more than 10 seconds between breaths)
- Loss of co-ordination
- Low body temperature (hypothermia)
- Pale or blue-tinged skin
- Seizure
- Slow breathing (less than eight breaths per minute)
- Unconsciousness or passing out
- Vomiting.

– Source: drinkwise.org.au

It is important that young people know exactly what to do and not to do if a young person has become unconscious. Many myths are still driving the choices that young people make when a young person slips into an alcoholic coma.

If someone has drunk too much, DO NOT:

- **Leave them to sleep it off:** the amount of alcohol in someone's blood continues to rise even when they stop drinking.
- **Give them coffee:** alcohol dehydrates the body, as does coffee. Having both can lead to severe dehydration and permanent brain damage.
- **Make them sick:** alcohol can interfere with a person's gag reflex causing them to choke on their own vomit.

- **Walk them around:** alcohol slows brain function and affects co-ordination and balance. Walking around might cause accidents.
- **Put them under a cold shower:** alcohol lowers body temperature. A cold shower could make them colder than they already are and lead to hypothermia.
- **Prop them up on the edge of the toilet to be sick:** see next page for more on this.
- **Force them to drink lots of water:** let them drink it at their own pace.
- **Let them drink more alcohol:** the amount of alcohol in their bloodstream could become even higher – which could put them in more danger.

Please educate your teens about what not to do, and then encourage them to take decisive action: put the young person in the recovery position, stay with them and immediately call 000 in Australia. Reassure your teen that they will never get into trouble for calling you or for calling 000. Even better, get them to download the Emergency Plus app so they can be located via GPS.

There's a great episode on the podcast *The Real Deal on Drugs with Paul Dillon* in which he explains when to call an ambulance – great to put on in the car with your teen one day!

Paul Dillion says: 'No one ever gets taken to hospital after having one drink. It's unlikely that anyone will end up on life support after having a couple of drinks across a night. People end up in hospital when they drink too much, too fast. So if you're with someone who you even remotely care about and they're drinking too much, too fast – you just need to say two simple words – *Slow down!*'

Remember everyone mucks up and makes mistakes. Everyone deserves a second chance. Monitoring your teen is about loving guidance, not policing and controlling, threatening or punishing. Please avoid using the disappointment card because it can trigger shame, and most teens who have had a problem experience with alcohol, already experience self-shame.

What to do when your teen comes home seriously drunk

The first thing is to take care of your son or daughter. Do not try to give them food or put them in the shower or any of the things listed previously. Sit with them, while they vomit with a plastic bucket and a 'cloud of tissues' (as per the tip about the toilet bowl below).

It is important to keep an eye on them because some teens have suffocated on their vomit when lying on their back in bed.

> Never prop a drunk person onto a toilet bowl to be sick! They can slip and crack their skull or their teeth.

If you have any concerns about leaving them by themselves in their bedroom, stay with them.

How to have a conversation about alcohol with your teen after their drunk experience?

Firstly, make sure your teen has recovered from the hangover. **Then take a look at 'Before you have the conversation' on page 171.** Once you feel like you're ready, prepare your opening questions.

Possible opening questions

It is important not to have this conversation while they are still hungover. Look after them and reassure them that you will chat about what happened when they are feeling better. You may like to preface this conversation by reassuring your son or daughter how much you love them, no matter what. Next, remember not to assume anything. Teens can do some silly things by adding extra spirits to drinks without an individual knowing or they can encourage them to do drinking games that seem quite benign to start with, however, the overloading and the speed of the alcohol in their system can make them drunk very quickly. Another thing to consider is whether there was any pre-loading of alcohol before they went out. When you can explore all of these without judgement and with loving concern, your teen may be able to learn something significant from the experience that may help them make better choices in the future.

- Bud, I was super frightened when I saw how drunk you were when you came home the other night. Are you okay to tell me what happened?
- Hey sweetheart, being drunk feels awful doesn't it, and I was really frightened that you could have had alcoholic poisoning. Are you okay if we explore how you got to be so drunk so that hopefully it might be the first and last time?
- Ava, my love, I'm curious as to how you got so drunk the other night because that was pretty awful for you and potentially dangerous. Can you tell me what you remember drinking?

Next steps

Together, collaboratively explore some key information that they may not have had before and allow them to consider their future experiences with alcohol.

It can be helpful to use a 'what if' strategy once you have an accurate picture of what led to them becoming really drunk. For example, if they became drunk because they drank spirits rather than lower-alcohol drinks, you might ask, 'What would you do if your friends were encouraged to play a sculling game with vodka?' Or 'what would you do if your friends were drinking much faster than you feel comfortable with?'

Maybe listen to Paul's podcast together – there's plenty of good episodes, but maybe at this stage Episode 8 on mixing drinks and hangovers might be a good choice!

Please keep in mind that punishment does not teach anything, and it can potentially damage the relationship. If you feel a consequence would be helpful, like no parties for a period of time, you make that call. For them to truly become wiser and more capable at making better decisions around alcohol, they will need to step back into the same scene going forward.

Remember the power of the concern for their friends. If you have the opportunity when they are together, remind them how important they are to each other when they are out in social settings. This can be deceptively powerful at helping them take better care of themselves, however, they are far more likely to watch out for their friends first.

Research shows that, as a parent, you're one of the most important social influencers in keeping your child safer when it comes to alcohol. Keeping connected and maintaining lines of communication through adolescence can be challenging but building a strong foundation nice and early can make all the difference. Talking about the alcohol issue and believing that you do have the power to make a difference in this area is vital.

For more resources on this topic, such as books, podcasts, websites and helpline information, see the Resources section at the back of the book (page 380).

14

What to do when your teen is experiencing significant bullying, including cyberbullying

WHAT HAVE YOU FOUND MOST CHALLENGING AS A TEEN?

- Having lots of pressure being put on me to decide my future when I'm not thinking about that and being bullied.
- Peer pressure and bullying.
- Trauma and bullying and adults telling me a certain way of dealing with it that wasn't helpful to me.
- People are much more brutal and mean in high school. People I've known all my life have said horrible things straight up to me in high school that they wouldn't have ever said in primary school. It's created a lot of new insecurities for me and has made me much more anxious coming into school because I know by the end of the day someone's words will be replaying in my head.
- The bullying that comes from other girls.

Background

Bullying and physical violence seem to have increased in our schools and communities and definitely in the cyberworld. I believe this is partly because of decreased emotional literacy, increased stress levels, poorer self-regulation, less resilience and a desensitisation to violence, mainly from the influence of screens. It can be really hard to find a movie or a series to watch today that is not incredibly violent.

These are common nasty teen behaviours that are technically not bullying, and yet can be hurtful:

- Showing off
- Being silly: 'it was just a joke!'
- Being dumb
- Laughing at others
- Attention-seeking because you feel left out
- Speaking without thinking
- Trying to be funny
- Trying to make yourself look better
- Dumping your negative feelings, like being angry or jealous, on others.

Bullying has been around possibly since time began. There will always be people who use power over other people. Serious bullying, especially during the teen years, can scar an individual permanently. It can go from a 'small t' trauma to a 'large T' trauma over time. Often teens who are being bullied don't want to tell their parents because they feel embarrassed, or they don't want to worry them or they are seriously afraid that their parents will make things worse.

> I had a smelly penis because I wasn't washing it properly and wasn't masturbating and hadn't been taught about either issue – it led to bullying at school.

Childhood nastiness, being rude and being mean don't necessarily constitute bullying. Bullying is when there is an intention to cause harm, usually with the use of power over another, and it is repeated behaviour and it threatens an individual's wellbeing. Bullies can be deliberately manipulative and plan their actions and they can also be triggered to bully when they feel inadequate, unsafe or rejected in some way. Often, they will target an individual who they perceive as weaker than them. Sometimes they target individuals who they are jealous of because they have popularity, high grades, loving parents or even live in a nice house.

Bullying can include:

- Name-calling
- Public shaming online or in real life
- Targeting a person based on their gender, sexuality, race, religion or disability
- Sending mean messages
- Spreading rumours
- Deliberately ignoring and excluding others
- Deliberately embarrassing others
- Harassment or physical intimidation
- Singling someone out to make them feel isolated or that they are different in some way.

It is important to remember that bullying can be happening in front of your teen or indirectly behind their back. It can also be overt and really obvious or covert, which is much harder to notice and to prove. Social bullying is when things are done to hurt your reputation and sadly cyberbullying has taken this to a whole new level of concern.

It is important to keep in mind that bullying is a learned behaviour. No one is born a bully. As your child is growing towards their adolescent years, it can be helpful to be mindful of certain things as you can possibly nip a problem in the bud before it becomes a habitual pattern.

In your circle of family members or friends have you noticed any of the following:

- Significant teasing inside or outside the family
- Anyone forcing people to do things they don't want to do
- Deliberate exclusion of individuals from activities
- Obvious gossiping, or spreading of rumours that are untrue
- Taking frustrations out on others and blaming others
- Trying to force people to adopt only their point of view
- Shouting or yelling frequently
- Any physical aggression.

I created an e-book for teens call *Taking the High Road* so I could explain some of the things that teens could do when they are struggling. There are some things that a teen can do in the heat of the moment that can de-escalate a bully, rather than escalate them. When I was counselling, I worked with a number of teens who were being bullied and the first thing I would teach them was how to have a power stance with their body. That meant that they would walk with their shoulders back, their chin up and a positive look on their face. We would practise standing and walking in a power stance because it sends a message to a bully that the teen is feeling confident and strong. Bullies tend to target more vulnerable teens who look weaker to them. There's actually some great information online about power stances these days, including a TED talk, so look it up for some more information.

Next, teens have to choose an automatic reaction and a few words that they will say if a bully calls out something mean or disrespectful. They get to choose the response and they have to practise it with their power stance frequently so that it seems natural when they need to use it.

Helpful things a teen can do or say if someone is mean

- Just nod, smile and walk away
- 'Whatever you reckon'
- Give them a wink and walk away
- Wish them a good day
- 'Sorry can't stop, the teacher wants to see me'
- Pause and then say 'Thanks for sharing.'
- 'Thanks for noticing my red hair. I love being different.'
- Call it out, e.g. Frown and say, 'Oh wow, that was actually really mean!'
- Pretend to agree with them (to show you don't really care), e.g. 'You're right, I am a loser. Thanks for being so open and honest with me.'

Another strategy that I would teach teens who were being bullied was to remember it's not what happens or what is said to you. *It is what we say to ourselves afterwards that really matters.* If we have an ANT attack following an altercation with a bully, those negative thoughts will create even more shameful negative feelings and emotions. These feelings and emotions were created with the conflict that happened. Teens can choose one of the following to repeat silently to themselves immediately after the bully has tried to bully them:

- My mum and dad love me
- My dog loves me
- Gee, someone is having a bad day
- No matter what they say or do to me, I am always going to be a worthwhile person
- It's obvious who has the problem here
- I am okay exactly as I am
- Their spark must be asleep.

Sometimes teaching teens about the power of being an active bystander can be really helpful. It is similar to being the secret guardian at parties; you step into the role of a protector and it automatically gives you more confidence to help protect someone being attacked.

> **WHAT HAVE YOU FOUND MOST CHALLENGING AS A TEEN?**
>
> Bullying that occurred – initially I had friends who would stick up for me but they were told by the school not to and everything went sour from there. This occurred from Year 7 to 10. I couldn't turn to anyone. Parents were very supportive but were a little lost at times. They attended the school and advocated for me but it fell on deaf ears. Basically, school wasn't supportive. I am now in another school and am feeling like myself when I began Year 7 before the bullying commenced.

Cyberbullying

One of the great things about being the host of the ABC podcast *Parental as Anything* is that I get to chat with all sorts of fabulous experts. One of those was Rachel Downie who has worked in school-leadership teams and as a high-school teacher for many years. Following the death by suicide of a Year 9 student, she began to question the role of friends in the prevention of suicide and that led her to explore one of the most significant factors that can impact a vulnerable teen – cyberbullying. She then went on to create an anonymous reporting app called Stymie. One of the most difficult things about cyberbullying is that it's not face-to-face bullying; it's anonymous. Cyberbullying is 24/7 and not only is it relentless, it is especially cruel. If you have a teen, it would be excellent to listen to that particular episode together, maybe while driving in the car, because it covers so much that can help them navigate the digital world.

Rachel believes that families need to have significant conversations about cyber wellness, and how to behave as a responsible digital citizen. Have you established how you are representing your family online and what does that look like?

On the eSafety commissioner website, cyberbullying is described as 'using the Internet to make someone feel bad or upset' by:

- Sending hurtful messages about them
- Sharing embarrassing photos or videos of them
- Spreading nasty online gossip about them
- Leaving them out online
- Creating fake accounts in their name
- Tricking them into believing you are someone else (this is called catfishing).

Obviously any hateful or hurtful messages left in the digital space that target an individual is also cyberbullying. Another example of cyberbullying is called roasting and this is when someone has a photograph of you and they post it in a group chat, and they invite other people to say nasty stuff about you. Then when lots of awful stuff has been said, the bully will invite the subject of the photo into the group. Not only does the subject see what has been said, they will also know the people who have been writing the hurtful messages. How horrendous would that be for any of us, let alone a child or a teen?

Another thing that happens is that the bully will set up a fake profile online and use that profile to write awful stuff and to be a cyberbully. Everyone in the school will believe the victim is the bully because the fake account is in their name. With the rise of AI, this kind of thing will only become easier for bullies to do. For a long time, the eSafety commissioner has had concerns about deep fakes, doxing (sharing people's personal details online) and sextortion which, as I mentioned earlier, many young boys are falling victim to.

Fake accounts can be problematic in other ways too. Your teen may have agreed to have a safe person who has access to their Insta, Snapchat or TikTok account to monitor their activities to make sure they are safe. But your teen may simply create fake accounts where they will really have the freedom that they want, and it is the covert things that are not visible that can create the worst harm.

The most tragic consequence of being attacked and shamed online is that it has contributed to the suicide of many tweens and teens, some as young as 12. And sadly, it sometimes comes out following such a tragic death that parents often knew nothing about what their teen or tween was experiencing. One of the biggest concerns that teens have about sharing their cyberbullying experiences is that their parents will remove their devices or phones if they find out, so many stay silent and suffer alone.

Also, I previously was not aware that, in some places, **your kids are responsible for their thoughts and actions, in terms of Australian law, from the age of 10 in the digital space.** So there can be very real consequences for cyberbullies too.

When to worry

These may be signs to watch out for that your teen may be being bullied:

- Struggling with higher levels of anxiety and stress
- Getting upset more easily
- Ripped clothing
- School reluctance or school refusal
- Change in friendship groups
- Vague headaches or stomach aches
- Withdrawing from social activities
- Lost or missing belongings
- Having injuries they can't explain
- Having difficulty sleeping
- Sudden drop in grades and subjects that they used to enjoy and do well in
- Depressive symptoms (see the chapter on whether your teen is just moody or depressed)
- Unexpected outbursts and meltdowns
- Seeming upset straight after they've been on their device/phone
- Being secretive about their online activities/phone use.

What to do when your teen is experiencing significant bullying, including cyberbullying?

It can be really helpful if you have sown the seeds of possibility around having a conversation about the bullying behaviour of teens in general, not just your son or daughter, *before you have the big conversation*. Remember your son or daughter may be the bully and this information will help you create that conversation. However, this outline is for the bullied teen.

Maybe something like:

- 'There were bullies around when I was at high school and they can make a life of misery. Have you noticed any bullies in your year group?'
- 'I saw something on my Insta page the other day where teens were telling other teens to go kill themselves! Yikes, that's a bit awful. Have you seen that on your pages?'

Or find an article to share with them. Many celebrities are cyber-bullied quite viciously, and talking about that with your teen may be a way to ease into the conversation. There is a lot of information in the media about the sharing of naked images without consent, so it shouldn't be hard to find a real example to ease into the conversation.

Having the conversation

Firstly, when it comes to bullying, if your child is being threatened physically, or they are indicating that they may harm themselves, you should get professional help. Call emergency services immediately in that case and contact a counselling service like Kids Helpline to help find them some emotional support.

If the situation is not life-threatening, firstly, **take a look at 'Before you have the conversation' on page 171.** Then, once you feel like you're ready, prepare your opening questions. Maybe mention this chat is not about taking phones or devices off your teen! It's a chat so that you can better understand what it's like being a teen in a digital world, a world you didn't experience when you were a teen.

Possible opening questions

- Bud, I've noticed that you seem to be struggling bit lately and I'm a bit worried about you – are you able to have a bit of a chat now or later?
- Hey, my mum radar is telling me that something is causing you some worries and I am a bit curious if there was anyone who's being a bit mean or nasty to you?
- Ava, my love, I noticed when you walked into school the other day that there seemed to be some other girls who didn't look very friendly and who looked like they were waiting for you – can we have a chat to see if everything is okay?
- I'm noticing whenever you get off your phone lately you seem agitated; is anything going on online to upset you?

If your teen does share stuff with you about bullying, please thank them and reassure them that it's never their fault. Never ever. With face-to-face bullying, it is handy to remember that you will only be hearing one half of the story and that it can be important to get as many facts as possible. Sometimes, your tween or teen may have contributed to the conflict, even though intentional bullying is still unacceptable on all levels.

If it is face-to-face bullying, explore the options above and see how you can support your teen going forward. If you feel it is serious enough, please contact the school. Never reach out to the bully or the bully's parents as that never ends well and often makes things worse for your teen.

Tackling cyberbullying

Once your teen shares that they are being cyberbullied, your next job is to gather the evidence and report image-based abuse. There is excellent information at esafety.gov.au that shows you how to gather evidence and how to block people. Rachel Downie says that some bullies will simply create other fake accounts and come back at your teen again. Your teen needs to keep blocking the bully and tighten their security by changing their privacy settings and putting limits on who can share their stuff and contact them. It can be really empowering for your teen to be able to take action against bullies in cyberspace, because that may allow them to be able to keep their other friendships and connections happening.

The apps and platforms have now become much more effective at combating cyberbullying with reporting processes in place. You do need to report to the app where the bullying is happening. For example, if it happens on Insta, apparently it is simply eight clicks and you can have an incident reported and they tend to respond really well, according to Rachel Downie.

For image or video-based abuse, the eSafety commissioner advises that:

> If you're under 18, you can use takeitdown.ncmec.org – a free online tool that prevents your image or video being shared on platforms such as Facebook, Instagram, TikTok, Yubo, OnlyFans and Pornhub.
>
> If you're 18 or older, you can use StopNCII.org – a free online tool that prevents your image or video being shared on platforms such as Facebook, Instagram, TikTok, Bumble, OnlyFans and Reddit.

Please be aware that if the cyberbullying involves sexualised images of a child under 18, then that behaviour may be a crime, 'even if you've just taken a screenshot for evidence purposes', advises the eSafety commissioner. Under 25s can get free legal advice from Youth Law Australia and you can report the incident at esafety.gov.au

It can be very difficult for schools to be able to resolve bullying conflicts of any kind, especially cyberbullying. Sometimes school staff are tied up for days just over one cyberbullying incident that happened in the middle of the night. Bullying of any kind will negatively impact learning in the classroom. Your teen simply cannot concentrate when their brain is in fight or flight.

Reducing the amount of time your teen has access to their phone is important. One of the most sensible steps initially is to put a new boundary in place that means that your teen has no access to the digital world overnight. It can be helpful if all the family participate in a cyber bedtime with the Wi-Fi turned off for everyone.

You might also remind them to focus on activities on the phone that bring them enjoyment. They may even agree to reduce the number of apps that they have on their phone. They need to be part of the solution to help build better protections for themselves. Have them read the chapter on anxiety as it has many ideas and strategies that can help them feel calmer and happier.

Parents and schools both have to work together to help overcome the negative effects of cyberbullying and bullying. This is a whole landscape that you haven't had to deal with, but your tweens and teens are.

Keep reassuring them that you will always have their back and that they can always come to you.

For more resources on this topic, such as books, podcasts, websites and helpline information, see the Resources section at the back of the book (page 381).

15

What to do when your teen's phone use becomes problematic

WHAT DO YOU FIND MOST CHALLENGING AS A TEEN TODAY?

- Having too much to do and not enough time. Social media, specifically Instagram, spending too much time on social media, thinking my life isn't productive enough, thinking about the examples I see online in comparison to my own life.
- The thing I have found most challenging as a teen is the exposure to videos of what's right and wrong (e.g. porn, sexualising videos); these videos have been shown in group chats.
- The social aspect definitely. Even if I bit my tongue and stayed out of whatever drama was going on around me, people always found a way to drag me into stuff and turn people against me. Especially with teenage girls. It's so mentally draining.
- Being exposed to sexualising videos and porn.
- Everything mostly
    - o School
    - o Family
    - o Friends
    - o Online world
    - o Mostly everything.

Background

Have you tried talking to today's teens when they are on their phones? Impossible, isn't it? It is almost like they are glued to their phone and that device can and does go everywhere from the classroom to the bedroom and yes, even the toilet. Many teens believe that if their friends don't answer them immediately, there is probably a problem or they don't care about them anymore. This means that their perception is that they need the phone by their side at all times or their friendships could be ruined! Many teens, mainly girls, are super vigilant with their phones in case their friends might need them or the very real pressure of FOMO.

If we keep in mind the three key needs of every human, connection, competence and control, you can see why teens are so connected to their phones. It gives them everything they need – well, that is debatable. They think it gives them everything they need. In Part One, I explained how there is a strong biological drive for teens to be connected to their friends and peers, even above their families. Connection is the juice that drives so much of teen behaviour. The opposite is exclusion which is what drives most teen suffering and mental anguish. So, let's be clear, as digital natives our teens need their phones. However, our job is to help them work out how to use them respectfully, sensibly and responsibly. Yes, I said all those big words in one sentence. And there are many adults who can't even do this! So, our job as parents is to lead the way, and to help our teens, to guide them and to educate them – not to ban them, punish them or endlessly lecture them.

Your modelling of your phone usage – and the same goes for any other grown-ups in the house – is a significant influence on your teen's behaviour. Ouch – I know the truth hurts.

Why do we need to worry about our teen's phone use?

The first concern is the displacement effect of the constant connection to a phone. What is your teen no longer doing that is good for their growth and development and general happiness because they are on their phones? Anecdotally, we know of many teens who no longer go out socially as often as they used to, preferring to stay in their bedrooms on their phones. This has created a higher level of social anxiety in teens, which is impacting their ability to transition to work. Not only that, when they are in work environments, many teens are struggling to engage without constantly checking the phone and some are even losing their jobs as a consequence. It is our job as the guides for our teens to ensure that their phones don't prevent them from growing in the best way possible.

The second concern is that the more time they spend on their phones, the more likely it is that they are going to come across harmful content or to be harmed in some way.

Many of our teens are being deeply impacted by negative content and inappropriate, disrespectful or hurtful messaging, such as:

- Cyberbullying
- Sexting and sextortion
- Phishing activities and being a victim of identity theft or fraud
- Misusing people's passwords and impersonating people online
- Making unauthorised purchases using other people's financial details
- Creating content that reveals private information about others
- Having trouble regulating online time, leading to problematic Internet use that can impact health and wellbeing, especially around sleep
- Being a victim of identity theft or fraud
- Inappropriate marketing messages or scam emails
- Intentional solicitation and exposure to sexual predation
- Deep fakes or AI that misleads, or misrepresents others
- Constant negative messages and/or highly sexualised content.

Some risks include encountering adults posing as children online, strangers who persuade teenagers to send them photos or videos of themselves or meet them in real life, and online scammers. Sextortion has become a significant problem, particularly for boys aged 14 to 17.

Parents need to have constant conversations with their teens around managing safety and privacy settings on their phone, such as checking that their social-media profiles are set to private and making sure they use facial recognition or a PIN to lock their phone. Many teens may reassure you that bad things won't ever happen to them and that we are being overly cautious, however, that's exactly how the teen brain works. They underestimate the likelihood of bad outcomes. I have found that many teens are very savvy about not entering personal details like the name, address or date of birth into online accounts – I have found it is adults who often make that mistake. However, just because teens are savvy in some areas doesn't mean they are always capable of being critically literate and accurate in their assessments, and they can make mistakes – it's important to remind them of that.

One thing that can be more difficult for teens to negotiate than grown adults is knowing not to accept new social media friend requests from people they don't know in real life, especially given all the fake accounts that exist with fake identities. Teens are so desperate to have people like them or join their online world, they will often let anyone in.

Also, another piece of sound advice for teens is to make sure that your teen turns off location services in apps rather than just leave them running in the background.

You will need to have many conversations about these key concerns – the more the better, even if they roll their eyes at you.

In their 2024 book, *How to Say No to Your Phone,* psychologists Brad Marshall and Lindsay Hassock share some interesting statistics about phone usage.

The world's smartphone stats:

- The average time a person spends on their phone each day is 4.8 hours.
- On average, people pick up and open their phones 58 times a day.
- Users worldwide spend an average of 95 minutes per day on TikTok.

That TikTok stat is interesting given that one in four TikTok users is under 20 years old, and 95 minutes a day is about four times more than the average time spent on Snapchat (21 minutes), and nearly twice as much as the average duration users spend on Facebook (49 minutes) and Instagram (51 minutes).

In the book, Marshall and Hassock explain that the reason that we all can struggle in our relationship with our phones is the intermittent reinforcement of the phone, which gives small hits of dopamine. It's not just teens. It's all of us.

The next area of concern is not just how much time your teen is spending online, but rather what they are doing online.

In a recent Roy Morgan research poll, they found that teens aged 14 to 17 were twice as likely as other phone users to use the device for playing music, videos and games. So that's good news, and we need to keep this in mind when we are helping our teen to manage problematic usage, as they often use phones for positive things too.

When teens use their phones mainly for social media, which tends to be our girls, that's when we can begin to have some significant problems.

In 2019, one US study of more than 6,500 12- to 15-year-olds found a link between using social media for more than three hours a day and heightened risk for mental-health problems. Another UK study that same year of 12,000 13- to 16-year-olds found teens who used social media more than three times a day had poor mental health and wellbeing predictions.

Further studies have linked depression and anxiety with high levels of social-media use. One 2016 study of teens found that using social media more, using it at night and being emotionally invested in social media were linked to worse sleep quality and higher levels of anxiety and depression.

Researchers have been arguing for a long time that there was no evidence that social media is responsible for the increase in the mental unwellness of our young people. There was a correlation but not causation. However, it seems the evidence has gotten much stronger, as a review of research from social psychologist Professor Jon Haidt and colleagues shows.

The recent collaborative review of more than 100 correlational, longitudinal and experimental studies around the influence of social media has concluded that the evidence is substantial that social media is a major cause of the epidemic of mental illness in teen girls. Haidt has written about the situation in the US where the CDC's bi-annual Youth Risk Behavior Survey showed that '*most* teen girls (57 per cent) now say that they experience persistent sadness or hopelessness (up from 36 per cent in 2011), and 30 per cent of teen girls now say that they have seriously considered suicide (up from 19 per cent in 2011).'

Another study that has come out in recent times has shown that the earlier a child gets a smartphone, the more mental-health challenges they will have between ages 18 to 24.

Despite all these concerns, which hit the mainstream in 2020 when the documentary *The Social Dilemma* came out, this information goes largely unheeded by the tech giants. At the time of writing this book, 33 states in the US and nine attorneys general had filed lawsuits against Meta complaining that Instagram and Facebook are deliberately designed to be addictive to children and harming young people's mental health.

One of the key reasons that excessive phone use can have such a negative impact on our developing teens is that most of the apps have been designed with very clever algorithms to ensure that every user sees more negative content than positive content. We are wired towards a negative bias because watching for negative things in our environment is how we keep ourselves safe. What that means is that our brains are driven to stay more engaged with negative content online. Sadly, this means that we are marinating our precious teens into the darkest, sickest and most violent content imaginable and that is definitely impacting their capacity to grow into happy, healthy adults who can access hope and optimism. Please explain this to your teens so that they can see that they are being used to make tech companies more money, because the longer you stay online the more advertisements you see, the more money they make. I suggest you listen to some podcast interviews/watch interviews with the author of *Stolen Focus*, Johann Hari, as he explains this very well. Johann Hari urges us all to put pressure on tech companies to demand that they change these algorithms. That's a whole other subject; in fact, it requires a big push of people power. It's not impossible, though, and I just want to plant the seed here that we could improve the wellbeing of our children and our teens significantly by demanding this kind of change. There are now initiatives around the world and in Australia to ban social media for under-16s. While banning anything with teens can be problematic, it shows we need to do more to keep kids safe online.

Our kids' wellbeing should not be at the mercy of making profits, especially our vulnerable and highly impressionable teens. For a deep, concerning exploration of the impact of phones, I also recommend Jonathon Haidt's new book, *The Anxious Generation*.

A little teen outrage can definitely help adjust problematic usage.

> Teenagers (especially my generation) have a large involvement with social media as we are surrounded with easy access to it. There is a constant pressure to send and respond, keep up 'streaks' and if you are not using your phone enough, you can find yourself quickly excluded by peers. Personally I find it extremely challenging to make sure I respond quick enough to people and give off a 'good impression'.

When to worry

- If your teen has an intense urge to use their phone all the time
- If your teen completely loses all track of time while on their phone
- If your teen gets panicked if the phone goes flat
- If your teen panics even if they temporarily can't see or find it
- If your teen neglects other more important things to use it
- If your teen is neglecting their homework
- If there is school reluctance or school refusal
- If there is a drop in your teen's school grades

- If your teen is unable to put the phone away during mealtimes
- If your teen experiences an increase in sleeping challenges
- If your teen spends an increased time in their bedroom
- If your teen gives up sport or hobbies to stay on their phone
- If there are excessive data costs
- If other people complain about how much time your teen is on their phone
- If your teen has increased meltdowns and outbursts
- If you find inappropriate photos and videos on your teen's phone.

Warning signs to look out for to protect your teen's mental health

How much social media connection is too much for your teen? Here are a few signs that it's time to log off to improve their mental health, according to Marshall and Hassock:

- Your teen spends more time on social media than they do with friends
- Your teen directs all of their attention towards capturing content for social media, and they don't enjoy the experience in real time
- They often compare themselves to their friends and feel jealous of what they are posting
- They experience hurtful harassment such as cyberbullying or trolling
- Your teen finds themselves getting caught up in hurtful conversations about others
- Your teen checks their social media feed again and again and again so they don't feel out of the loop.

– Brad Marshall and Lindsay Hassock,
How to Say No to Your Phone

We need to recognise that even grown-ups are struggling with their phone usage and so this is a conversation for the whole family, rather than just them.

What are your phone guidelines for your family?

Here are a few suggestions you might consider.

1. Phones are not to be seen or heard during family meals
2. Phones are not left in bedrooms overnight
3. There is a digital Wi-Fi bedtime agreed by the family
4. Phones and other devices are charged in a family area overnight
5. Phones need to be put down when you are talking face-to-face with each other.

Creating change from habitual behaviour needs to happen gradually and in small steps. It would be wonderful to change problematic behaviour by going completely cold turkey, but that would be extremely difficult and could possibly damage your relationship with your teen. You might mention that is a thought you have had so that they might have a buy-in to your tentative plan to reduce their usage. Aim to make some significant shifts over a four-week window and have regular monitoring in that time. An hour less of usage a day can make a huge difference in a teen's life. They might break that up into half an hour in the morning and half an hour after school or in the evening, or one hour after school, when they are most likely to want to be engaging. This is much easier to achieve.

In his writing and his work as director of The Screen and Gaming Disorder Clinic in Sydney, Brad Marshall recommends practising some screen-free time at the same time each day. Our brain loves predictability and so when we create a routine, it can help curb our hunger for the dopamine hit. Bearing in mind that one of the biggest drivers for using the phone for teens is connection with friends, then before school may not be a good time to go screen-free. Mealtimes, while doing homework, while at sport or while going for a walk or ride are great opportunities to practise screen-free time. Leave the phone at home when you go for a walk with your dog. Seriously, try it. Yes, it will feel uncomfortable the first few times, but then it will become your new normal.

It can be helpful to start with a good quality parental control app – one that ensures safety from inappropriate material, excessive hours online and a healthy bedtime – on all devices and screens. We also need to teach our kids about healthy boundaries around screens and agree on some guidelines as a family. However, many of our teens are very tech savvy, and they know how to get around most parental control apps. Education is the key to the prevention of harm in the digital world. Navigating this world that is forever changing is the most significant challenge for parents today.

Claire Orange from DiGii Social uses the metaphor of a busy highway when talking about preparing your children to access the digital world. We don't put our toddlers in the middle of a 10-lane highway where cars drive at 110kph. We gradually prepare them over time, so that they can learn to drive slowly, in the 60km zone. Having frequent conversations with your teen about being a safe and responsible digital citizen is important.

Much like in the question about problematic gaming, you need to explore what your teen used to be doing before their phone usage became problematic. There is an agreement in the Appendices section about tech, which may be helpful in negotiating with your teen around better managing their phone time.

There needs to be many conversations in your home around cyber safety and the impact of social media that is full of unrealistic images. Respectful behaviour online also needs to be an ongoing conversation.

Remind your teen that having a phone is a privilege in your home and not a right. And that if they are unable to use it appropriately, they can lose that privilege for a time.

Negotiating the limits around their usage needs to be done collaboratively. It can be helpful if they prioritise their favourite activities, so that they can ensure they continue to do the things they enjoy which are not causing harm. Many teens use their phones to wake them up or to use calming music that helps them go to sleep. You will need to work out alternative solutions to these things.

It can be really helpful to set a timer or adjust the 'screen time' settings on their smartphones to remind them how much time they are spending engaging with their phone, especially if they are playing a game. Doom scrolling can also be managed much better with the use of a timer because they can all lose track of time when they are in the state of flow with their phones or devices.

Another huge thing that can make a big difference for your teen can be to switch off the notifications and stop the blips and beeps – the sounds that mean something has happened. I have absolutely no notifications on my phone because I found I was forever picking up my phone to check what the notification was for. Having notifications turned off not only helps your teen stay more focused in the moment, they are less likely to want to respond to every message that they can see.

> The pressures of growing up with technology – yes there is a lot more opportunity and ability to educate oneself with the information available online, but I also feel because it allows people to spread their achievements, happiness and image of their 'best life' that constantly pressures one to be 'catching up' to whatever is ideal at the time. This ideal can be lifestyle, body image, food, money, family, relationships and all of the above.

It can be helpful if your teen can share their concerns about their phone usage with their circle of friends. They might suggest that within their friendship circles, they agree not to share harmful comments to anyone and that they will pause before they respond to what they see online. If a friend's use becomes problematic, your teen may notice their friend is not achieving as well at school, or they may be struggling with the negativity that permeates the digital space. Working together with their friends on how to navigate their phones in the most positive way possible can be incredibly empowering for all teens. It can really improve their wellbeing. They can have fun working together identifying the things that lift them up, and the things that pull them down. This helps them to be more mindful of their choices while on their phones.

What to do when your teen's phone use becomes problematic

It can be really helpful if you have sown the seeds of possibility around having a conversation about problematic phone usage in general, *before you have the big conversation*. Teens are very sensitive to being blindsided, especially around big topics.

Maybe find an article online or a podcast episode that explores the excessive use of phones, especially social media and how it impacts health and wellbeing. You might mention one of the studies above, and then just let it permeate before you have the conversation.

Having the conversation

Firstly, take a look at 'Before you have the conversation' on page 171. Maybe mention this chat is not about taking their phones or devices off them! It's a chat so that you as their parent can better understand what it's like being a teen in a digital world, which is so different from when you were a teen. Reassure them that everyone can struggle with using their phones responsibly and that you want to work together with your teen, so that they are in charge of their phone, and their phone is not in charge of them.

It can be helpful not to use the word 'addiction' or 'addicted' when you are going to have a conversation with your teen. It is better to use a word like 'problematic' or 'worrying' as it provokes far less pushback from your teen.

Possible opening questions

- Bud, I've noticed that you seem to be struggling with being able to put your phone down, even when you're around your friends and I wonder if you have noticed that?
- Hey, my mum radar is telling me that something is causing you some worries and I am a bit curious if your phone has become way too important in your life and you could be finding it hard to put it down?

- Ava, my love, I have been reading about some of the latest studies that show how problematic phone usage is in increasing teens' mental unwellness and I want us to have a chat about ways of using the phone in a positive way?

Next steps

If your teen is not convinced they have a problem with their phone usage, get them to turn on their screen-time settings on their phone (they have these on Android and iOS phones), so they can see how long they are spending on their phone and what they are spending most of their time doing on there. Then you and they will have clear evidence to bring to the table to help initiate change.

Once you have explored the challenges, you can collaboratively consider ways of improving healthy access to their phones. When we remind teens about the privilege versus the right of access to their phone, they can often be more motivated to participate in finding small steps to a solution. The very thought of having their phone removed permanently can be a wonderful motivation to work with you rather than against you. If you are talking to your son, it can be better to ask for his recommendations, and to give him a couple of days to come up with them. Girls tend to be much quicker at considering challenges and accessing solutions.

Another recommendation is that you aim high with your expectations as a parent, and that when you settle on the more moderate situation, your teen feels like they've had a win.

Once you have settled on some steps, give them a few days to ease into the new guidelines, and have a check-in a week after beginning. Remind your teen that there will be consequences if these first steps are not followed. Of course, they may need to be given a second chance; however, after that, they may lose their phone for a night or for 24 hours.

It can be helpful to write the new guidelines down and put them on the fridge so that there is visual clarity about exactly what was agreed upon. If you feel an agreement would work better with your son or daughter, go ahead. Yes, your teen is not going to be happy with you, because they would like the freedom to make all their own choices. That's okay. Our kids need parents not best friends and holding boundaries does far more to help than hinder your teen's development.

From time to time, remind your high-school aged teen that you can spontaneously check their phone as part of being a good parent. I find that if you warn them on a Sunday morning that you will be checking their phone that day, it gives them a chance to remove any images or videos that their friends may have sent them that you might find offensive. Sometimes, they just forget what is on the phone. It is likely that often it's material that is sent to them rather than things they have created themselves.

It can also be helpful to come to your teen to check on the privacy settings on your apps to make sure they are set appropriately. They then become the teachers, rather than the students, and trust me, most teens are far more tech savvy than parents. Have many conversations about how some apps change their settings from time to time, which can make it easier for sexual predators to access our kids and teens.

Older siblings or cousins are often incredibly helpful at helping younger family members to navigate the digital world more safely. Most of them have made big mistakes that they regret so encourage them to become guardians of the younger family members and maybe to offer a word of caution if they see their younger relative post something inappropriate, for example.

A great suggestion from my friend Dr Kristy Goodwin, who is a digital wellbeing expert, is that if we can't see our phone when we are around our family, we are much less likely to pick it up. Create a place in your kitchen, behind cupboard doors, where the phones can be put when the family is in the kitchen either preparing or eating food. This goes for teens as well as us!

Finally, banning phones in the bedroom can make a huge difference around some of the risky behaviour that can occur, especially at night. I know this is so hard because as a teen you probably spent a lot of time in your bedroom so it feels natural . . . but most of us as teens didn't have access to the Internet while we were in there. Given that they very rarely talk on the phone and mainly they message through apps or text, they can do that in the public areas at home. Teens don't seem to want to video call each other as much as we might think, until they have fallen head over heels in love with someone. It will be very difficult to implement a complete ban with your teen around phones in the bedroom, so negotiate a time when they need to disconnect from all digital highways to prepare for bed.

Gradual change, step-by-step, with lots of encouragement and enthusiasm can help change problematic phone usage. Creating many opportunities for your teen to connect with their friends IRL can also help reduce problematic phone usage. Organise 'overs' – they are sleepovers without the sleep and without phones. Maybe get yourself a fire pit. We need to rebuild real-life connectedness in the lives of our teens. They just want to hang out together and have fun so let's make it as appealing as possible for them to do this face to face.

For more resources on this topic, such as books, podcasts, websites and helpline information, see the Resources section at the back of the book (page 382).

16

What to do when your teen's gaming becomes problematic

Background

Gaming on a computer or device is a wildly popular pastime for kids, teens and adults in most countries in the Western world, including Australia. In a 2020 report from *Digital Australia,* 92 per cent of Australian households had at least one device to play digital games.

It is important to avoid demonising gaming because, much like physical play, it has some advantages in terms of the growth and development of children. It's even been shown to have some benefits in terms of mental health for many adults. Individuals are *still playing* and learning the social aspects of play and gaming can be particularly advantageous for neurodivergent children who can sometimes struggle socially in the real world. Having fun is a great part of being a kid and an adult. Not all video games are based on hunting and killing. There are many creative video games that can help develop problem-solving, creative thinking and strategising, and they are all good life skills to have. Learning to lose well is another possible benefit from online gaming, especially in multiplayer games, even though there would be some who would argue that you would learn to lose better with real humans than avatars.

- The fact my parents don't understand that not everyone online is a predator looking to lure in children but instead are genuinely decent people who are just looking to have fun or meet other similarly aged people on places like r/teenagers.
- The way people use online platforms. Some things are just so hurtful and fake. Also the lack of things to do, people just resort to the online world.

When gaming is a part of a balanced lifestyle, it is in essence not a problem. In the Appendix I have included an outline of an agreement that you could adapt with your child, preferably before they are 13, which can act as a template around gaming and other screen use. Many agreements do not work longterm, however, they do put a clear expectation out in the open which can help in the transition to teen gaming behaviour.

Over time, I've been contacted by several mums, in particular mums of boys, who say they have strict rules about time limits and content. However, they ask, 'Am I being paranoid or just plain unreasonable to want to limit the time my boys spend gaming, especially violent games?' My simplest answer to this is if they are violent games, then these mums are not being paranoid or unreasonable. I believe these types of games can influence the development of character in young people.

Both girls and boys can become very angry towards their parents when they have their gaming time limited, but it sounds like the most volatile responses are coming from boys. My sons behaved in similar ways around Nintendo when they were young, and they weren't happy that I banned access until the weekend – anger is just normal teen behaviour when they are unable to have their autonomy and choices respected!

It was easier when my boys were growing up to monitor them to keep them away from games that used senseless violence and other morally unsavoury activities such as stealing, verbal abuse or destruction of property. Later, they told me they would play these games at other people's houses anyway, but at least at home, they had a healthy balance. And given they spent most of their time at home, I felt there were boundaries in place that were helpful.

Teen boys tend to display a few characteristics that can lead them to be more competitive, more physical, more impulsive and more prone to hunting dopamine – the fun, focused, engaged neurotransmitter, the feel-good brain chemical. The reasons for this are varied, but basically, our boys are socialised into behaving this way and perhaps that's because this expectation goes all the way back to a time when the male role was to protect against predators and hunt for food. Genetics, hormones, brain development, cultural expectations, the way boys are treated compared to girls – each of these factors comes into play in regards to gaming. The proportion of teens who have problematic gaming behaviour is much higher in boys than girls. Our girls tend to struggle far more with problematic social-media use.

Boys are potentially more at risk of becoming addicted to gaming because playing triggers that competitive reward system in the brain by releasing squirts of dopamine as they pit themselves against adversaries, something they seem generally driven to do, and their game preferences reflect that.

Brad Marshall is known as the Unplugged Psychologist. He is the director of the Screen and Gaming Disorder Clinic (Sydney) and author of *The Tech Diet for Your Child and Teen: The 7-step plan to unplug & reclaim your kid's childhood and save your family's sanity*. When I asked him how much gaming is too much, he explained that it is more a question of asking is the gaming interfering with their lives, whether that be their social lives, their sleep, their sporting lives or creative lives. These other things need to be still happening as well as the gaming.

Too much fun or problematic?

Internet Gaming Disorder (IGD) is the technical term for problematic gaming and it first made an appearance in the Diagnostic and

Statistical Manual of Mental Disorders in 2013. So how do you know when your teen's use is becoming problematic? Well, it is definitely becoming that way when your child is not getting a good night's sleep because they are gaming late at night or setting alarms and gaming early in the morning before school. It is also becoming problematic if their behaviour is becoming more aggressive and even violent when they are reminded of the boundaries around gaming. Brad also cautions parents about being totally trusting of parental controls, because teens tend to be able to find ways around them.

Australian research suggests that between 2 and 3 per cent of teens could be classified as having IGD. However, Brad points out that the study that provided that statistic was self-reported, and he would be curious as to how many of the survey responders were being completely honest. Based on his clinical experience and research, Brad feels there is a strong possibility that the number of teens who experience risky or hazardous gaming prevalence would be closer to 10 per cent. It is important to note that excessive use of gaming has been culturally normalised, especially among teens.

We do need to be concerned not just about what they are doing in much of their spare time but about what they are not doing that will help them grow into happy, healthy, strong, kind human beings. There are five developmental domains that are important in adolescence: social development, educational development, behavioural development, emotional development and health development. To mature into a healthy adult, all of these domains need to be nurtured and encouraged during adolescence.

When to worry

- If there is increased difficulty in getting them to follow the boundaries
- If there is more frequent swearing and verbal aggression at home
- If your teen is increasingly or regularly breaking things at home
- If they exhibit physical aggression of any kind

- If there is a decline in invitations from friends to hang out
- If they distance themselves from old friendship groups and don't replace them with new ones
- If your teen has difficulty sleeping
- If your teen refuses family meals or showering due to screen time
- If there is an increase in emotional volatility and intensity over small things which may mean they're experiencing an overloaded nervous system
- If your teen has poor conversation skills (which, to be fair, is common to many teens)
- If your teen has difficulty losing when playing with real people
- If your teen disconnects from the outside world – if they drop out of sports or other activities they previously enjoyed
- If your teen has posture problems
- If there is a significant drop in school grades
- If there is school reluctance or school refusal.

What to do when your teen develops a problematic gaming issue

If a few of the things listed above are happening, and things seem to be getting worse rather than better, it is time to take action. Sooner is probably better than later in terms of having these conversations.

How to have the conversation

Firstly, take a look at 'Before you have the conversation' on page 171. It can be helpful to have sown a seed of possibility by mentioning what you have heard from other parents or something you have heard on TV or read in the media or by saying 'Do any of your friends seem to be gaming more and more over time? I've heard it's becoming a real issue for lots of teens'.

Make the initial conversation about their wellbeing and then lead gradually into time spent gaming.

You need to choose your biggest concerns before you have your conversation. Are you worried most about the offensive language you are hearing, or the angry and aggressive language you are noticing that is being directed at you, the parent? I would avoid mentioning school grades even if you are worried, because they don't tend to be very high on the motivation list for a teen who has problematic gaming, especially boys. He just doesn't care.

Possible opening questions

- Bud, you seem to be losing interest in school more than usual? I have noticed you have been pretty tired lately. Can we have a chat about how you been spending your time because I'm worried about your health and wellbeing?
- Hey sweetheart, I have been a bit worried that you have pulled out from playing netball and you have declined going to catch up with your friends of late. I am worried that your online time might have a part to play?
- Ava, my love, I have been a bit worried about you lately, and you are spending so much more time in your bedroom, especially online. I wanted to chat about how we can work out how you can have fun gaming with your friends as well as spend time doing things you used to do.
- I have been reading up about things that can impact teens' health and wellbeing. I wonder if we can have a chat about some of the changes I've noticed in you that I am a bit worried about so we can make a plan to help you navigate your off-line and online world.

Next steps

It can be helpful to tell your teen that some parents have chosen to make their kids go cold turkey, removing all technology from the home. Your teen may then be a little more enthusiastic about working collaboratively with you on small steps that can help create long-term change. If they have some ideas to try to initiate change, maybe try that as plan A and your idea is plan B. Review the effectiveness of plan A after a week, and if things are still the same, it's time to try plan B.

Maybe start with a common-sense plan that says that their gaming needs to fit in after chores and homework, and that there will be a firm bedtime going forward. Marshall recommends making sure there's time to consolidate these small steps before adding any more.

Some of the considerations that you might put on the table for you and your teen are having a locked box for all phones and devices after a certain time at night, having a clear endpoint to the availability of Wi-Fi for everyone in the home, or you can go along with your teen's suggestions about cutting back their time, with a clear consequence for when they are caught out. Some of these things have worked in some homes, however, there is no guarantee they will work in yours. They are merely options to consider as you are negotiating with your teen to create a healthier relationship with the amount of time they are spending gaming. If your teen breaks the rules, Brad recommends that you aim for a 25 per cent consequence rather than 100 per cent consequence. This means that if they haven't met the boundary on a given day, they simply lose half an hour the next day. If they break that boundary again, after you have cautioned them that the next consequence will be longer, maybe 45 minutes. This will work better than a total ban of 24 hours or longer.

For more resources on this topic, such as books, podcasts, websites and helpline information, see the Resources section at the back of the book (page 382).

17

What to do when your teen hates their body and you suspect their eating habits might be disordered

WHAT HAVE YOU FOUND MOST CHALLENGING AS A TEEN?

- I find many things challenging as a teen. One of them is body image. With the multiplicities of social-media platforms and attention they draw, especially to youth, I find myself habitually comparing my body to other bodies I see, whether they are real or fake, and most of the time you don't know, which is even more problematic.
- Not knowing what I'm going to do with my life after school, feeling really lost in that way. Also body image – everyone says it doesn't matter what you look like but I'm not comparing myself to other people, I just don't like the way I look. It has a bigger impact than people realise.
- Mental health and body image/eating.
- I struggled with my body image, and how I looked. I was also bullied for just being me. The relationship I had with my father became strained and I've since gone no contact with him, but it was a challenge to get people to listen to me and say you've made the right choice for you.

Background

When I did a survey for my book *Girlhood*, 71.9 per cent of the responders to my question 'What societal pressures on our little girls worry you the most?' selected 'the focus on how they look, rather than who they are'. Early childhood educators I've worked with have reported fat shaming among girls as young as three and a half to four. Research suggests that increased screen usage, particularly social media, can influence body image, either in a positive way or a negative way. If we want to build healthy teens who have a healthy relationship with their bodies, the foundations are laid early.

Our body image is formed by the thoughts, attitudes, feelings and beliefs that we have about our bodies and how we look. It can include our shape, size, physical weight, gender identity and the way our body functions for us.

Writer and activist Taryn Brumfitt was Australian of the Year in 2023 and is known for her documentary film *Embrace*. **One of her strongest messages is that no one is born hating their bodies.** Body hatred is not innate; it is something we learn to do, much like bullying. Body dissatisfaction has been very common for teen girls for as long as I can remember. I lived in a time without magazines, TV, or the digital world, and I hated my body intensely during my teenage years.

Australia's national eating disorder charity, the Butterfly Foundation, says research shows a majority of young people are experiencing body dissatisfaction, which significantly impacts all aspects of their lives.

For the first time in Australia, in 2022 Butterfly conducted research among 12- to 18-year-olds to better understand what they think and how they feel about their bodies and the impact that body dissatisfaction has on their lives. Butterfly's Body Kind Youth Survey (BKYS) found that:

- Nearly half (45 per cent) of young people are dissatisfied with the way their body looks
- Nearly 70 per cent of young people said they had experienced

appearance-related teasing, with 73 per cent of these saying they'd experienced it at school
- Nearly two-thirds of young people say their body image stops them from doing physical activities.

Why is body image important?

Poor body image can lead to:

- Low self-esteem
- Obsessively thinking about your body and appearance
- Putting too much emphasis on your weight, shape or size
- Frequently comparing your body and appearance with other people
- Changes to your eating and exercise behaviours in an attempt to change your weight or muscularity
- Withdrawing from things you enjoy, such as sports and social activities
- Relationship changes with your friends, family members and intimate partners
- Other mental-health concerns such as depression or anxiety
- Engaging in risky and harmful behaviours, such as smoking, abusing substances or increased sexual activity.

– Source: butterfly.org.au/body-image/can-body-image-issues-be-serious/

Body dissatisfaction is one of the strongest risk factors for a teen going on to develop an eating disorder (ED) or disordered eating. In her book, *When Life Sucks*, Dr Jo Prendergast reports that some degree of disordered eating affects around 30 per cent of teen girls, 15 per cent of teen boys, with possibly even higher rates in transgender teens. She writes that ED is the third most common chronic illness in teens.

A UK researcher found that 36 per cent of young women and 24 per cent of young men sometimes avoided taking part in certain activities such as sport because they worried about the way they looked.

I worked with two boys who developed disordered eating coupled with excessive exercise, and they were only 14. Thanks to social media, they had become fixated on what the perfect male body looked like. It was difficult to convince them that they were physically underdeveloped because of their age and that to develop the sixpack they yearned for, it would take significant targeted exercise as they grew older. One of the lads took many weeks before he owned up to his binging and purging cycle, and when we were able to explore how long-term vomiting can damage his beautiful teeth, he became motivated to change the behaviour that had become automatic.

Some teens are at higher risk of developing ED:

1. Girls and gender-diverse youth
2. Those who struggle with perfectionism and rigid thought patterns
3. Athletes, especially dancers, gymnasts or wrestlers
4. Those with a history of trauma, particularly emotional abuse and neglect
5. Those with anxiety, OCD and mood disorders
6. Neurodivergent teens, especially those with autism
7. Individuals who have focused on appearance, especially influenced by excessive social-media use.

There are a few different kinds of eating disorders

The most commonly known are:

Binge Eating Disorder – eating a lot of food over a short time, out-of-control eating episodes.

Bulimia Nervosa – binging then purging, vomiting, taking laxatives or over-exercising.

Anorexia Nervosa – restricting food due to fear of becoming overweight, often regardless of their current appearance. Can cause low weight, failure to grow.

Avoidant/Restrictive Food Intake Disorder (ARFID) – avoiding food for sensory reasons rather than body image concerns.

As well as these, your teen may experience behaviours that may not point to a full-on eating disorder, but which can become very serious, such as disordered eating, which is effectively disturbed and unhealthy eating patterns. On the other hand, there is emerging concern about people who are obsessed with 'clean' eating, called orthorexia.

You would have noticed if your teen has been displaying some of the concerns listed above. I am sure you would have been giving them encouraging messages about their body image and their body, and they would probably have been ignoring you or rolling your eyes at you because 'you don't understand!' That can be so frustrating.

When to worry

The most common signs of an eating disorder are the following.

- A noticeable change in what they are eating, whether they have new intolerances and avoidances, become picky eaters, suddenly become vegan/vegetarian, are limiting what they eat, only eating healthy foods, cutting food into tiny bits, becoming rigid in eating patterns.
- Drinking large amounts of water and chewing sugar-free gums or mints.
- A change in how they are eating, whether that be skipping meals, food going missing, saying they are not hungry, repeatedly saying they've already eaten somewhere else, not finishing their meals, taking longer than usual to finish their meals, wanting to eat alone.
- They may begin disappearing, going for walks or going to the bathroom during or soon after meals, running water in the bathroom to hide noises or spending large amounts on food with lots of food wrappers in the bin.
- Obsessing about certain parts of the body.

- Continually comparing their body to others.
- There may be a noticeable change in their emotions around food and eating – seemingly more anxious/angry/feeling guilty or more irritable at meal times, especially about high-calorie foods or unhealthy foods.
- There may be a significant change in their thoughts about eating that you can tell by how often they are talking about food/weight/body shape/perceptions that they are fat, or suddenly interested in cooking and baking, but not necessarily eating it themselves.
- They may talk about wanting to have surgery or other cosmetic procedures, spend a lot of time looking in the mirror or taking photos and looking for changes or imperfections.
- There may be a noticeable change in their appearance and a preference for wearing baggy clothes to hide their appearance.
- There may be a shift in their attitude and activity around exercise where they will seem to be exercising excessively, secretly.
- There may be other behaviour changes such as wanting to use laxatives or diet pills, signs they have vomited, spending more time on weight-loss websites/blogs and following social-media accounts with fitspo content – perfect athletic bodies or pro-ana ideologies (which is the promotion of anorexia) – and withdrawing from other people.
- Often there is a shift in their moods where they will tend to focus on more duality thinking, where things are either good or bad, feeling judged by other people and finding it difficult to talk about their emotional state.
- Some new health concerns can occur – dizziness, fainting, stomach pains, constipation, menstruation stopping, feeling colder, hair loss, sore throats, really bad breath and tooth decay, or even a strange, sickly sweet smell from starvation because the body is in ketosis.

These are signs that your teen could be really struggling with an ED, and all the experts in this field recommend a trip to your family GP for a full check-up. Your GP may recommend your teen to a specialist ED unit for ongoing professional support. Early intervention gives a better chance of a full recovery from an ED, and we must keep in mind that eating disorders, alongside substance abuse disorders, have the highest mortality rate of all psychiatric disorders (often due to cardiac complications).

What to do if you suspect your adolescent's eating habits might be disordered

Firstly, take a look at 'Before you have the conversation' on page 171.

Secondly, sow a seed of possibility around your concerns in a general way BEFORE you have a chat – 'I saw an advertisement on the side of the bus today that was advertising perfume, and the image of the model was so obviously digitally altered that she didn't even look like herself. How crazy is our world that we need to use filters and alter photos, and we just can't be ourselves?'

Or 'Did you see the video on YouTube of Lady Gaga when she took off her make-up at the Oscars? How incredibly gutsy and brave. There should be more of that, you reckon?'

Or 'I was listening to a podcast yesterday called Eat the Rules, and it is a podcast dedicated to empowering girls and women to break free of societal standards and body shaming and live life a life without rules – it was so good I wanted to toot the car horn!' Then leave it for a couple of days before the conversation.

Next, as parents, we have all probably said something that wasn't helpful for our teen around their body image. We may have over-praised them on how good they look in a certain outfit, or we might have told them to stop eating all those chips and eat something healthier! Before you continue reading this chapter, let go of the guilt and regret because it's only when we know more that we can do better. Since I wrote *Girlhood*, I have been so much more mindful of not greeting little girls, especially my granddaughters, by always commenting on their appearance or clothes. I do not want them to grow up to think they are defined by how they look because that's exactly what can create problems with body image in their teens. I remind them much more often about what their body can do than how their body looks.

I once worked with an incredibly bright and bubbly teen who developed Anorexia Nervosa and who needed long-term intensive care. It had started around the age of 14 when, following an illness, she had a few people comment to her how good she looked since she had lost some weight. That message quite quickly became her mindset, and she realised many years later that she had consciously decided that if she looked good losing a little bit of weight, she might look even better losing more. Then things turned into a mental illness. I met her again when she was around 22, and she had recovered despite still having days where she struggled with her body image. She thanked me for being someone she could turn to during her darkest hours. Her mum and I kept in touch so that I could keep her spirits up as well because as a parent of a teen who has a significant ED, it can be really heartbreaking and hard.

Possible opening questions

Please preface this conversation by reassuring your son or daughter how much you love them, no matter what.

- You know, I read a book called *The Anxious Generation* and the author wrote about how social media can target girls especially with content around being thin – that's so wrong, eh? Have you noticed that?
- Hey sweetheart, I know we all have days when we don't like our bodies, but I have noticed that you seem to have changed the way you eat and even seem to be avoiding eating, and I want us to have a chat about what might be happening for you.
- Ava, my love, you seem to have changed of late, and I am a bit worried that you are struggling with something pretty big.

I wonder if we can have a bit of a chat about some of the changes I have noticed.

- David, I have noticed that you've increased your exercise a lot lately, and I wonder if there's something you are aiming to achieve with this shift. Can we have a chat, do you reckon?

Next steps

This is a sensitive topic because it is about a teen who has really big feelings about themselves and their body in a really negative way. Shining a light on that can be quite scary and a common response when you first bring it up is that they can become angry and defensive. This may take many little conversations rather than one big conversation. For many who are struggling with an ED, they believe that their plan, whether it be starving, binging and purging, or excessive exercise, will change their body so that they can like themselves and accept themselves in a positive way. In so many ways, the ED is in control of your teen and their behaviours, even though your teen will think they are in control and they are going to fix it by making the choices they are. We can't simply call EDs mental illnesses, because on top of the psychological impairment and distress they bring, they can impact every organ in the body through a vast array of serious medical issues. EDs are complex, and often they start quietly and go undetected until they become quite severe.

There are some more things that you can do that can help, especially for girls. Modelling a healthy attitude to your own body is important. Encourage and embrace the diversity of all bodies and keep reminding your daughter that it is not what her body looks like; it is what her body can do that is the most important thing. Avoid talking about diets and challenge the endless messages that happen on our screens about dieting, losing weight and looking fantastic! Feeling happy within yourself, with a healthy sense of self, is an inside job, not an outside job.

The words to use around food really matter as well. Everyday food and occasional food are much better than good and bad or healthy and unhealthy. Food in moderation can also be a helpful attitude to model in your home. Another key message is listening to your body, and when it gives us a hunger signal, that's when we can choose to eat. When our body gives a satiated feeling, we can choose to stop eating. Emotional eating is something that can become habitual and problematic, or we can address it and create a plan to change it.

Following your initial chat or your many chats with your teen, research some of the resources that are available so that your teen can have good information going forward. The great news is that parents are in an incredible position to make a difference and create a home environment where all bodies are treated with kindness and respect.

In my experience, teens who were really worried about their parents knowing about their struggles definitely felt that they were not struggling alone after they shared their story.

For more resources on this topic, such as books, podcasts, websites and helpline information, see the Resources section at the back of the book (page 383).

18

What to do when you discover your teen is intentionally self-harming

'We just had no idea what to do! It's incredibly confronting to find out your child has been secretly self-harming and it can leave you feeling completely helpless to know what to do next. My initial reaction as her mum was that I was a failure and that I felt I had failed her.'

– Mother of a 12-year-old daughter who was self-harming, from the ABC podcast *Parental as Anything*

Background

Over my years of teaching and counselling, I only came across a few students who were self-harming, also known as self-injuring. That does not mean there weren't many who were struggling in secret. Things have definitely gotten worse, sadly. Recent figures from the Australian Government's *Growing up in Australia: Longitudinal Study of Australian Children* (LSAC) estimate that one in four girls and one in 10 boys are self-harming.

As I have already explored in the first part of this book, being an adolescent today is more challenging for most than in previous generations. When teens are struggling with heightened levels of stress and challenging and intense emotions, they can experience distress. The nervous system is like an emotional barometer and, at some points, it can reach a tipping point. When some people reach their tipping point, they turn to family and friends or they simply make choices to shift the distress in the knowledge or hope that this will bring them a sense of calmness or joy. Others may engage in choices that can release the same distress via pain. So while this is incredibly worrying for all of us who live with or work with teens, we need to keep in mind that the choice a person makes – such as self-harm – is a coping mechanism they have developed. Some of the ways a person might self-injure themselves are by cutting, burning, scratching or scraping skin, pulling hair out, hitting or punching themselves. Many of these behaviours occur in private. There is even digital self-harm, which is when a teen creates a fake account that they use to cyberbully themselves.

Learning more about how to be a supportive parent is one way to help our teens when they have a sense of overwhelming distress and an inability to cope. In her excellent book *When Life Sucks: Parenting Your Teen Through Tough Times*, Dr Jo Prendergast stresses how important it is to be an 'askable and tellable' parent – someone your teen can ask anything and tell anything to. This is one of the main reasons why I am writing this book because you, as a parent, with your loving connection and your compassion, can be the safe base that your teen needs as they ride this really bumpy road to adulthood. Parents and teachers are powerful influencers on the neurochemicals in our kids' brains. When teens get stuck with intense feelings and overwhelmed with all the changes in their lives, warm connectedness – especially with some laughter and lightness – can shift the distress for a time. Reassure teens often that you will love them no matter what and no matter how difficult things might get, tell them you will always love them.

- My parents didn't know I was feeling like this; heck, I barely even knew what I was going through at the time, but they were always there for me to have good conversations even if they had no idea how to help.

- That it's okay to feel this way and that they still love me and will always help me.
- Sometimes the casual check-in if I was okay. Hugging me and saying it's okay to feel sad.

Some of the key risk factors that can contribute to a teen turning to self-harm as a way of coping can include poor-quality sleep, anxiety symptoms, depressive symptoms, being a victim of bullying, failed grades and poor school achievement, friendship challenges, trauma, gender or sexuality confusion, the challenges of being neurodivergent, family violence and having less supportive, disconnected parents. I interviewed Professor Jo Robinson from Orygen (a mental health advocacy not-for-profit organisation) about self-harm on the *Parental As Anything* podcast. She explained that even when teens who are engaging in self-harm have been asked what an episode of self-harm means for them, they can find it hard to describe. This is important to keep in mind for parents who discover a child is self-harming – you may find that your son or daughter can find it difficult to express why they are resorting to this behaviour. Every single young person who self-harms will do so as a consequence of multiple possible causes rather than just one cause.

Michelle Mitchell, author of the book *Self Harm: why teens do it and what parents can do to help*, has worked to support self-harming teens for more than 20 years. One of her key messages is that teens are really good at hiding behaviour they don't want you to know about, so self-harm behaviours can be difficult to identify, especially in the early stages. Behaviours and signs Michelle recommends parents should be on the lookout for include:

- Unexplained scratches, cuts or burns
- Bald patches in the hair
- Biting nails until they bleed
- Covering their bodies up more, especially when it's hot
- Avoiding situations where they might need to change in front of others, such as for PE or swimming

- Punching themselves or hitting themselves
- Unexplainable presence of sharp objects (for cutting) or unusual objects like a lighter (for burning) in their room or bag.

A significant message that Michelle highlights is that voluntary self-harm – when a young person makes a deliberate and conscious choice to self-harm – is very different to habitual self-harm. Habitual means it happens without your teen giving it any thought – almost like an automatic response to release big emotions. It is important to remember that the action of causing yourself pain is a way of shocking the nervous system that releases the stress hormone cortisol very quickly. The result can be a sensation of calm throughout the body. At this point, if you can identify with your teen that self-harm is one choice they could make to feel better, they may be open to considering some of the other options that are available to them. Sadly, however, habitual self-harm can develop quite quickly into voluntary self-harm. This is when the behaviour becomes a choice and a routine which is rewarded by the sense of relief the person experiences.

Before you have a conversation about self-harm with your teen, it will be important to understand some of the strategies that may be helpful to discuss together. Mitchell recommends creating safety plans so that parents can help create guardrails depending on the self-harm behaviour your teen is choosing. These safety plans are tailored to the teen themselves and will respond to their specific expression of self-harm. If you remove one form of self-harm from the house (such as blades), then teens may use another form (such as burning) instead, so many families are best to temporarily remove any items that could potentially be used to self-harm.

If a person is using medication inappropriately, the medication will need to be locked up or removed from the house. Dr Prendergast recommends discreetly removing or locking away ropes and extension cords, alcohol, blades, lighters, firearms, car keys, hoses, vacuum cleaners, toxic garage chemicals and cleaning products, and ladders. If your teen discloses that they are really struggling, it can be helpful for parents to do shifts throughout the night to be close by. This can mean sleeping outside the room or sleeping beside your teen in their bedroom. Don't ever hesitate to call an ambulance or any of the online help numbers if you are worried about your teen.

If you or your child are in distress you should contact:

Triple Zero (000) – or the equivalent emergency number in your country

Lifeline for support and advice in a personal crisis for people of all ages. 13 11 14 or visit lifeline.org.au (they do online text chat too)

13YARN for Aboriginal and Torres Strait Islander people who are going through a tough time and feel like having a yarn. 13 92 76 or 13yarn.org.au

Kids Helpline for a chat about any challenges, from age 5 to 25. 1800 55 1800 or kidshelpline.com.au (online text chat is an option too)

What to do when you discover your teen is intentionally self-harming

Firstly, take a look at 'Before you have the conversation' on page 171.

Secondly, recognise that you won't be able to get all the answers in one conversation and seeking connection and information around their behaviour as calmly as possible is important as this will avoid making things more worrying or stressful for your teen. It might be best not to use exact terminology like, 'intentional self-injury' or 'self-harm' with teens – rather talk about hurting oneself or finding ways to manage the tipping point of their emotional barometer. A professional may be the best person to work out this distinction. Keep in mind that self-harm, and all that it entails, sits on a scale – it's not black and white. However, it will be important for your teen to be offered and supported to engage with professional support, especially if self-harm has become habitual. Even if your teen doesn't want to talk with someone, it can be helpful for you to see someone and get some guidance about how to support them.

Thirdly, your teen who is choosing self-harm is not doing so because you have failed as a parent. Do your best to calm your own inner critic and any tendency to catastrophise or awfulise. Your teen needs you to be as calm and grounded as often as possible. For some parents and their teens, this can be an extremely scary and confronting journey. Again, please consider seeking professional help for yourself as well as your teen as caring for a family member who is self-harming can be really difficult to navigate without support.

Finally, reassure your teen how much you love them and that there is nothing that could ever change the way that you love them.

Possible opening questions

- Bud, I noticed that you had some cut marks on your forearms and I have been reading up about self-harm – can you tell me if that's been happening for you?
- Hey, sweetheart, I have noticed that things have been a bit rough for you lately and you seem to be struggling and I am wondering if you've considered hurting yourself as a way of coping?
- Ava, my love, I have been a bit worried about you lately and I know how life can really pull you down at times. I'm just curious if you've thought of hurting yourself as a way of coping?
- Sometimes it can really help talking to a person who knows more about coping and managing hard feelings other than your parents – so we can explore some of the helpful sites online, or would you be okay if we looked for some professional help?

Sometimes writing a letter of concern can work well. There is a sample in Appendix 1 that you could adapt to suit.

Next steps

Never diminish or dismiss what your teen has said by saying things such as:

- Don't be so dramatic.
- Just cheer up. We all have bad days.
- You need to sort yourself out!
- Just stop doing it!

The first conversation needs to be about truth-telling and building connection. Most teens who are self-harming don't talk much, especially to adults. It's often connected to deeper issues such as depression so getting the conversation started and helping them find language to explain a crazy experience can be really difficult.

Then you can begin to discuss strategies such as how a young person can acknowledge and integrate into their life aspects of the four recognised pillars of being healthy physically and mentally: good sleep, healthy diet, exercise and therapy.

Gaining a change of perspective from self-harming to self-caring can be really difficult for a teen who struggles with low self-esteem and a low sense of self. However, it is a helpful distinction to attempt to make.

The following suggestions may be helpful in your follow-up conversation with your teen.

Distracting from self-harm

ReachOut Australia has some good advice for a young person on distracting themselves. These ideas from ReachOut, Michelle Mitchell and others include:

- Delay the self-harm: When you feel the urge to self-harm, choose to pause and talk to someone. If talking to someone isn't possible, ReachOut suggests you: 'make the decision to wait for 15 minutes. If you make it to 15 minutes, congratulate yourself for waiting, and then try waiting for another 15 minutes, etc. It might not feel like it at first, but the urge will gradually pass.'
- Encourage your teen to make a self-harm distraction box, self-soothing box, a green box . . . whatever you want to call it. This

is a box or bag where they keep stuff that they can turn to when the urge to self-harm comes over them. It's kind of like a 'first-aid kit' and the idea is that your teen puts activities and prompts in the box that will give them something to do that requires concentration and does no harm. For example, you might have a crochet set and wool, a colouring-in book, a bead-making kit, a photo album, face/body paint, and anything that carries favourite childhood memories – anything that will bring them comfort.

- Exercise is wonderfully beneficial for our mental and physical health, and when it comes to fighting off urges, especially vigorous exercise can really help (whether that be star jumps, sit-ups, dancing, running or a cardio workout).
- Gaming – this can really help if it's something your teen enjoys. Research has also shown that playing video games with your teen can help build your relationships, so if it's something you enjoy, perhaps suggest you do it together.
- Writing down thoughts and feelings can really help a teen to identify triggers for self-harm and process their feelings. Perhaps buy your teen a beautiful journal and pens to encourage them to write down their private thoughts.
- Teach your teen some breathing, movement and other relaxation strategies. There are lots of calming audio visualisations they can listen to online. I have a couple on my website, and there are some great ones on the Smiling Mind and ReachOut apps. There are also some great apps to help with breathing strategies and short yoga routines that may be helpful.
- Consider a pet if you don't already have one. I am a firm believer in the power of a good dog to support kids with stress, but any pet can be helpful. If it works for your family (and please do your research to make sure it is right for you), perhaps consider getting a dog.

Some good apps and sites that your teen may benefit from

- Calm Harm app: this free app is designed for teenagers and is available on Google Play and App Store.
- MindSpot Clinic: this free online mental-health support service is particularly good for PTSD symptoms, improving self-harm and managing night times.
- Virtual Hope Box Mobile App: this app is a great distraction option, which could be a helpful addition to a self-care kit or 'distraction box'. The app includes tools to help with coping, relaxation and positive thinking.
- Beyond Now is a suicide safety planning app created by Beyond Blue; this seven-step plan will include what a person has found helpful in the past, what they have found unhelpful, and what to avoid. It offers ideas from others, and further information for support.
- The Sleep Ninja App: an evidence-based smartphone app created by Black Dog Institute, this app has been designed to support young people with sleep challenges.
- myCompass online program: this free and confidential online tool aims to help a young person keep track of their mental health, providing immediate feedback and learning activities.

At a recent conference, I met an amazing woman, Jo, who is an occupational therapist. She has helped her neurodivergent son to create fidget toys that can help calm the nervous system. These toys have been especially designed for teens. She demonstrated for me some harm-minimisation fidgets that mimic the same sensation of cutting without damaging the skin. If you google 'Kaiko Fidgets', you can find the 'spiky' versions for this purpose.

Jo explained to me that the pain sensation was very similar to cutting. I tried it and ouch, it really hurt – but it doesn't damage the skin. She explained that the reason that using the fidget gave the same release of emotional tension and distress was that it gave the nervous system a shock as I mentioned earlier in this chapter. Using a metal fidget that doesn't break the skin but has exactly the same effect is a relatively new concept. Other nervous system shocks that can help a teen who has been self-injuring include the use of ice – suggestions include chewing ice, putting their face in iced water, or holding ice in their hand. This is similar to doing some vigorous exercise in that it can also trigger the nervous system to spontaneously release tension.

Another excellent piece of advice from Dr Prendergast to help your teen make big changes in their behaviour is to support them in finding a key to their motivation – identifying 'their why' not 'your why'. A teen may be able to realise that by choosing not to self-harm, they will feel better, they will be less tired or they might be able to participate in activities that they haven't been able to take part in because of their self-harm. Big change needs little steps gradually over time and, yes, this can be frustrating for you and your teen.

The influence of the digital world can either be harmful or helpful for your teen if they are self-harming. Some self-harm groups celebrate the 'wound of the week' and for a teen who is struggling with a sense of identity and worthlessness, being validated for that behaviour might encourage further self-harming. In one of your follow-up conversations with your teen, you could consider exploring the socials of some helpful and positive individuals whose messages could help your teen overcome their habitual self-harm.

If you are still worried, keep reaching out for professional help.

For more resources on this topic, such as books, podcasts, websites and helpline information, see the Resources section at the back of the book (page 384).

19

What to do when your teen's school grades suddenly plummet

> My parents always said they love me no matter what and that a grade does not determine who I am.

Background

In the early years of high school and middle school, it is quite common for grades to be lower than they were in primary school, especially for boys. This disengagement can be the result of boredom, a sign a student is adjusting to the very different world of high school, or that other variables are impacting their motivation.

A sudden drop in grades, though, is cause for concern for parents. Given the reports are usually done by semester, it can mean that whatever has been happening that has caused this drop has been going on for a while. Many schools now have a digital portal that parents can access to keep track of their kids' school achievements and even find out when major assessments are due. This can be helpful as a drop in grades can be caught a lot earlier.

Both as a parent and as a former counsellor, I would be concerned when a significant drop in grades across the board occurs. Single-subject low marks are common and can often be the result of a disconnect between the student and the teacher, a missed major assessment or a student's complete disinterest in the subject.

In my experience, a sudden drop in multiple grades will mean something is going on for the student. If we bring back into our mind the metaphor of the tipping point, I would suggest that a student whose grades have dropped is really struggling to manage their world in some way. The most common reason for a significant drop of this magnitude is that the student may be struggling with major life challenges. Some of these can be in the family home, and I have seen this happen when there has been a significant experience of family violence, regular criminal activity in the home, ongoing bullying either inside or outside the school, a major loss experience of a loved one or a special pet, or a major health concern that has not been addressed for the student.

Sometimes, a student will deliberately underachieve, not hand in work and appear disinterested in class because being smart and achieving well means you are uncool. A drastic drop in grades could also mean a student has been rejected from the friend group they want to belong in and, remember, belonging is a fundamental human need, but especially for teenagers. Being known as the class geek or nerd can be an uncomfortable reality, and so a student consciously chooses to underachieve.

Problematic anxiety that may have been previously undetected can also be a reason for a sudden drop in grades. Struggling to juggle all the demands of high school, possibly extracurricular activities like sport or music, as well as navigating the strong pull of their digital lives, can also create a drop in grades. It's like juggling too many balls at the same time. Teach your teen about the metaphor of the emotional barometer, the tipping point and the ways that we can shift the needle on the dial in a different direction.

Some students may have been able to mask or compensate for a learning challenge they have up until high school. As the work gets harder, the need for more focused concentration also increases, and so students who may be neurodivergent, especially with dyslexia, ADHD, autism or any sensory processing challenges, will struggle more significantly. I had a student whose grades dropped drastically in his first year of high school, and on investigation, it was discovered that he had a significant hearing loss that had been undetected for seven years at school.

> As we near the middle of the year, due dates start looming, assessments start piling up, and exams get closer and closer. Sometimes having so much to do can drown you and you start to have a really negative outlook on everything. I know that I just get really overwhelmed and stressed, and everything sort of just seems slightly impossible or far scarier than it actually is.

When to worry

If it's just one subject, it's pretty common, and a casual chat with the subject teacher may be all that's needed. If it's across the board and is significant, you need to respond (note the word respond, not react) as soon as possible because it is a sign that your teen's world is challenging them. Be careful not to overstress the importance of high grades compared to good-enough grades. In the 2023 Mission Australia Survey, the number-one personal challenge for almost half the students (49.0 per cent) was listed as 'school concerns'. This included academic pressure, high workload, challenges with teachers, general school challenges and learning difficulties. This challenge was listed significantly higher than the second biggest personal challenge of young people, which was mental-health challenges (24.2 per cent).

Checking in with the year coordinator discreetly can be helpful before you have this conversation because, on your behalf, they can check in with all the teachers who teach your child to see if you can get some feedback that can help you going forward.

What do you do when your teen's school grades suddenly plummet?

Firstly, take a look at 'Before you have the conversation' on page 171. Then, once you feel like you're ready, prepare your opening questions.

Possible opening questions

You may like to preface this conversation by reassuring your son or daughter how much you love them, no matter what.

- Bud, your school report has shown that many of your grades have dropped, and I want us to work out what's been happening to see if we can make things better so that you can get some good-enough grades next semester.
- Hey, sweetheart, I know the last six months have been pretty hard for you, and I know that your grades have been dropping. Can we have a chat to work out how we might sort things out going forward?
- Ava, my love, I have been a bit worried about you lately, and you haven't been enjoying school much either. I'm just curious as to why your grades have been dropping so that we can work out how to improve them next semester.

Next steps

Sometimes, a teen may need some help to identify why they are struggling.

Then, you may need to seek some more guidance from allied health professionals while reassuring your teen that you are working on a plan to help them get back on track.

Once you have been able to identify some of the key concerns, it can be helpful to work out a plan going forward with your teen, with some realistic goals that they can achieve. If your child ends up diagnosed with learning difficulties, the school should be involved in working up a formal, individualised plan of support.

Remember, if grades have been dropping over a number of months, they will take time to recover, and your teen may need some extra support from within the school and possibly from outside. An excellent resource that could help with this is a book called *ROC and Rise* by Claire Eaton, a former teacher and now teen coach. *ROC and Rise* is full of wonderful guidelines and strategies to help teens be better organised and more optimistic in their journey through high school.

- The most challenging thing would be having to be enough as in trying to keep up with everything that is happening in friend groups, at home with sport and also trying to keep up with school.
- Parents' expectations around grades.
- School, keeping up with parents' expectations.
- Time management.
- Finding a balance between all aspects of life. Sometimes, I make myself feel guilty about hanging out with friends when I could be with my family, or if I'm stressed about school, I feel like I can't see anyone and I should just be at home studying all day.

Homework is important in high school because teachers are unable to cover the full curriculum in class time. Creating healthy homework habits is important, and it can be helpful if parents can help review it, if a teen requests it. Please do not do their homework for them because that does not facilitate their learning in the classroom, and you will not be there when they do their next assessment based on the homework that you completed. It can be helpful if, after school, teens are able to complete homework before they are able to use their devices for fun and connection. However, negotiate rather than command how both can be possible. **As a parent, being overly invested and too enthusiastic can have the absolute opposite effect intended.** So please, temper the choices you make around supporting your teen doing homework. The last thing you want is for your teen to feel pressured overtly or implicitly by a loving parent. I have had teens tell me that they feel their parent's love *only* when they do well academically.

It can be important to check in with the year coordinator every few weeks to see how things are going within the school environment. It's best to do that discreetly and to acknowledge any improvements in attitude or effort.

In my experience as a high-school teacher and counsellor, I found that boys were much harder to motivate to improve grades than the girls I worked with or taught. I worked with a number of boys whose grades had plummeted, and their parents were extremely frustrated at their obvious disinterest in improving those grades.

Firstly, let's acknowledge that boys' engagement in education worldwide is an issue of concern, and there is much research in that area. Many boys told me that when their parents told them to do better, to improve their grades or to try harder at school, they actually had no idea of how to do that because those phrases lacked the serious specifics on how to do it. Boys do better when we identify a target: how will I know if I've hit it and what's in it for me when I do hit it? Aiming to improve across multiple grades just seems ridiculously too hard for many boys. To focus on improving one grade, which would require a shift in attitude and behaviour, can be deceptively powerful, and is likely to lift other grades as well. I created a process called 'The Deal', which I explored in my bestselling book *From Boys to Men*. It shows a step-by-step approach that can be quite successful.

The Deal

1. **Set the target** – lift his maths grade from an F to a C. Avoid aiming too high, too soon.
2. **Draw up the plan** – map out what afternoons he has maths homework, and his maths assessments, if possible. This way, he has a clear, visual reminder of important things so they have less chance of being forgotten.
3. **Support him** – get in the habit of providing a snack, a drink, shoulder rub or a non-verbal thumbs-up of encouragement to support him anchoring in his new habit.
4. **Ask for help** – normalise your son asking a teacher for help if there is something he is struggling with. Maybe consider a tutor.

5. **Feedback** – ask your son to ask his teacher for feedback each fortnight on how he is going and what else he might do to improve.
6. **Reward** – help your son to choose a significant-enough reward so that he has something to look forward to at the end of this deal, and which includes his friends or mates. Maybe a movie night, or a night out tenpin bowling or even better, a weekend camping trip. If he doesn't achieve the specific target, even though you can see that he really did try very hard, it's okay. You might be surprised how well boys can accept this – and knowing that failure can teach them something and that it doesn't define them also helps. He just needs to make another plan or goal.

Maggie Dent, *From Boys to Men*

I once had a class of Year 8 boys who were considered to be struggling, and I noticed that all of them had a very poor attitude and mindset around learning and school. Many of them were convinced they were just dumb, and they would always stay dumb. I created a closed-eye exercise called My Best Report Ever, where the boys had to visualise taking home a report card that had good grades and positive comments written on it. We did that every week for over a month, and then some unusual changes started to happen in their behaviour. Firstly, their maths teacher came to me and asked me what was going on because some of the boys were handing in homework when normally they didn't. Things change when behaviour changes and the expectations of both students and teachers changed at the same time. Gradually, over a term, these boys started improving their grades. Given that the brain can't tell the difference between what's vividly imagined and what's real, their brains had come to believe they had already taken home a good report card. Reading their greatly improved report cards at the end of the term was quite emotional for them and me. This visualisation may be helpful for both girls and boys, and there are many others out there, I'm sure.

It can be helpful to focus on your teen's wellbeing before you focus on their grades. Stressed brains do not learn well.

Lastly, keep reminding your teen that they are not defined by the grades they get at school. That inside them are some unique gifts and strengths that aren't always able to shine at school. The world is full of good humans who didn't do brilliantly academically at school and who have changed the world for the better. I had a student who failed my English class and never graduated, and he managed to sell his software company for over $2 million when he was just 22.

For more resources on this topic, such as books, podcasts, websites and helpline information, see the Resources section at the back of the book (page 385).

20

What to do when your teen's anxiety becomes problematic and prevents them from doing things that matter

WHAT HAVE YOU FOUND MOST CHALLENGING AS A TEEN?

- Getting all the school assessments done to get good marks when they are all due at the same time. Why can't they spread them out so you can do your best and not be so stressed? It's like they want you to do bad by stressing you out and putting pressure on you. If they spread them out, you can put more effort in to each one.
- Too many assessments and tests due at once and trying new things like getting a job and learning to drive. Finding time to relax among the workload of school and outside-school activities.
- Dealing with stress – teenagers go through a lot at such a crazy age and some of it we aren't prepared for well enough. We are expected to be adults but we still are children technically. Big thing about being 17–19 is we are either seen as adults or children – it's hard.
- As a teen, I struggled most with my mental health. I did not think I would survive adulthood's many pressures and expectations, nor the ones weighing on teenagers. It's difficult to see a positive future

when the issues of climate change and unaffordable housing exist. On top of this, I struggled with maintaining my grades, balancing my relationships, finding an academic pathway, finding a job, maintaining my mental and physical health and learning how to navigate the feeling of being burnt-out as a 'high-achieving' student. My mental health continues to be a struggle, even in young adulthood.

Background

If you are human, you will experience both stress and anxiety in many different ways on any given day. Our brain loves predictability and, unfortunately, it's impossible to have 'predictability' all the time. Our teens are going through massive transformation that means lots of change, and all change triggers a degree of stress. As you will know from Part One of this book, the teen brain is still maturing and the part of the brain that helps manage stress does not finish maturing until a person's mid-twenties. Stress is often described as a sense of feeling pressured, wound up tight, tense and, for some, a feeling of being out of control. To be honest, all parents who have been raising kids and teens through the COVID pandemic, followed by cost-of-living pressures and higher rents and mortgages, are all living with heightened levels of stress and anxiety. Many of us have been impacted by global events such as natural disasters, the war in Ukraine and the current war in Gaza. Our amygdala is doing its job. *It is not a sign that we are weak, and that there is something wrong with us – we are merely humans responding to our environments.* In many ways, we're living in more stressful times than we have before because of our awareness of what's going on around us. Thanks to the 24/7 news cycle and our social feeds, the threats feel closer than they may have when we lived in simpler times.

Remember, as I mentioned in the background chapter, anxiety disorders are the most common mental-health challenge for adolescents. Prior to the pandemic we were looking at rates of around 15 per cent, but this has risen to almost one third of young people between 16 and 24 who have experienced an anxiety disorder. The numbers are even higher for our girls and our LGBTQIA+ teens.

However, there is such a thing as healthy stress. This can be when we experience a feeling of stress ahead of an exam, a deadline or a performance. Your body can feel 'wired up', and if that tension is channelled positively, it can improve a person's performance. For some, a level of healthy stress can improve focus and can give a person a boost of energy which can be used in the pursuit of achievement. It can be really helpful for a teen to know that stress can be used in a positive way, and that everyone feels stress in their lives – not just our confused teens. I know that your teens may not appreciate you reminding them that some anxiety before exams, or before their driving test, or before their graduation ceremony can be a good thing! However, please keep reminding them because it is an important message for them to realise that not all stress and anxiety is problematic.

Stress can look and feel similar to anxiety, especially in how it feels in the body. Anxiety brings with it more worry, more apprehension and more irrational fears that something bad or something that you will be unable to cope with is going to happen. Anxiety can also arise without the presence of a challenging situation or event. Our stress response occurs when our amygdala has perceived a possible threat to survival, which is commonly known as the fight-flight response. Sometimes this occurs when our thoughts trigger the perception that we are under threat. Technically, however, we are just imagining the threat.

I really love the way that Australian psychologist Karen Young explains how even though anxiety can feel awful, it's coming from a strong healthy brain that's 'doing exactly what brains are meant to do – protect us and keep us alive'.

When the brain perceives that there might be a problem, it surges with a cocktail of neurochemicals and hormones, especially cortisol, which are designed to motivate you to go faster, be stronger and more powerful, feel more alert and be more able to physically deal with the threats. This is why it's called the fight-flight response. Anxiety can be seen as the amygdala being overenthusiastic in its job of protecting us!

Once the threat has been neutralised or tamed, the brain then shifts into a different response called the rest and digest response. There are two parts to our nervous system and both of them have a role to play in keeping us mentally healthy. If we are constantly in a state of distress – flight, fight or freeze – the body can become fatigued, our immune system can be negatively impacted and it can become difficult for our brain to function at its best, especially in our classrooms. The pressure to do well at school is a leading concern among teens because a sense of failure can be perceived by the brain as a threat to survival. Staying constantly in fight-flight makes it harder to concentrate and self-regulate big feelings as they materialise. Given the normal human biological drivers of needing to belong with our peers and friends and trying to work out our identity in a very confusing landscape, is it any wonder that many of today's teens are struggling with high levels of anxiety?

Educating your teen about anxiety can support them to understand it and better manage any experiences of anxiety in their lives.

Nervous systems

The autonomic nervous system is made up of two parts: the **sympathetic nervous system** and the **parasympathetic nervous system.**

Both systems control the same body functions, in a process we're quite unconscious of, but they have opposite effects. The sympathetic nervous system gets our body ready to undertake physical activity. This is often referred to as the **fight-or-flight response.**

The **parasympathetic nervous system** relaxes the body and puts the brakes on those intense, high-energy functions. It's more commonly associated with the term '**rest and digest**', as already mentioned.

Anxiety

Teens struggle with misinterpreting non-threats as threats, especially in the emotional world and when interacting with others. I was once asked to work with a school that reported higher levels of bullying.

When I asked for some specifics about incidents of bullying, one Year 9 girl reported that she felt bullied when other girls rolled their eyes at her! Another reported feeling bullied when people turned their backs to her as she approached. Now technically, these are not incidences of bullying; they are just girls being nasty or unkind. Given the greater importance of belonging with their own age group and the increased vulnerability to misinterpreting social cues or the intentions of friends, there is an increased risk of conflict, exclusion and friendship dramas that create a breeding ground for increased anxiety. The friendship dramas are particularly potently troublesome for girls. In the survey I conducted for my book *From Boys to Men*, many men expressed that they had struggled with anxiety from being bullied by other boys, moving schools and homes throughout high school, unstable and unpredictable home environments and family violence.

Unhealthy thinking can sometimes be called 'stinking thinking' or 'ANT attacks' – you'll recall that phrase from Chapter 3 where I explored the influence of automatic negative thoughts and how they can contribute to overloading the emotional barometer of our teens. The 'tipping point' is often a sign that anxiety is playing out in a teen's world rather than just stress. It can be helpful for a teen to simply pay attention to the somatic signals from their body, and to take small action steps to shift their focus consciously like taking some deep, intentional breaths.

One way is to **measure it:** Create a 0 to 10 stress scale – maybe use a visual like this below, which, can be adjusted easily:

0______________________5___________________________10

You could put this on the side of the fridge, a mirror or even on a window. As teens often struggle to find words to express their emotional world, this simple scale can be insightful, helpful and deceptively simple. If 10 is feeling very stressed for example, then once a teen reaches five, it may be time to employ some calm-down strategies. If they find they're consistently reaching above five on the scale, then it might be time to seek some help.

Every individual has different ways of experiencing anxiety in their body. It may be butterflies in the stomach, a dry mouth, a racing heart, difficulty sleeping, chest pain, feelings of dread/fear/panic attacks, shaking, feeling pins and needles or dizziness. As you have conversations with your teen around anxiety, make sure you share your experiences with them as well. How do you feel when you are feeling anxious? Are you aware of your inner critic drowning you in lots of negative thoughts of potential failure or danger? What have you learned over the years that has helped you? What are your biggest triggers for anxiety?

It can also help to understand why we experience anxiety. Our amygdala is a pretty amazing thing, even if it can be overenthusiastic at times; it drives our early warning system and tells our body that there is a threat or danger before we realise it consciously. When I was working with teens, I made sure they came to understand why tuning into the sensations in their body was really important. Everyone's early warning system works a little differently and when we are able to sense our body is trying to warn us of something, we can start to be more conscious of our anxiety. It can be really helpful to get in the habit of asking these three questions.

- Am I in an unsafe place?
- Am I with an unsafe person?
- Am I about to do an unsafe thing?

Even though teens can make impulsive and risky choices, just bringing their awareness to these three questions can give enough of a pause that their inner compass, or their higher self, can be heard. It is always trying to be heard. However, it is a very quiet whisper compared to the loud voice of the ego mind. Taking a pause when anxiety starts to flow, asking these three questions or directing a question to the anxiety can be really helpful.

Given that many of the thoughts that drive unhealthy anxiety are of the catastrophising nature, it can be helpful to pause and simply ask – is that true? How do I know that thought is true? Sometimes these were questions I asked teens and when they thought about it, they realised that some of the irrational fears for the future were just irrational fears and not facts.

Most importantly, teens need to learn to manage their anxiety side-by-side with a loving parent or a caring mentor. We cannot leave our teens to flounder in a world of uncertainty or frightening immediacy when we could instead offer some calm, grounded support.

When to worry

An important requirement when exploring your teen's anxiety is to help your teen to identify when they may be experiencing *unhealthy levels of stress or anxiety* (i.e. having three of these main symptoms for a prolonged time).

1. Headaches, other aches and pains
2. Upset stomach, indigestion, diarrhoea
3. Changes around eating habits – either excessive or no appetite
4. Anger, irritability, entrenched moods
5. Lethargy, low energy
6. Racing heart/palpitations and/or hyperventilation
7. Tension in muscles and/or excessive perspiration
8. A dry mouth
9. Often feeling restless, apprehensive or on edge
10. Panic attacks
11. Noticeable changes across multiple settings (at home, online or at school)
12. Difficulty concentrating or feeling scattered
13. Difficulty getting to sleep, disturbed sleep
14. Avoiding usual activities, especially friends
15. Feeling frightened for no obvious reason
16. Morbid thoughts regarding people close to them
17. Constant worry/apprehension about the future.

You should worry when these changes are impacting your teen's ability to do the things they need to do and the things they like.

> Getting angry at most times in the day where I can feel my mental health taking a slow turn in the wrong direction. Not sleeping enough during the night because I spend too much time over-thinking many things that have or have not happened. Getting really, really anxious and worried that something is going to happen if I do or don't do something.

If a teen seems to be struggling with too many things to do, feeling unprepared or overwhelmed by tasks over a period of time, this can be a sign that they are struggling with anxiety. The longer it continues, the more difficult it can be for a teen to work out ways of managing that are more effective.

School reluctance that can lead to school refusal is also a sign that anxiety has become problematic for a teen who is attending a high school. It is important to reach out for some support as soon as possible before avoidance becomes their only choice. Sometimes the reason a student may become reluctant to go to school can be quite a small thing that their mind turns into a very big thing. Remember the saying, 'don't make a mountain out of a molehill'? Well that definitely is the case for many teens.

Neurodivergent teens, teens who have experienced trauma, and teens who are experiencing confusion around gender identity and sexual identity can struggle deeply with anxiety, especially in high school. Relational safety is one of the most important things to lower stress and anxiety in any environment so in a large, busy school, it can be hard for students to find safe grown-ups who can help them develop the skills and capacity to manage what they find difficult.

It has been excellent to see many wellbeing programs introduced into our high schools that are helping teens develop skills. Smiling Mind in Australia runs programs in schools and also has a brilliant free app, where mindfulness audios are available for all ages. When these programs go across the curriculum, everyone has an opportunity to benefit. Just talking about mental health is not enough to build the skills that our young need.

Our brain learns best through experience, and we need to have opportunities to experience strategies and techniques to be able to make a real difference.

What to do when you are worried that your teen is suffering from problematic anxiety

Firstly, take a look at 'Before you have the conversation' on page 171. Secondly, sow a seed of possibility around your concerns in a general way BEFORE you have the chat – e.g. 'Gee, stress can be tricky. I've noticed just how impatient people have been lately on the roads and in shopping centres. You noticed of any of your friends struggling with stress at the moment?'

'I was listening to a podcast yesterday and the person talking about anxiety was explaining that it's not always a bad thing and that you can use it as a bit of a superpower? Did you know that?' Then leave it for a couple of days before the conversation.

Next, resist the temptation to say things like, 'Everything will be okay'. Or 'there's nothing to worry about!' Platitudes like this are particularly invalidating and show your teen that you are really not listening to them and even worse, not really hearing what they are saying. Reassure your teen that struggling with anxiety is really common and that there is not something wrong with them.

Possible opening questions

Please preface this conversation by reassuring your son or daughter how much you love them, no matter what. It could be worth revisiting the chapter about the secrets of effective communication before you have your conversation. You really want to be able to give this the best chance of success, and teens are not the easiest humans to communicate with.

- Bud, I know the last few months have been pretty hard for you and you seem to have been angrier and a bit more volatile than normal – and I wonder if you have noticed. Is that how you have seen it?

- Hey sweetheart, you seem to have been walking around a bit in the middle of the night lately and I want to check how your sleep is going? Is there anything that is bothering you that we can talk about?
- Ava, my love, I have noticed you have been a bit more stressed and anxious over the last few weeks and as the exams are still a fair way away, I feel I need to check in to see if we need to be worried?
- David, I have noticed that you seem to be a bit more stressed of late. You seem to have lost your sense of humour – even I can't make you laugh. Can we just have a chat about what's happening for you?

Next steps

Teens can feel quite alone when they are struggling with anxiety, and they often think they are the only one who is struggling. It is interesting that when I have presented to groups of teens in high school about stress, anxiety and wellbeing, I have had feedback afterwards that teens then reached out for help from their parents or the school student services. They just kept struggling on their own because they didn't really know if they needed to worry. They just kept on feeling awful and stumbling through each day. Awareness and education can really help all of us in understanding the struggles that our teens can experience, especially living today in a digital world.

In her book *The Emotional Lives of Teenagers*, Lisa Damour explores a situation with a teen who is struggling with anxiety about a school trip. She asked him what was the worst-case scenario? Then she asked what he would do if the worst-case scenario happened. Interestingly, he had some strategies.

When teens cannot change an unwanted situation, they can sometimes change how they think about it.

I have found that to be true and that is why having conversations with them can help them navigate their way through their anxiety.

Another excellent strategy from Damour is helping teens take the third-person perspective. So, if they are expressing anxiety about the possibility of failing a major exam and they are expressing deep self-doubt such as 'I am gonna fail' or 'I am dumb or stupid', Lisa asks the teen, 'If your best friend just said something like that to you, what would you say back to her?' The shift in perspective can be quite illuminating. They are always much kinder to their friends than they are to themselves!

Many of our teens are deeply concerned about the future of our planet, and rightfully so. Rather than just worrying about climate change and the impact of waste on our beautiful earth, it can be really helpful to encourage agency for your teen. This means we help them explore ways and things they can do to make a positive difference to their world. The war on plastics is something every human, including our kids, can take action on. Maybe watch documentaries together and have conversations about what you learn. Not only can they be proactive in their reducing, reusing and recycling they can also join groups that are helping to clean up beaches or waterways. They can also become informed about clothing waste and become advocates for recycling clothes and avoiding buying cheap disposable clothes. It is so good to see that op shops are quite trendy among many teens. They could also adopt a koala or any other wildlife charity to help save them from extinction. Rather than just focusing on the problem, our teens can be active participants in creating the solution and they can be very passionate about it.

Headspace has some excellent free resources on their website for managing anxiety, including animations and activities. One of their resources shows four steps that your teen can cultivate when anxiety visits.

- Recognise the signs that anxiety is visiting (some people even name their anxiety)
- Be curious
- Have faith in your ability to cope
- Be kind to yourself.

How to help our teens handle stress and anxiety

Our job as parents and lighthouse figures is to help our teens find, practise and then master techniques that help them lower the cortisol their brain is producing so they can shift from fight-flight and return to rest and digest.

In my counselling sessions with teens who were struggling, I gave them a relaxation audio that they needed to listen to three to four times a week. Due to the neuroplasticity of the brain, in around three weeks their brains had created new neural pathways that supported calmness. Many of the teens told me years later that they used these audios to help them later in life when they felt challenged. Once a neural pathway is built, it can be accessed anytime. But if your teen has a ten-lane highway to anxiety and stress, without an alternative pathway to calmness, they will struggle to allow their parasympathetic nervous system to find a place to rest, even when they are asleep.

When I was teaching, I identified that stress was impacting my students and we did many calming activities including creative visualisation, and not only was I surprised with the improvement in classroom engagement, I found students were more socially cohesive and friendly. The biggest surprise was their grades improved. As Daniel Goleman discovered in his research, 'happy calm students learn best'. This became my mantra as a high-school teacher and as a mother.

I learned in my early twenties that being late is one of my biggest triggers for anxiety. I made a choice then to be early and sometimes I am half an hour early or even an hour early in case I get lost. Often, I have cuppa in a nearby café, or I sit overlooking a park or a lake until it is time for my commitment. I learned a strategy that accommodates one of my main triggers for anxiety and even today I know that that choice I make each time prevents me from being flooded with cortisol and anxiety. *Rather than leave our teens to feel paralysed with stress and anxiety, we can also help them explore it and to work out ways of becoming a little bit braver or how to temper our biggest stressors!* In the chapter about resilience, I explained the importance of keeping a balance between stressors and protective factors. Strategies that help around anxiety are protective factors that we can learn all through life.

Some other techniques that work well to help tame automatic pathways of anxiety are doing some breathing exercises, a mindfulness activity or some yoga or tai chi. Not only do these things increase the oxygen in the blood with deep breathing, they distract the brain from ANT attacks (see page 70). The brain can only focus on one thing at a time.

There are lots of videos on YouTube and apps that demonstrate short calming yoga routines or techniques like square breathing to help alleviate feelings of anxiety. I have some 'Maggie Soothers' on my YouTube channel and website, which can help. Beyond Blue also has a great page called 'Relaxation Techniques'.

As well as relaxation techniques, there are many lifestyle factors that we can support our teens to attend to: good nutrition, exercise, good sleep hygiene, minimising caffeine (especially in energy drinks!), avoiding alcohol and other drugs – all these things can support them to feel less anxious.

Top tips for helping teens cope with stress and anxiety

- As a parent, it is important to be mindful that your teen will have more stressors during this window of their life, with fewer tools to manage them. And that's okay.
- Help your teen to identify the main causes of their anxiety and plan ways to recognise their triggers while taking small steps to soothe their amygdala if it is being overenthusiastic. This is particularly helpful if they experience panic attacks.
- Work with your teen to create a sense of calmness around your home with possibly less noise, calming music and even using essential oils like sandalwood and lavender.
- Explore fidgets to see if there is one that may work for your teen that they can use discreetly in their hand.

- Model the power of the pause: teach your teen about intentional breathing – three breaths in, each with a longer outward breath – as it really works and needs to become a habit.
- Practise moments of lightness or, even better, be deliberately stupid. Wear a fluoro wig, flashing glasses, a tiara or a cape – not when you're picking your teens up from school though. Being silly at home is one thing, but embarrassing them in public will simply add to their stress!
- Search together for good resources to promote calmness. Try the free app Smiling Mind or any other closed-eye relaxations that can work at calming 'stinking thinking'. There are many calming visualisations on YouTube and your teen may respond to ASMR. Headspace has a series of 'be kind to your mind: online self-care videos' that can help.
- If your teen is spiralling, another technique that can help ease anxiety is asking your teen if they notice when panic starts to arise what can they see, smell, hear and feel right now?
- Find the feel-good neurochemicals. When a high level of stress is present, the feel-good neurochemicals of serotonin, dopamine and endorphins are often low. Help your teen work out the top three ways to create more positive neurochemicals to help them feel better.
- Your teen could spend time with people they love.
- They could go for a walk, go to the beach, swim, surf, connect with nature.
- Your teen could do something they love – shoot some hoops, dance wildly, sing loudly, cook, watch fainting goats/funny cat videos, have a bubble bath.
- Your teen could have their favourite snack/hot chocolate/smoothie.
- They could call and chat to a friend rather than text/message.
- They could put on their favourite playlist (encourage them to create an anxiety-busting playlist of songs that they know will help shift their mood).
- Your teen could focus on improving sleep.
- Ask your teen 'How can I help support you?' Offer to go for walks together, give them a shoulder or foot rub if it works for them, be

a safe place to vent verbally, give them a hug, take them for early breakfast before school once a week. Ask your teen to give you feedback on what you can do that might help!
- Practise small acts of kindness and give peace offerings after a heated moment. A cup of Milo/juice and a home-made biscuit always meant 'it's okay' in our home. Be kind.
- Remind them often that you love them fiercely and unconditionally – no matter what happens on this bumpy ride to adulthood. Write them notes/write on their mirrors and tell them you love them and you are here for them. They can struggle so much with feeling they do not deserve or are not worthy of your love. Give them hope that one day things will get better.

Stress can be distracted, even tamed, and these habits can support them throughout life. Have your teen choose three things from this list to focus on and maybe create a visual reminder for their room, mirror or phone. Positive actions are deceptively powerful in creating new habits for wellness.

Depending on your teen's response, you may explore the Brave program as it has a questionnaire that may be helpful and which can be done at home (brave4you.psy.uq.edu.au/teen-program). This questionnaire can be helpful to work out if your teen's anxiety is in the normal range or problematic, and they have online support.

If the same concerns continue, please encourage your teen to see their school counsellor, family GP or a mental-health professional. Remember, even if they do have a mental-health professional or a counsellor, your role as a caring parent is still just as important. What you do every day in your home makes a difference. Make it positive.

If your teen is struggling with anxiety, you have not failed as a parent. Well respected psychologist Karen Young has shared in her work, especially her excellent picture books, that learning to take tiny steps of bravery is needed, more than avoiding things that cause anxiety.

For more resources on this topic, such as books, podcasts, websites and helpline information, see the Resources section at the back of the book (page 386).

21

What to do when your teen experiences a significant loss experience or a death

WHAT CHALLENGED YOU MOST AS A TEEN?

The death of one of my best friends out the front of our high school. We were talking one morning when he realised he had left his science project at home, so he quickly ran home to get it. He was hit by a car and died a few days later. I was the last person to speak to him before he died. I was lucky enough to be a pallbearer at his funeral, which was an eye-opening experience. It was the first funeral I had been to, the first dead person I had seen (it was open casket) and I hadn't experienced that kind of grief before. I had a great year group, a great group of friends and we all helped each other through one of the most significant events of our lives to that point.

Background

Let's be honest – death hurts those loved ones who are left behind. Grief can impact people who have never met someone that they have come to love and trust. Most of us adults will remember the day we learned that Princess Diana had been killed in a car crash, or when Shane Warne, David Bowie or, more recently, Sinéad O'Connor died.

There were outpourings of grief the world over. The loss of someone we value triggers major emotional, cognitive, physical and spiritual challenges as we come to terms with living in a world without someone (or a pet) we love and value.

I have supported teens who have experienced the sudden death of a parent, the death of a friend by suicide, the sudden death of a friend who contracted meningitis overnight and – in the most difficult scenario – I have supported teens who have lost multiple friends in a car crash.

Sudden, unexpected death is particularly difficult as it comes with a huge degree of shock that stuns our psyche and body as our survival instincts struggle to ensure our survival. Not only do our brain and our instinctual human biological drives kidnap much of our logical processing capability, they also reduce the spaces for new learning that normally grow daily. That means academic learning can be derailed for quite some time no matter how hard a teen may try.

> 'A traumatic experience impacts the entire person – the way we think, the way we learn, the way we remember things, the way we feel about ourselves, the way we feel about other people, and the way we make sense of the world are all profoundly altered by traumatic experience, especially the loss of someone we love.'
>
> – Noga Flory, 'Residence Directors as Residential Crisis Workers'

The time of bereavement is an unpredictable journey where we process the grief and sadness, sometimes fear, anger and a crippling sense of vulnerability. Teens are sensitive and immature in many ways – cognitively, socially and emotionally, and they are living through a time where their emotions are even more intense. The loss of someone they love can seem insurmountable and paralysing. Many I've worked with have expressed that they believe they will never be happy again. Every human being processes grief differently and depending on your capacity for resilience, you will rebuild your life in your own time and your own way. One thing we cannot do for someone who's grieving, no matter how much we want to, is to take away that pain of loss. However, there are things we can do that can support them to recover and heal and there are some things we need to avoid doing.

In our death-phobic world, we seem fearful of saying the wrong thing so we often say nothing at all. I wish we called death by its correct name – instead of saying things like 'passed over' or 'gone to sleep'. I believe such terminology adds to the fear and phobia that we experience around this life transition that is death. Often, when I was working with a grieving teen, allowing them the space to sit in silence without asking questions gave them time to really get in touch with the emotions stirring inside them.

The physiology of adolescent grief

For teens who are already experiencing the confusion, angst and stress of coping with life changes on all levels – in a tougher, less caring world – a major loss experience can have long-term detrimental effects on their wellbeing.

The executive functioning part of the human brain that allows us to make sensible, sound decisions, plan for the future, manage impulses, feel empathy for others, have patience, and an ability to manage conflict and stress does not complete its construction until around the mid-twenties, as we have explored elsewhere in the book. The heightened emotional intensity in adolescence creates emotional instability, especially when a teen perceives a threat, and it increases the difficulty they have managing moods. They can also struggle with their emotional barometer. It is common for teens to resist asking for help and that can create a cluster of unique challenges that can make grieving the loss of someone significant especially difficult. Sleep is often seriously disrupted in the first months after a major loss. As most teens are already struggling with sleep debt, this can increase their emotional suffering and can increase chances of illness as the immune system is compromised with serious patterns of insufficient sleep.

Significant loss can be like a death too

Broken friendships and broken hearts

Friendships are incredibly important during adolescence as teens are biologically driven to pull back from their parents and draw closer to peers. This is partly to help them grow in their ability to become independent and to create their own life pathways. Good friends are seen as a protective factor during this journey to adulthood and when friendships end, or are a source of conflict, they can cause enormous emotional angst.

When a good friendship ends, it can feel as painful as a death in so many ways. When two friends break up, teens can struggle with grief and confusion as their social connections are often destabilised. It can be so helpful to have older teens or siblings to help them navigate the breakup because often there is painful 'stuff' that happens via social networks, which can make the loss even more painful – and many adults are really unaware of all the ways teens connect in the virtual world. Nasty messages or false rumours can shatter a teen's confidence for years and, sadly, some of these messages have been the trigger that has tipped a young person into attempting suicide. Careful, supportive monitoring without interfering is a difficult task; however, it is the best way to guide a wounded teen through a friendship loss.

Do you remember your first love? Many people still hold strong memories of their first love and this is because of the intensity of the emotional domain of adolescents, especially under 20. Infatuation is common and again the intensity of feelings of attraction can be amazingly strong and often the subject of an infatuation may not even know about it. I was 'madly in love' with a student in the class above me when I was in high school. I would stop breathing when he walked past, and I struggled with lots of big, ugly, sad feelings when I realised he didn't even know I existed.

All parents and teachers need to be mindful of the loss of that first love that is mutually reciprocated during the teen years. The massive spikes of serotonin that adults feel when they fall in love are so much more intense (is that possible?) for our teens. The higher they fly with these feelings of affection and attraction, and the longer they are together, the bigger the sense of desperation and grief when it ends.

Often the first love is a time when we have opened ourselves to a place of deep vulnerability with the expression of our sexual desires and often our first time being sexually intimate. I have read some anecdotal accounts of sensitive teen boys who have suicided after the end of their first love because the sense of loss was too much. Again, parents and teachers need to treat this breakup like a death and avoid offering advice or making light of their intense feelings. Validate that love hurts the most when we lose it. Someone once said that it's important to remember than when we feel badly hurt by loss, it's good to remember that that is because we have loved. Nurture your teen by allowing them to grieve in the safety of their family.

Numbing with drugs and alcohol

Over the years many teens have shared with me the physical pain they have felt in their hearts and sometimes in their stomachs in the weeks that follow the death of a friend. The intensity of feelings can be very frightening, and many turn to food and/or alcohol, or mind-altering drugs to ease the intensity of their feelings as well as to give them a break from feeling so distraught. Sadly, they have found that after drinking excessively or smoking cannabis or taking ecstasy or MDMA, their temporary relief was often followed by even stronger depressive feelings because alcohol and cannabis are depressants and there is often a significant crash after taking ecstasy.

Grief consumes enormous amounts of physical energy and I encourage both teens and their parents to consider taking some vitamin supplements to help the body manage the extra work it has to do during this stressful time. This is even more important if your teen doesn't have an appetite and is struggling to eat healthy food. Smoothies and soups are a great way to help your teen get some nutrition into them while they're grieving. Thankfully, family and friends tend to be very generous with donations of home-cooked food to help keep those most traumatised nourished. It is important to accept these offerings of kindness because those around are helping in any way they can. Accepting offers of kindness stops people who are trying to support you from feeling helpless and powerless, so accept with thanks.

It is recommended for all teens and adults to avoid driving for the first few days after a death, as the mind and body are in a state of shock. Your normal mental processing can be disrupted so you can miss cues like stop signs and red lights. It is handy to keep in mind that we are wired to survive as our first instinct – being smart or happy again only happens once our brain decides our survival is secure.

Talking with safe people about irrational feelings following a loss can also be helpful. Sometimes teens can have fears and sources of guilt and shame which they feel they cannot talk about in case of upsetting someone, or because of shame. For example, they may think they have done something to contribute to the loss, or that they could have done something else. Sometimes, teens can feel that something they are doing is making the situation worse for people in their family. Also, they may have a secret fear that there will be more losses. I have worked with a teen who was struggling with survivor guilt, as his best mate was killed in the car that he was supposed to be travelling in to a party. He felt he was responsible for his mate's death.

These secret fears and guilty feelings make young people feel worse. We can help adolescents feel better by asking them about some common fears/sources of guilt and reassuring them.

If parents are impacted by the death of someone close to a teen, the teen can often be concerned that sharing their grief and emotional pain will burden their already suffering parents. Often, with teens, their circle of friends and support people are all struggling at the same time, so this is where the role of significant adult allies, 'lighthouses', is incredibly valuable. Within our school systems, students often have favourite teachers and making these teachers available for students to spend time with can help struggling teens enormously. It is incredibly important to just be beside them, listening and supporting them, rather than giving advice or telling them how to grieve. Unfortunately, I have seen many well-intentioned schools hire outside counsellors to come in and offer support, but these outsiders have no connection at all with the teens. This often doesn't work in isolation because there is no relationship, no sense of trust.

Sometimes teens just need to be held and 'allowed' to cry and sob. I often had teens in my office who just sobbed until there were no sobs left, and very little talking happened. Releasing big emotions from the nervous system helps all of us to heal. I taught many teens how to use 'tapping' to release big feelings around grief. For many boys, I encouraged them to run the grief into the ground so that it could leave their body. This does not mean they are over it because it takes a long time for us to integrate the loss of someone we love into our lives. It merely releases some of the tension they experience in a way that they have control over. It is far better than numbing the pain. I have found many well-meaning adults want to talk too much or offer platitudes that can be patronising and unhelpful. Statements like 'time will heal' and 'I know how you feel' or 'they are with God now' may feel like the right thing to say, however, to a teen, those statements are about you and not them. This young person is really sad and feeling vulnerable and frightened – *validate that how they are feeling is normal and okay.*

In my experience, other teens, especially girls, often benefit from journaling or writing in diaries when they feel overwhelmed or are processing major life transitions. This can be a good time to give a special teen in your life a beautiful new notebook and/or pens to plant that seed in their mind.

Another way to channel the big ugly feelings of grief is to engage students in writing memorial booklets, creating photo displays or digital memorials, using an art teacher to help them create a memorial plaque, a figurine or their own personal piece. Many schools have encouraged students to be part of a quilt-making activity or a knitting activity to create something substantial to gift to the family of the person who has died. Students who are talented musically can write a song that can be performed at the funeral. Using the arts is a powerful way to help channel painful emotional energy into something that has the potential to heal. In a way this is like channelling the grief energy into something positive. One of the reasons this works so well is that it gives teens agency and an opportunity to do something with their grief. Channelling it towards hope can be deceptively powerful.

Close friends have also been known to do a group symbol to acknowledge their friend. While a group tattoo may seem like a really 'cool' idea, it can be one that, as an adult, one may regret – not so much because they don't want to remember their special friend, but tastes change as we get older. Instead, I've known some close groups to make a special piece of jewellery that all the friends wear, maybe even wearing a wristband or choosing simply to all dress in a certain colour that was a favourite of their friend. Or getting matching t-shirts printed with a symbol or saying that reminds them of the deceased. Planting trees or creating memorial gardens or creating a plaque to be placed at one of their favourite places are other ways that close friends and families can honour their loved one. This allows for a collective expression of love that also respects the autonomy of the young people in grief.

I once worked with a high school that was struggling with the aftermath of losing two of their young lads in a car crash. It was a few months after the funerals and the staff were concerned that they were finding 'graffiti' around the school and the community. On further enquiry, I found that the 'graffiti' was the deceased boys' names being drawn with pictures of flowers and skateboards. This was a clear sign that the teens felt there was a lack of collective expression to acknowledge their friends in a public way, so the school and community worked closely with the teens to create a more appropriate memorial. Having a place to visit to acknowledge the deceased person is helpful, and temporary memorial sites can be set up in a school until a permanent site is created. Park benches, tree plantings, large rocks or logs with memorial plaques are all ways of creating a special place nearby.

A healthy grieving process can acknowledge the journey of accepting the loss, allowing the human psyche to express the sometimes irrational emotions and feelings while rebuilding our expectations of life without that special person. This then allows loved ones to re-invest in living by turning back towards life while being grateful for the gift of life. I know some teens who have travelled to the parts of the world their friend had planned to travel, and who have jumped out of perfectly good aeroplanes because it was something their friend had planned to do. There are also those who have gone on to name a child after their friend.

- Recently a family member close to me passed and I've been feeling low for a while. I get sad but also feel empty. I'm getting more and more anxious over small things which then stops me doing stuff. When I'm trying to sleep, I sometimes get scared thinking I might not wake up. I go into dark thoughts and I struggle with basic things like brushing teeth and brushing my hair. I've been getting more agitated at small things that I usually wouldn't and I don't know why. That's how I feel when I'm struggling emotionally.
- Last year I finished primary school and was going to a school where I knew no one. At the time we were also moving to my grandma's house to be closer to this school, so being isolated from my friends other than online was hard for me mentally.
- Broke up with girlfriend of two years which made me sad quite often especially when I wasn't busy doing other things.
- I recently went through a breakup with a boyfriend. I had liked him for a while but he was interested in me for much less time. He ended up breaking it off after a month and didn't give me many reasons apart from 'needing someone to do his hobbies with'. This made me feel unworthy and like I had somehow messed up because he thought I didn't enjoy doing the things he did. Later on I found out that he had talked about how he was feeling with another girl who was one of his close friends. I was confused and hurt and somewhat betrayed. I felt really anxious about the future as I couldn't imagine liking anyone else as much as I liked him. I stopped eating food and drinking water for a couple days because I completely lost my appetite.

In the survey of men I did for *From Boys to Men*, when I asked them what had most challenged them as a teen boy, a lot of respondents listed moving house, states or schools while they were adolescents. In my work with teen boys, I identified that so much of the challenge they experienced in moving and in losing touch with people they really cared about was about grief. *No one had spoken to them about grief.* Going to boarding school is an enormous time of adjustment that involves many layers of grief. It is not just homesickness, and I have long been an advocate for preparing our teens about the grief they may feel when they are first transitioning to boarding school.

- Moving interstate from my friends and starting again.
- When friends left for boarding school to the city for Year 11 and 12 but I was left behind in a country town to get a job.
- We moved often, so fitting in with new groups at new schools was a daunting task to say the least.
- Moving schools in Year 8 was a big challenge.
- Moving from the suburbs to a country town when I was 15.
- Moving house and changing schools was a bit of a challenge, finding new friends and trying to fit in.
- My siblings moving out.
- Moving countries, from South Africa to Australia. Changing a whole world, getting used to a new culture and different perspectives.

When to worry about your grieving teen

If after six to eight weeks you are seeing the following things happening, there may be room for concern. Certainly, if these things are persisting after three months, your teen may find it helpful to see someone experienced in grief counselling.

- Depressed mood, feeling sad or low most of the time, especially after the first six to eight weeks
- Social withdrawal, especially from friends
- Marked fall in school work, particularly grades

- Changes in usual sleeping or eating patterns
- Reluctance to go to school or take part in normal activities
- Fearfulness and heightened anxiety
- Restlessness, fidgeting and trouble concentrating
- Fatigue, lack of energy or significant lethargy
- Irritability, especially intense anger for boys
- Numbing behaviour with alcohol or drugs
- Crying a lot, especially while at school
- Feeling hopeless or worthless
- Suicidal thoughts/thoughts of death. (Please see Chapter 24 on suicide for more information.)

What to do if you feel your child is really struggling after experiencing a loss or death?

Firstly, reflect deeply and ask yourself – am I the right person to have this conversation? If you have been impacted by this loss, or you have had a significant loss elsewhere in your life, you may not be the best person to have this conversation. This does not mean you are not going to support your child, you are, you just may not be the best person to have this conversation. If you feel like you're ready, then **take a look at 'Before you have the conversation' on page 171.**

Possible opening questions

Please preface this conversation by reassuring your son or daughter how much you love them, no matter what.

- Bud, this last month has been really hard since David died and I just wanted to check in to see how things are going with you and your mates?
- Hey sweetheart, I know the last few months have been pretty hard for you and your friends since your favourite teacher died. I know grief can be really confusing for everyone. I wonder if we could just have a chat to see how things are going for you and your friends?

- Ava, my love, I know it's only been a month since Buffy – the best dog in the entire world – died and I have noticed you seem to still be struggling with sadness. I wonder if we could have a chat to see how I can support you while you grieve and your heart heals?

Tips for parents supporting teens in grief

- Don't take it personally or react harshly if your grieving teen lashes out at you. TLC, non-judgement and patience from you are required.
- Encourage your son or daughter to have a friend/s stay with them especially during the early days of grief. The companionship can help soothe frazzled nerves.
- Small gestures of kindness can make a huge difference.
- Let your teen know that during grief, intense feelings are normal and will get easier in time. Help them see these intense emotions as energy that they can discharge through crying, humour and physical activity.
- Keep them hydrated and offer easily digestible, nutritious food. Also consider getting them to take supplements to help the body with the extra work it's doing.
- If you are involved in organising a wake, discourage drinking alcohol. Offer light beer for over 18s and other refreshments, and keep an eye on young guests to keep them safe.
- Let your teen cry without too much talking from you. Validate that how they are feeling is normal and okay. Check in with simple statements like 'How can I best help you right now?' Or 'please tell me what I can do to support you?'
- Use guided relaxation or creative visualisation audio tracks to give the teen and their mind a break.
- Seek out 'lighthouses' – loving adult allies who can support your son or daughter when you can't, or they prefer not to share with you. Also be a support yourself to your child's friendship circle.
- With your teen, create a spot at home, like a mini 'altar', where you can have a photo of the deceased, flowers and a candle that can

be lit whenever they want to reflect in silence. Pretending they can still have conversations with the deceased has been helpful for many teens.

- Seek professional help if the person who's died did so by suicide as there is a high risk of copycat suicides.

Funerals

Reassure your teen that grief is unpredictable, irrational, hard and it takes time and many tears. That is okay. That is normal. We grieve deeply when we have loved deeply.

Please be honest about your own grief and do not be frightened to cry in front of your kids of any age. Involve your kids in funeral preparations, and the funeral itself if they want to be involved. As a celebrant, I have conducted funerals after the sudden death of the teen, where up to 500 people were there and most were under 18 years of age. Funerals are an important part of accepting and acknowledging the loss of someone we care about.

Today's funerals focus much more on the celebration of the life lived rather than the loss of that life. There are many warm moments, and they tend to land on hope and joy.

In many ways it's a tough thing for a parent to witness their teen buried in grief and yet it is one of those life experiences that will happen at some point. It is an inevitable part of life. With awareness and understanding, grieving can be a journey that enables individuals to mature and grow as well as to recover and heal. Despite how hard it can be, we can validate this process and accept the times of emotional turmoil as a part of being human. Human connectedness gets us through hard times, including significant loss experiences and the death of loved ones. We must never leave teens to grieve alone.

For more resources on this topic, such as books, podcasts, websites and helpline information, see the Resources section at the back of the book (page 387).

22

What to do when your teen experiences sexual harassment or sexual violence

Background

As parents, we are biologically wired to want to keep our kids safe, and when anyone hurts them, even when they are a young adult, our response will be pretty much the same. We may feel furious and upset, and deep down we may want to go and hurt the person who hurt our child. Thankfully, because we are mature grown-ups, when we calm down, we realise that what we need to do, above all else, is to look after our child and help them heal and recover.

Sexual violence

According to 2020–2021 figures from the Australian Bureau of Statistics, an estimated 14 per cent of people aged 18 years and over (2.8 million) have experienced sexual violence since they were 15 years old. That includes both sexual assault and threats.

Women were more likely than men to experience sexual violence, with 2.2 million (22 per cent), experiencing sexual assault or threat:

- 20 per cent (2 million) who experienced sexual assault
- 5.5 per cent (544,700) who experienced sexual threat

Of men, 6.1 per cent (582,400) had experienced sexual violence, including:

- 5.1 per cent (483,800) who experienced sexual assault
- 1.4 per cent (137,900) who experienced sexual threat.

Sexual violence or sexual assault is defined as when an individual is pressured, forced, coerced, tricked or manipulated into doing something sexual that they don't want to do. The key message is that sexual assault is any unwanted and forced sexual behaviour that happens without consent. Research shows that the easy and frequent exposure to pornography has been linked to an increase in teen dating violence, including things like hitting, being hurt with objects or slammed against something, and being forced to have intercourse. Sexual harassment, sadly, has also been increasing in our schools, even in primary school. This is when individuals use sexual gestures, make sexual groaning noises, rape threats and disrespectful and demeaning sexual name-calling. This is also a form of sexual aggression and needs to be taken seriously.

Early sexual experiences can be confusing and scary for anyone, even when consensual and respectful, let alone when things go wrong. I am sure that as a parent, you can remember an awkward and possibly uncomfortable moment in your teen years as part of your own emerging sexuality.

Director of Collective Shout, an anti-sexploitation movement, and author of *He Chose Porn Over Me*, Melinda Tankard Reist wrote about how porn is damaging our young people for *Eureka Street*.

> Choking, bruising, bondage, whipping, rape-play: p*rn-driven expectations . . . Exposure to pornography has been linked to an increase in sexually aggressive behaviour and adolescent dating violence. Boys

wanting to enact the signature acts of pornography on girls has also become more common. More young men expect facials (ejaculation on the face), anal and oral sex.

Debby Herbenick, a leading sex researcher at Indiana University, advises students: 'If you're with somebody for the first time, don't choke them, don't ejaculate on their face, don't try to have anal sex with them. These are all things that are just *unlikely* to go over well.'

Adolescent sexual maturity

Evidence is now showing that today's children are beginning puberty earlier than ever, sometimes as young as eight. There are so many changes on this journey – physical, emotional, cognitive and hormonal – and one of the drivers on this journey to adulthood is sexual awakening. This is normal; however, it is problematic if our young people are learning how to express their sexuality through watching pornography or by following certain websites like content/fan connection website OnlyFans. Why? Firstly, because they are watching porn during a stage in which they lack the cognitive capacity to understand and make sound choices through reasoned decision-making using a fully formed executive functioning brain (remember – this doesn't develop until the mid-twenties or so). Overwhelmingly, porn is not modelling healthy sexual intimacy between consenting adults.

Secondly, during adolescence, they are biologically driven to belong, and to be liked and validated by those of the same age so they're more prone to being influenced by what they're seeing. So we can understand how this could become problematic. There is plenty of research that indicates that our young people's sexual behaviour is being shaped (negatively, more often than not) by porn.

The influence of porn works both ways. Both boys' and girls' violent behaviour has increased but it is still more often girls than boys who are the victims of sexual violence. There is a problem of male entitlement where boys demand that girls meet their sexual needs, or where boys think there is no problem with raping a sleeping or unconscious girl, which has to come from somewhere. Yes, it has been a part of traditional patriarchy for years but it seems to be reaching a tipping point for teen boys today – attitudes aren't shifting as we might hope and expect. This is not just about the lack of consent education and the influence of what they see online. This is a lack of character building from not only their family and society at large, but also their school community, and the communities that surround them, whether that be sport, faith or the arts.

In recent years there has been some serious light being shone on the dark underbelly of inappropriate sexual behaviour and abuse and most specifically rape perpetrated by boys and men in Australian schools, communities, businesses and parliament. Something shifted from the moment that the courageous advocate for survivors of sexual assault Grace Tame became Australian of the Year.

Sexual violence among adolescents particularly came to light when, in 2021, former private school student Chanel Contos created a petition which has since been signed by more than 44,000 people.

Chanel started the petition after asking followers on Instagram if 'they or someone close to them had been sexually assaulted by someone when they were at school'. More than 200 people said 'yes' within 24 hours and the testimonies they left are harrowing and distressing to read, however, the light needs to shine on the stories so that we collectively know the truth of this violent culture and stop it happening to other girls.

Chanel's petition called for 'more holistic and earlier consent education in Australia', and she launched a website where people can share anonymous testimonies of sexual assault.

This a message from teachusconsent.com:

> Those who have signed this petition have done so because they are sad and angry that they did not receive an adequate education regarding what amounts to sexual assault and what to do when it happens. These are uncomfortable conversations to have with young

teenagers but it is far more uncomfortable to live knowing that something happened to you, or a friend, or perhaps that you were even the perpetrator of it, and it could have been avoided.

Many of the stories shared are about appalling behaviour from boys from elite private schools. Since then, stories have been shared that include government schools so it is safe to say this is problematic for many adolescents, not just in Australia but around the world.

I want to acknowledge that not all boys behave in these disgusting ways, but many decent boys stand by and do nothing, and that has to stop too.

In Chanel's words:

> 'The following testimonies were sent to me by those who passionately believe that inadequate consent education is the reason for their sexual abuse during or soon after school.'

It should be no surprise to us that things seem to have gotten worse since the digital world arrived. Earlier in the book, I explored how access to smartphones and the Internet has disinhibited many of our teens. There has to be some cost for the loss of childhood innocence much earlier than our children are cognitively, emotionally and psychologically capable of comprehending. Indeed, most children and tweens have smartphones which give them access to content that can be shattering their child-like innocence and feeding a notion of a 'hook-up' culture where sex without intimacy is almost the norm. **We need to keep in mind today's children, teens and young adults DID NOT create the digital world.** It is a massive experiment that was created by adults and, sadly, it is our young who are paying the price. There has been a significant upswing in extreme right-wing views that are based on traditional patriarchal values and many of our boys are being influenced. Much as I hate to draw any attention to him, the case in point is influencer Andrew Tate who has managed to spread unhelpful messages about how to be a man today, which includes the control, manipulation and mistreatment of women for his own benefits. At the time of writing, he's awaiting trial in Romania on rape and human trafficking charges, which he has denied. He has been enormously influential among tween and teen boys and, despite being banned from most social-media platforms, he continues to make headlines.

Melinda Tankard Reist, who works with thousands of students at schools around Australia, shares what she is hearing from girls in schools now:

> Please ask the boys to stop telling us about the porn they watched last night. Please ask the boys to stop ranking us according to the bodies of porn stars. Please ask the boys to stop making jokes about our bodies. Please ask the boys to stop rubbing up against us in the corridors. Please ask the boys to stop sending us dick pics. Please ask the boys to stop pressuring us for nudes.
>
> These everyday sexual affronts tell us a great deal about how entrenched the objectification of girls is. They also tell us how widespread is the callousing of our young men, the erosion of empathy, the decay of civil behaviour, and the social arson caused by mass pornography saturation.
>
> – melindatankardreist.com

Kirra Pendergast from Safe On Social reports that she is hearing more and more from parents of kids in Year 5 and 6 about flirting via devices that is bordering on sexting. We are seeing more and more instances of revenge porn (distributing nude images of people without their consent) and 'sextortion' (blackmailing someone by threatening to send images) and often young people are involved – this can get very serious. Please educate yourself about having conversations with your kids about this and what to do when things go wrong (the chapter on cyberbullying has some helpful tips).

When I was counselling, many teens disclosed things to me about sexual violence or abuse that they had experienced. However, it was the disclosure from men in their forties that I found more surprising. We need to keep in mind that our teen boys are often targets of sexual predators too, and their deep and profound sense of shame can keep that hidden for years. The impact of that trauma plays out in their lives in so many unhealthy and unhelpful ways, just as it does for our girls and gender-diverse kids.

This is why we must educate our teens about what constitutes sexual abuse, and that they are never responsible for being abused in any way and that you will always believe and support them. This message needs to go to all of their friends as well. You never know what is happening in the lives of your son or daughter's friends.

Sexting and nudes

Research from the eSafety commissioner indicates one in three 14–17-year-olds in Australia 'had some experience of sending, sharing or being asked to share nudes'. Even though this may be considered quite normal among teens, it is still illegal, and it can still cause harm to an individual. Sending unwanted 'dick pics' and harassing girls for naked images needs to stop. Harassing and pressuring anyone in any situation is a form of coercive control. We must call this out and stop it because this is often a dark underbelly in family violence. Many teens do not experience a sense of sexual violence around sexting, however, some definitely feel violated with what happens with the image afterwards if it is shared without consent.

So many schools tell me how much valuable time they lose during school hours managing the fallout of sexting or the unwanted sharing of nudes. This is not the job of schools and much of it happens at night.

> Please delay giving your kids smartphones for as long as possible and definitely have tight boundaries around access to phones and digital devices at night, especially in the privacy of bedrooms or bathrooms. Really, don't be complacent.

The legal system must change

Sadly, so few sexual assault cases end in convictions and this needs to stop. Further, the victim-blaming rhetoric must stop. The legal process needs to focus on the perpetrator and the wrong they have done, not on what a woman was wearing or why she was walking alone at night or whether she was drinking! Victim blaming is a part of unhealthy patriarchy, and we must all educate ourselves about it and name it when we see it.

Unfortunately, consent education will not be enough to transform some of the social conditioning that teen boys have experienced and may hold as truth. US writer Peggy Orenstein interviewed more than 100 boys for her book *Boys and Sex*, and she discovered that it is still fairly common for groups of boys to demean and shame girls (aka 'slut shaming') all in the name of good fun and male bonding. Hopefully, consent education provides the opportunity for teens to fully understand what constitutes sexual harassment and assault. Making sexist slurs in a classroom, yelling out rape threats and spreading intimate images without consent are all a form of sexual harassment. **Sexual harassment, verbal and online, is illegal, and it is a criminal offence.** Maybe we need to start charging students who are behaving in this way, so that they can see there are consequences for their behaviour – regardless of whether they were trying to be funny! It is not just the criminality of rape, cyberbullying, possession of child pornography (i.e., in the case of asking for nudes from underage girls) and other forms of sexual violence that needs to be considered as being serious.

Parents are responsible for educating their children and teens around protective behaviours and healthy sexual awareness from a young age. Of course, schools can play a part. However, the many conversations that you have over many years can better prepare your teen to understand what constitutes sexual violence. Yes, we do need to talk to young children about what constitutes sexual abuse and about the potential for sexual predators, especially from grown-ups who are close to them. Over 90 per cent of sexual abuse is perpetrated by someone the victim knows. Generally, it is not strangers.

Sadly, despite the Australian government previously rejecting calls for age verification around online pornography, it took an increased number of women dying in family violence incidents in 2024 for them to change their mind, and they will now trial it. Even with responsible parents who have careful parental controls on their devices, monitor screen time closely, and who have had conversations about seeing 'bad' pictures and videos, many children get exposed to porn by other children. Often this happens on the school bus, in the playground or on a play date or sleepover. Education will help your child if they are sexually violated or abused.

Grace Tame used a significant catch cry during her year as Australian of the Year: 'Evil thrives in silence'. That is so true, especially around sexual violence and sexual assault. Interestingly, I have never told anyone about a challenging encounter I had with a large, powerful, popular young man at a twenty-first birthday party. He tried to pull my knickers down and pushed me against the wall with his erect penis in full view. I am a strong, feisty female with very clear boundaries even as a then-16-year-old, and maybe thanks to having older brothers, my impulse was to punch him hard in the face. Thankfully for me, it was enough for me to escape. I have often wondered why I have never shared that with my nearest and dearest, or even the therapists I've worked with over the years. Speaking up must be encouraged from a young age and keeping secrets should be discouraged.

I have also known two men in their forties who have disclosed being raped and sodomised by clergy and a boarding master at a boarding school. This has gone on around the world and, here in Australia, the Royal Commission into institutionalised sexual abuse found that many children, especially boys, went on to keep sexual abuse secret for over 20 years before they found the courage to disclose. The profound shame is again the main reason for this. One of the men I supported was worried that if his wife of 25 years knew that he had been raped, that somehow she would not be able to love him. Trauma, especially around sexual abuse, can cause really long-term mental and emotional damage and this needs specialised professional help to cope with. Sometimes the trauma and the shame are too much to bear – the last thing we need is the suicide of more young people.

Why consent education matters

There is a grey area around consent that even adults can misread at times and so our teens are naturally more at risk of making poor choices. It's not as simple as 'yes' or 'no'. Men in my surveys have expressed regret about poor choices they made as teen boys.

Consent is basically free and voluntary agreement. A lawyer explained to me that there are two types of consent – explicit and tacit. From state to state and country to country there are different requirements around ascertaining consent such as 'affirmative consent' and 'enthusiastic consent'. Basically, this means you can't assume someone's consent, you need to explicitly ask their permission. There are also certain situations in which someone legally can't be considered to have given consent (i.e., when they are under the age of consent, asleep or intoxicated).

> 'Consensual, enjoyable sexual activity is about constant communication. Sometimes one person will be asking for consent for something, and sometimes they'll be giving it. If teenagers can communicate openly and freely during their sexual experiences, these experiences are likely to feel good. They're also likely to be equal, respectful, legal and safe.'
>
> – 'Getting and giving sexual consent: talking with teenagers', raisingchildren.net.au

When to worry

Sexual violence can impact individuals differently but it is a form of trauma. The impact on your teen's system can show up in different ways. It can be very much like the impact of a sudden death or an overwhelming anxiety that makes it hard for them to get out of bed in the morning. In my experience, teens show quite obvious signs that something big and confronting has happened immediately afterwards or in the days that followed. Stay tuned to your gut instincts around any sudden change.

If your teen comes home obviously distressed, crying, angry or in denial, you would not have had enough chance to prepare what to say. Calm yourself as much as you can and be what your son or daughter needs – listen, believe them, reassure them and seek help.

However, these are some of the things that may also become more obvious following an experience of sexual abuse if they haven't been able to disclose it to you immediately.

- Freezing up, shutting down, avoiding communicating
- Incidents of self-harm
- Unexplained bruising
- A urinary tract infection
- Headaches, other aches and pains
- Upset stomach, indigestion, diarrhoea
- Changes in the way they dress
- Changes around eating habits – either excessive or no appetite
- Anger, irritability, entrenched moods
- Lethargy, low energy
- Racing heart/palpitations and/or hyperventilation
- Tension in muscles and/or excessive perspiration
- A dry mouth
- Often feeling restless, apprehensive or on edge
- Panic attacks
- Noticeable changes across multiple settings (at home, online or at school)
- Difficulty concentrating or feeling scattered
- Difficulty getting to sleep, disturbed sleep
- Avoiding usual activities, especially friends
- Feeling much more frightened about leaving home
- Constant worry/apprehension about the future
- Engaging in risky sexual behaviour.

Worry when these changes impact your teen's ability to do the things they need to do and the things they like.

Having the conversation

Firstly, take a look at 'Before you have the conversation' on page 171.

Start by reassuring your teen how much you love them and that there is nothing that could ever change the way that you love them. There is nothing under the sun they cannot tell you about.

It can be incredibly hard not to want to jump in immediately if you suspect something big has happened, however, you need to temper that with knowing that the sooner you know sexual assault or rape has occurred, the better. So rather than just focus on **when** to approach your teen – because you really want to tackle it immediately – it can be wiser to focus on **how** you are going to approach them. Maybe imagine yourself in your teen's shoes, and think, how would I like my mum or dad to approach me if this had happened to me?

Possible opening questions

- Bud, I have noticed a pretty sudden change in you, and I know that something big has happened. I want you to know that there is nothing you could ever tell me that would stop me loving you. When you're ready to let me know what's going on, I will be ready too.
- Hey sweetheart, I'm really worried as I have heard you sobbing in your bedroom, so I know you're upset. I want you to know that there is nothing so awful you can't share with me. I am here for you and want to know how I can support you right now?
- Ava, my love, something is really bothering you and I wonder if something has happened to really upset you. No matter how big it is, how awful it is I want you know that I will always have your back. So do you want to chat about it now or maybe later?
- My mum radar is going crazy right now and I think something awful has happened. I want you to know that nothing is too big for you

to overcome with me by your side – shall I make a cuppa and you can tell me what has happened? Or do you want to chat a bit later?

Next steps

Believe what you are being told, even if it doesn't make sense, or it might be hard to believe.

Your next priority is to validate their distress and soothe them in any way they prefer. There will be so many emotions swirling around, and sometimes a teen will feel guilty for getting in that situation, or they can feel really angry at themselves and many will struggle with a deep sense of shame. Sometimes their sexual activity may have been something that they were keen and enthusiastic about, which then became hurtful and harmful. I have had emergency doctors tell me that they have had teen girls admitted to their departments with internal injuries or anal tears when a sexual encounter went bad.

Thank them for sharing this difficult information with you and tell them they're incredibly brave to do so. Also reassure them that telling you is absolutely the right thing to do and that together you'll work out the steps to go forward.

Reassure them that it is not their fault, and they are absolutely in no way to blame for what happened. You also need to remind yourself that you are in no way to blame for what has happened as well! When your teen revisits an experience of sexual violence or sexual assault as they tell you what happened, it can often bring up more trauma for them and more distress. Sometimes, focusing on the sequence of events, rather than the specifics of what happened, can be easier in the first conversation.

Remember, it can be really difficult for a teen who has experienced sexual violence to decide whether to report it. It's important to know though that while you can report an assault to police at any time, the earlier you report it, the more likely the police will be able to collect evidence.

You can help your teen make an informed decision about this by seeking advice yourself. I suggest you start by calling 1800 RESPECT or 1800 FULL STOP in Australia to talk through what might happen next. They should also be able to connect you with local support services.

If you elect/need to take your teen to the doctor or emergency department (or a sexual health centre) for an examination, the health professionals will likely talk with your child and assist with emergency contraception, testing for potential STIs and examining and treating any physical injuries. If it's within around 72 hours of the assault, they may offer for your teen to have a forensic medical examination and take samples that can be passed on to the police if your teen does decide to go to the police.

In the days following the disclosure, your teen can still be experiencing shock and if you can, it can be helpful to keep them at home with a loving parent as you support them to get back on their feet.

It can be incredibly difficult for a parent to care for a teen who has been sexually violated, especially if you have very little awareness or understanding about sexual violence. Keep in mind caring for them emotionally, physically and psychologically needs to be your first priority.

I cannot understate the importance of considering counselling for your teen and yourself in the wake of a sexual assault. Even starting with calling a sexual assault crisis line can help. It is a very sad indictment of our world that there is the need for so many support services around sexual violence and sexual assault. As soon as you can, check them out online and become better informed. There are many helplines that you can call immediately, and they are very experienced at helping people just like you.

For more resources on this topic, such as books, podcasts, websites and helpline information, see the Resources section at the back of the book (page 388).

23

What you need to know about supporting your neurodivergent teen through the challenges of adolescence

I would like to dedicate this chapter a wonderful human called Lou Kuchel who was a passionate advocate for neurodivergent kids and their families here in Australia. Lou was host of the Square Peg Round Whole *podcast, through which she gave people a space to discuss diversity, and how to embrace our neurodivergent kids at home, at school and in the workplace. Through the podcast and her advocacy work, Lou spoke with dozens of experts, and she was instrumental in bringing internationally renowned clinical psychologist Dr Ross Greene to Australia to help up-skill and educate parents and teachers in neuro-affirmative practice. I supported Lou in many of her endeavours and was a guest on her podcast. Sadly, we lost Lou due to a battle with cancer, and I wish to acknowledge that her work and her passion will continue as she has left such a legacy. I like to think Lou is still cheering us on from the other side because as a passionate social-justice campaigner and an advocate for all the 'square pegs' among us, her spirit will never be dampened.*

Background

I would like to encourage you to read this chapter whether you have a neurodivergent teen or not. We all need greater understanding of neurodivergence, and I can guarantee your teen has classmates and friends who are neurodivergent. We are responsible for learning how to better understand and support neurodivergent people in our lives – rather than just expecting them to fit in.

Everyone has a different neurotype. No two brains are the same. However, not everyone is 'neurotypical'. The word neurodiversity was coined by Judy Singer to describe the identity of having a brain that works differently, due to a wide array of reasons including neurotypes, mental-health conditions and trauma. Neurodiverse is plural which means the family, the classroom, the workplace and the world are all neurodiverse. However, one person cannot be neurodiverse.

The word neurodivergent was coined by Kassiane Asasumasu, a biracial, multiply neurodivergent activist, as a word to describe an individual whose brain diverges from the 'typical' or 'neuro-normative' expectations. More and more teens are identifying as neurodivergent as they recognise differences in their emotional and behavioural processing, executive functioning, social and communication styles and highly activated threat responses.

Formerly considered problematic, abnormal or a disorder, there has been a significant shift in our understanding about neurodivergence; in neuro-affirmative language, it just means different.

WHAT HAVE YOU FOUND MOST CHALLENGING AS A TEEN?

- School pressure with ADHD/anxiety, in a selective school and I didn't do as well as extended family expected but still got into uni to do the course I wanted.
- I feel extremely anxious. I have panic attacks. When I was three, I was diagnosed with Selective Mutism, at nine ADHD and dyslexia and at 11 with OCD.
- ADHD & Dyslexia – conventional school is hard. Homeschool is better & I can work outside.
- Dealing with bullying, a bad home life, no friends, and sensory overloads/meltdowns when I didn't know I was autistic. And I had chronic depression and anxiety with no one to help.

Most common divergent neurotypes

- Autism, or autism spectrum conditions
- ADHD: Attention Deficit Hyperactivity Disorder (ADD isn't an official diagnosis anymore)
- Dyscalculia
- Dyslexia
- Dyspraxia, or Developmental Coordination Disorder (DCD)
- Sensory Processing Disorder.

When I was teaching and counselling, I was aware of many students with ADHD who were all boys. At the time, I didn't understand that it can be very difficult to diagnose ADHD in girls from primary to secondary, because they are so good at copying other girls' behaviours so they can fit in, thus masking their needs. At that time, autistic teens tended to be schooled in special-needs schools and were excluded from mainstream schools. These days, our neurodivergent (ND) kids tend to be integrated into mainstream schools. Surprisingly, though, despite this I have spoken with many primary and secondary teachers over the last year, and none of them received any training at university about teaching ND students. This has to change.

Some common characteristics of divergent neurotypes include the following:

- Inflexibility or inability to adapt or change interests
- Passion about a specific interest
- Learning challenges that may be related to difficulties with focus and concentration, reading, calculation
- Hyper focus on tasks they enjoy
- Difficulty following verbal instructions or other neuro-normative dialogue at times
- Problems with executive functioning, and cognitive flexibility
- Some impulsivity in social situations like calling out, blurting, yelling
- Social communication differences
- Speech and language differences
- Unique responses to sensory input, especially overload
- Unique physical behaviours such as stimming, flapping or expressing tics
- Often have high energy for physical pursuits they enjoy.

In order to confirm someone's neurocognitive status, they need a psychological assessment. This can be helpful in gaining extra support and information. Sadly, waiting lists are very long and in some places, it can take over two years for an assessment to take place. Child and family counsellors and occupational therapists who specialise in self-regulation may often *infer* a child's neurotype from observation of their behavioural, social and emotional characteristics. In the absence of a formal assessment, this can give families a starting point for better understanding their child's support needs. Self-identification of neurotypes is also widely accepted within neurodivergent communities as a valid form of identification, and many teens are gaining a sense of clarity and greater capacity for self-regulation due to self-identification.

Supporting our neurodivergent teen requires becoming aware of our own ableism, which refers to the beliefs we hold around what our teen 'should be able' to do. If our expectations are based on what we would expect of a neurotypical teen, then we are often expecting too much.

We are still basing so much of our knowledge around behaviour on behaviourism and the role of rewards and punishments, especially in our schools, even though the science of child development has clearly shown this to be ineffective. Is it any wonder, then, that many of us have internalised ableism? So many of the assumptions we have been led to believe around autism and ADHD need to come into the light and be reassessed. I certainly have been bringing some of my ableism up to be re-examined and I'm really grateful for that.

Changing our perspective

Over the last five years I have been working with Allison Davies, an autistic woman with sensory processing and executive functioning difficulties who specialises in music and the brain, and I have come to a much deeper understanding about neurodivergence. She argues very strongly that if autistic children and people were allowed to actualise and embrace their own unique way of life, and to live in ways that make sense to them while accommodating their own needs along the way, autistic lives would improve significantly. We need to change the lens that sees autism and ADHD in particular as just problematic. Constantly seeing autistic culture as a 'lesser-than' way of being and that the ideal is to fit into neuro-normative culture needs a cultural change. We need more neuro-affirmative conversations, education and a significant shift in awareness.

One of the corrections that Allison has helped me with is that autism DOES NOT exist on a spectrum from high to low. It is way more complex than that and she sees it better represented as a sphere, not a continuum. Another good reminder that came from my good friend is that if you have met one child with autism, you have met one child with autism. Every individual who is ND is completely unique and different and we need to be mindful of not making assumptions when we interact with them.

Another perception I had that needed correcting was that ND individuals lacked empathy. In fact, many ND people struggle with an overwhelming sense of empathy, which can cause them to become just dysregulated and shutdown.

A significant shift in understanding is needed so that as a society we stop seeing ND individuals as 'less than' or disordered. They are different and they are often disabled because of our society's inability to accommodate their needs. We also need to stop trying to change them to act less neurodivergent. We definitely need to better understand how we can accommodate their unique needs so they can become their own competent selves in our homes, schools and communities. This is an incredibly important message to give to all teens so that they can grow up to be more inclusive and caring than previous generations.

At a recent conference, I got to meet an amazing neurodivergent woman named Em Hammond who is better known in the social-media world by the handle @NeuroWild. Em creates the most beautiful, articulate graphics that explain how we can better understand ND children and adults. One of the key concepts she explains is fluctuating capacity in ND kids, especially in the classroom. Sometimes, they are quite simply unable to do something that they normally can do. For a neurotypical child, you might be able to push them to do hard things. However, to a dysregulated ND student that can feel to them like you are pushing them off an edge which can be terrifying. In a way, this concept of fluctuating capacity is similar to the way Lisa Feldman Barrett explains the body budget and interoception. This means that an individual's brain and body are working hard to ensure they have enough energy to keep the body working well and the brain working well. When the body budget is depleted, there is less energy to regulate behaviour, feelings and emotions. Sometimes the body does not have enough energy which may be due to one thing or a combination of things – poor sleep, poor nutrition, experiencing conflict, feeling unwell or exhausted, having trauma or feeling incredibly overwhelmed or unsafe in the environment they are in. When a

ND student refuses to do a task, *it is not because they won't do it; it is because they can't do it at that moment in time.*

When you weave in that teens are particularly sensitive to being told what to do and need to have their own agency, this situation in classrooms can become very difficult very quickly, without a better understanding of what's happening. This graphic from Em shows some of the possibilities around why a ND student/teen/child may not be meeting expectations.

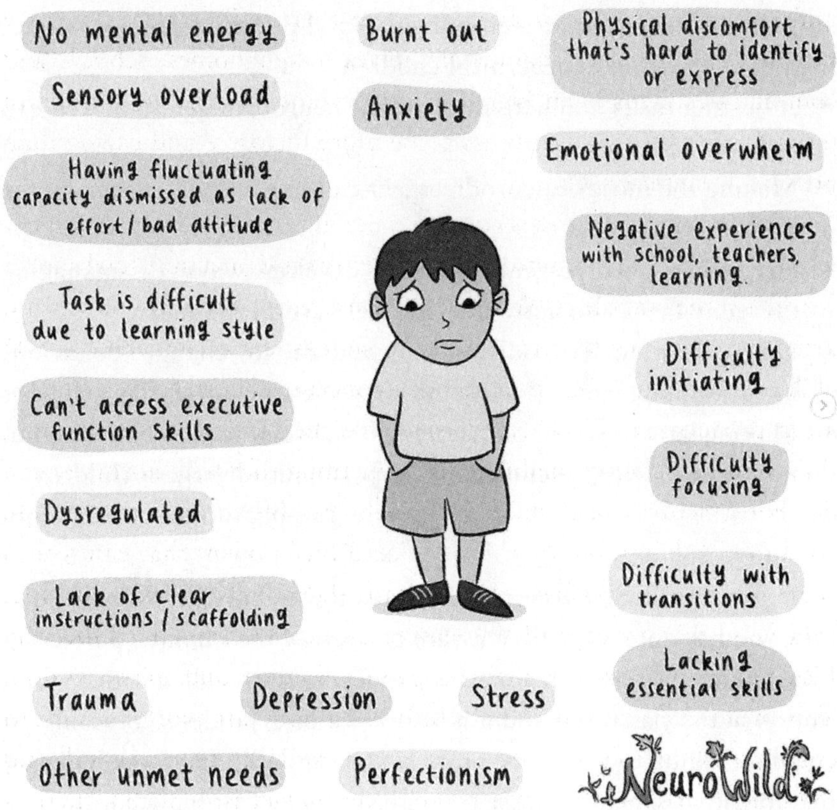

Sometimes, when adults ask an ND teen to make a better choice, they are missing the understanding that, in that moment, the ND teen is unable to make a better choice – they are not deliberately being difficult or disrespectful.

Embracing neurodiversity

Embracing neurodiversity is about **accepting, including, celebrating and supporting neurodivergent children the same way you would all children**. Their differences are part of natural variation and don't need to be treated or changed. However, they may need us parents to advocate for them and to educate others around them.

According to the Raising Children Network, embracing neurodiversity involves:

- Acknowledging that neurodivergent children might do things differently from neurotypical children
- Adjusting tasks and activities so that neurodivergent children can fully participate
- Making the most of neurodivergent children's skills, especially the skills they're proud of
- Helping neurodivergent children develop ways of managing everyday tasks and activities that feel natural to them
- Not expecting neurodivergent children to change behaviour like stimming, which doesn't interfere with their everyday activities
- Making sure that schools, sports clubs, social groups and community organisations include and support neurodivergent children.

Source: raisingchildren.net.au/autism

If you suspect that your teen is ND or if they have been identified as ND, you have probably been aware of some of their unique differences over a number of years. If you have a teen who is struggling with concentration in the classroom and it is impacting their grades significantly, it could be helpful to seek some professional support (even though I know that might be difficult). Please reassure your teen that the school system is the problem, not them. Accessing a neurodivergent mentor for you or your teen can also help you more deeply understand your needs and ensure you support your teen through a neuro-affirming lens.

Keep reminding your teen that they will have some unique and significant strengths within them, as well as some of the challenges they may have identified. Together, keep searching for the things that they feel passionate about and that they do well and pursue them.

> 'The key to a successful, rewarding, happy life with the neurodivergent adults I know seems to be finding their niche and their people. Harnessing their hyperfocus, finding a job they love and accepting themselves for who they are all seem really important ingredients with things going well.'
>
> – Dr Jo Prendergast, *When Life Sucks: Parenting your teens through tough times*

What can be helpful parenting a ND teen:

- Regardless of the temptation, avoid over-praising and toxic positivity – your teen will see through it and will often feel more invalidated.
- Create positive connection experiences one-on-one that you both enjoy and prioritise that.
- Keep your focus on their strengths and seek out other interests that may bring a 'spark' into their lives.
- Autistic women are significantly more likely to be victims of sexual abuse and to experience sexual coercion so make sure you pay special attention to educating your ND teen about puberty and sex. There are lots of resources out there these days to guide you in this so do seek them out.
- Work together to create plans to overcome some of the biggest challenges like being late, disorganised, or even more forgetful than most teens can be!
- Normalise adolescent development and its unique challenges so that they can appreciate that even neurotypical teens are finding things challenging.
- Have conversations around stress and anxiety and explain the emotional barometer to them and work out ways to keep it at a good level.

- Explore Chapter 14 about bullying and help them navigate these experiences if they happen. Prepare and educate against the nasty kids.
- Explore the use of calming strategies including fidgets that they can use discreetly in a classroom when they are dysregulated.
- Negotiate routine and structure that feels comfortable for your teen in the home.
- Be a gentle reminder if they need specific feedback about their social skills – remember timing, tone and intention matter.
- Recognise that sometimes ND teens will need mental-health days because coping with school can be particularly draining and exhausting, even if they have appropriate scaffolding to help them.
- Support them if you can around homework; however, avoid doing it for them.
- Help them to work out how to create a study environment that works for them – even consider a desk outside.
- Remind your teen about their wise voice within and get them to practise listening to their instincts and the messages their body is telling them.

Finding your tribe of supportive ND humans is incredibly important. If there is one thing that we need to be grateful for in the digital world, it is that you can find a digital family of support. Be mindful of choosing one that does bring you comfort and support. It can be especially helpful if your teen can find their own ND network.

An excellent book for those who live with or work with autistic girls is called *Supporting Autistic Girls and Gender Diverse Youth: An essential neuro-affirming guide for parents, teachers and allies* by Yellow Ladybugs, an autistic-led not-for-profit that supports autistic and gender diverse youth.

> Autism is the lens in which we see, process and experience the world. It is a part of who we are. It is our identity and our culture.
>
> – Yellow Ladybugs CEO Katie Koullas

A key message of that book is that Yellow Ladybugs are passionate about promoting the social model of disability in which ND folks do not need to be fixed. However, some ND kids and adults may need extra support or accommodations to live happily and function in the world that is built for the neurotypical majority.

If your teen is struggling with any (or multiple) of the issues in this book, such as school grades dropping, increased anxiety, self-harm or substance abuse, and you are having trouble working together on solutions or finding the root cause, you might want to consider if there are underlying neurodivergent needs that aren't being met.

All teens struggle navigating the bridge to adulthood and given the additional challenges that many ND teens experience, parents simply need to be vigilant when things get really hard for them.

Having the conversation

In all the other chapters I have given suggestions about how to communicate your worries with your teens from a neurotypical lens. Out of my deep respect to those in the ND community, I am not offering suggestions on how you can speak to your ND teen, because I am not neurodivergent, nor have I parented a neurodivergent child. The range of possibilities with neurodivergence is so large as well that advice about talking to one ND teen will not work for another.

Some of the suggestions above, the 'Before you have the conversation' section on page 171 and the resources on page 389 may be helpful in shaping your conversations, as many have come from resources created by ND folk.

I'd like to end this chapter with a message of hope. As Allison Davies said to me once, the whole Internet was created by autistic people because they were the only ones clever enough. And there is a much higher representation of people with ADHD among elite athletes than in the general population. The world is a better place for the neurodivergent among us.

For more resources on this topic, such as books, podcasts, websites and helpline information, see the Resources section at the back of the book (page 389).

24

What to do when you are worried your teen may be considering suicide

Background

The death of a child for any parent is tragic, however, the death of a son or daughter to suicide is one of the toughest traumas imaginable for any parent and to those who love that individual. Sadly, in the Western world, we are losing far too many of our young people to suicide. In Australia, suicide remains the leading cause of death for young people in the age group of 15 to 19. Even more concerning, from the ages of 18 to 24, the death by suicide rate has increased by around 50 per cent over the last 10 years.

Another concerning statistic is that the suicide rate for Australian female young people, aged 15 to 19 years, has almost doubled since 2010.

Young people outside capital cities are significantly more at risk of dying by suicide than their peers in capital cities.

The rate of suicide among Indigenous young people is significantly higher than among non-Indigenous young people. Over the five years 2018 to 2022, the suicide rate of First Nations Peoples aged 24 years and under was more than three times as high as non-Indigenous Australians in the same age group.

One in six young LGBTQIA+ people have attempted suicide and one-third have harmed themselves: 16 per cent of LGBTQIA+ Australians aged between 16 and 27 have attempted suicide and 33 per cent have self-harmed.

I interviewed Associate Professor Mat Coleman, who is a child and adolescent psychiatrist and also a previous commissioner with the National Mental Health Commission, on an episode of the ABC podcast *Parental As Anything*. He explained that many of the risk factors that can contribute to a teen completing suicide are linked to the complexity of adolescent development in general and the stress it can cause individuals. There is still a strong sense of stigma in adolescence around seeking help when they are struggling. There is also the problem of the significant lack of services for those who choose to seek help, especially in rural communities. Professor Coleman mentioned that the disruption in family environments can have a really adverse impact on teens during this time of massive development and transformation. When teens are impacted by bullying – which can now follow them 24/7 in the form of cyberbullying – their sense of self-worth can be significantly impacted and they can experience an increased sense of despair, which is considered a significant risk factor. Adverse childhood experiences and trauma can certainly be factors of risk for children and teens. Professor Coleman explained that some mental illnesses like depression and psychosis, if untreated and the teen is left to cope on their own, are directly proportional to the amount of suicidal ideation that can occur and subsequently increase the person's risk of self-harm and suicide. He explained that there's never just one issue, and that having supportive parents or lighthouse figures who walk alongside our often confused teens can make a critical difference in the prevention of suicide.

Dr Claire Kelly is a director of research and curriculum at Mental Health First Aid in Australia. She helps to coordinate the Teen Mental Health Program in high schools which encourages parents and those who work in schools to complete some form of mental-health training if possible. When I interviewed her for the same episode of the podcast, she expressed clearly that even without any training, through caring, compassionate curiosity, parents and lighthouse figures can make a notable difference. Every teen wants to be seen, heard, accepted and supported without judgement. If you are concerned about a young person and want to have a conversation checking if they have any suicidal ideation, one key message to keep in mind is that we need to be careful *not to guarantee confidentiality*. No significant adult should be managing a teen who has expressed an intention to self-harm or to end their life on their own. It is a duty of care responsibility to seek professional help. Seeking help can start possibly with student services in the high school, or we can encourage the young person to go to their local GP. If neither of these work, then reach out to:

- Lifeline: 13 11 14
- Suicide Call Back Service: 1300 659 467
- Beyond Blue Support Service: 1300 22 4636
- Kids Helpline: 1800 55 1800

When to worry

Here are some common warning signs. But if you're unsure, reach out for support.

- Withdrawing from others
- Not doing things they used to enjoy
- Self-harming
- Looking up ways to suicide, stockpiling pills, buying scalpels, razors
- Hints they're thinking about suicide such as 'I'd like to go to sleep and never wake up'
- Talking about feeling worthless, hopeless, alone, being a burden to others or having no reason to live
- Talking about death or suicide (even as a joke)

- Dramatic changes in mood including being suddenly excessively happy
- Reckless, dangerous behaviour without any regard for self-wellbeing
- Increased drug or alcohol use
- Giving away possessions or saying goodbye
- Having the means to end their life such as medication or weapons.

– Source: kidshelpline.com.au

> It was a couple weeks ago and I was really depressed and anxious, about work, life, uni etc. and I couldn't sleep, didn't eat, didn't talk to anyone, just sat in my room by myself with my headphones blasting music to make me feel less alone.

If you have not read about the emotional barometer and the 'tipping point' in the first part of this book, please do so. You will find it easily by using the index. This concept of when life gets too much, or too difficult or too hard to bear, can be really helpful when you have the conversation of concern with your teen. When done empathetically, checking in with how they are feeling when you are concerned can be helpful for them as well as you.

Professor Coleman explained that for some teens who die by suicide, there may have been few or no signs that they were struggling. Indeed, many seemed to be thriving. These are known as spontaneous suicides. I believe, and I have absolutely no research to support my belief, that some of these spontaneous suicides are the consequence of teens reaching a tipping point. The last thing that triggered that moment could be quite small and normally not a significantly challenging moment.

Obviously, if the warning signs listed above aren't there, sadly a parent is unable to recognise the urgency that a teen may feel. Hopefully, though, if you have enough open conversations with your teen about mental health (and help them be aware of what the tipping point is and when they might be reaching it), then they may have some tools to take a pause and make a better choice.

In my counselling experience with boys suffering despair, depression or even ideas of suicide, I found these lads often feel overwhelmed by their emotions triggered by shaming. Emotions were unidentified and unresolved, lying buried inside them. Many of these boys felt deeply flawed and like a failure; they believed that those closest to them did not love them. This deep sense of alienation and feeling separate came up so often when listening to these troubled lads. They were starving for deep, meaningful connection, not only with their parents but also with other significant adults in their life.

– Maggie Dent, *From Boys to Men*

What to do if you are worried a teen may be considering suicide

When you first begin to have concerns about your teen's wellbeing, it can be helpful to have a discreet chat to one of their favourite teachers to see if they've noticed any shift in how they are at school. It can also be really helpful checking in with your teen's friends to see if they have any worries or noticed any changes.

If your son or daughter has lost a family member or a close friend to suicide, this can be a significant risk factor, especially in the first 12 months following the death.

It is common to feel really angry – especially if you are beside them in an emergency department after your son or daughter has made an attempt to end their life by suicide. It is usually a fear-based response that is quite automatic but, sadly, can further isolate a teen in times of great distress. Much like the panic response, you need to recognise that it is a reflexive response, and that it would be helpful for you to take a few moments to re-orientate yourself, so that you can be the warm, safe base your teen needs. This is also a very common response following a completed suicide.

When you feel like you're ready, **take a look at 'Before you have the conversation' on page 171**.

Possible opening questions

- Bud, I know that this question might seem like it's come completely out of the blue but given that you have been so upset and down in the dumps lately, I feel I need to ask if you've had any thoughts about hurting yourself or ending your life?
- Hey, sweetheart, I have noticed that things have been a bit rough for you lately and you seem to be struggling. Do you ever feel like checking out of this world completely?
- Ava, my love, I have been a bit worried about you lately and I know how life can really pull you down at times. I'm just curious if you've had any dark thoughts about hurting yourself or ending your life?

Sometimes writing a letter of concern can work well. There is a sample in Appendix 1 that you could adapt to suit.

Next steps

Never diminish or dismiss what they have said by saying things such as:

- Oh no, you're just making that up. You'll be fine.
- Don't be so dramatic.
- That's ridiculous, you would never hurt yourself!
- That's so selfish, just thinking about yourself. Something like that will ruin our family forever.
- Just cheer up. We all have bad days.
- You need to sort yourself out!

Professor Coleman suggests regular check-ins with a teen are important. He says asking them to respond, even if it is just with an emoji, can be helpful for both the teen and the parent. It is important you make an agreement with your teen about regular check-ins and that you ensure checking in is more about reminding them of your unconditional love and connection. Remember that checking in is an important opportunity to remind your son or daughter how much you value them, even if they have been struggling. Messages like, 'Your mum and I aren't perfect, but we reckon you are incredibly special and worthwhile'; 'Times can really suck, but we will be here for you whenever you need'; 'Just thinking about you and hope your day is okay?' can be helpful. You need to be careful to temper the helicopter tendency and maybe suggest to your teen that they let you know if your messages are helpful or not.

One of my dear friends is an early responder to teen suicide and they check in with a number of teens who have made an attempt to end their lives with simple text messages two to three times a day, every day. She said that these teens have told her how important those messages are.

Explore making positive brain chemicals – what things bring joy? It is different for each teen and these are all possible ways:

- **Athletic success & sport** – team and individual
- **Artistic & creative expression** – drama, art
- **Deep relaxation and stillness** – calming audios, yoga, quiet time in nature, bush walk or at the beach
- **Safe, honest human connection** – deep human connectedness, family, friendship, community
- **Listening to music or podcasts** – make favourite playlists
- **Singing or dancing**
- **Taking a refreshing shower/soak in a bath**
- **Watching something you like** (such as a film, YouTube video or TV)
- **Games and puzzles**
- **Connecting with a pet**
- **Significant immersion in nature** – walking, surfing, fishing, pets
- **Acts of service** – helping others
- **Discovering new purpose and meaning** – starting something
- **New hobby, fitness program**
- **Nutrition** – eat good food
- **Create a vision board of life dreams** – places to visit, things to do.

If they are reluctant to seek professional help, maybe start with Orygen's #chatsafe suicide prevention program. It's available in multiple languages from orygen.org.au and is designed to guide parents and carers when they're having conversations about suicide or self-harm with the young people in their lives.

Some suggestions Orygen makes are to:

- Thank your teen for trusting you and reassure them you have got their back.
- Check in with them about who else – other than an online support or a health professional – you can share their struggles with. Respect their wishes.
- If you are still worried, keep trying to reach professional help.

If you are seriously concerned about your teen being at risk, please call one of the emergency numbers BEFORE you take them to an emergency department. Many EDs are under huge pressure and waiting in a room full of sick and distressed kids and adults for very long hours could escalate your own teen's distress.

Organisations that may be able to offer counselling/mental health services include:

- Community health centre
- Local council/youth counselling service
- Private psychologist or psychiatrist
- School/TAFE/university psychologist or social worker or well-being counsellor
- Public mental-health service such as Orygen Specialist Program.

> REMEMBER most teens do not want to die – they want the pain to go away. Just because a teen doesn't ask for help doesn't mean they don't want some help so they can feel better.

For more resources on this topic, such as books, podcasts, websites and helpline information, see the Resources section at the back of the book (page 390). For immediate support, contact one of the services on page 373.

Conclusion

Ever since I stepped into a classroom over 44 years ago, I have been passionate about supporting our emerging adults to navigate all the changes that are happening to them, often invisibly, so that they can land safely in their twenties as unscarred as possible. The mystic and philosopher Joseph Campbell called major life transitions like adolescence the hero's journey because it is a metaphorical journey of loss, challenge, growth and renewal. Campbell argued strongly that you will meet metaphorical demons, as well as allies and mentors.

As with any major transformation journey – getting a job, leaving home, getting married, becoming a parent – there is no certainty on how we will get to the destination, or on exactly what the destination is. Adolescence is a similar journey of uncertainty.

> Every teen is unique, and every journey into adulthood is different; however, every one of them will have experiences that challenge them and bring them to their knees. Just as you – the parent – did on the same journey.

Our job as parents is to not be the demons. Our job as parents is to be the allies and the mentors for our own sons and daughters, and for the sons and daughters of those around us in our families, our neighbourhoods, our schools and our communities. This does not mean we do not call out inappropriate behaviour, or that we let them smash boundaries. Allies and mentors are the rails on the bridge and rather than shame and punish teens who challenge boundaries and make impulsive choices without much thought, we guide them by being firm and yet fair. Just like with toddlers, having boundaries helps them feel safer even when they push up against them.

We don't want our teens to just worry about whether they might get caught. We want them to worry about whether they might get hurt or hurt someone else.

Raising our kids to adulthood is not meant to be a competition, and yet that is what many of our teens are experiencing. The number of responses in the survey that expressed anguish around the pressures to perform well at school, and that their number-one priority was marks and grades was quite frankly heartbreaking for me as a former teacher.

> I have found the most challenging thing about being a teenager to be academic stress. I'm a star student and receiving even an A- can be detrimental to my mental health, another issue which affects my day-to-day life. This then affects my grades and leads to a cycle of self destruction and criticism.

Some of the significant shifts in our culture over the last 20 years have been increased competitiveness in every area of life. Parents tell me they feel like parenting is a form of competition. Our little ones begin being assessed and tested well before they even start school and the amount of testing that happens in schools is beyond ridiculous. Increased competition in early childhood means there will be increased competitiveness for our tweens and teens, rather than *a focus on nurturing connectedness and belonging.*

If we want to be really serious about shifting the crisis of mental health of today's teens, we grown-ups, those who live and work with them, need to sing from the same song sheet. I believe we could take a lot of stress off their shoulders by constantly affirming to them that their wellbeing is more important during this time of incredible change and confusion than their endless assessments and that they are not defined by their final grades. There are so many pathways to further education and given that many of today's teens are taking longer to launch from the family nest, wouldn't it be a great idea to destroy the holy altar of high grades once and for all. Those who are academically capable and who are part of the 80 per cent who are not struggling with high levels of anxiety and depression will still be able to succeed without the pressure to be number one.

Not only that, many teens and young adults are losing hope for the future of the world, particularly since the 2022 UN Climate Change Conference in Glasgow. Feeling disconnected, like no one cares, and feeling unheard and misunderstood have always been common cries from young people on the bumpy ride to adulthood. However, when they see the adults around them not acting for the future of the world – their future – it validates their feelings of being insignificant, invisible, unworthy, powerless and that they don't matter. When this happens, without enough support, life can seem hopeless and dark. Maybe while they are still in high school, we can help them determine their own sense of agency in how they can be a part of the solution to the challenges they are deeply concerned about. They could take time off the school curriculum to help remove plastic from beaches, clean waterways, plant trees and learn how to grow vegetables. They could take part in recycling programs, help at animal rescue centres and even help raise money to save endangered species. Imagine how that might pick up their weary and defeated spirits.

Another recommendation I have for you as a parent of today's teens is please search for that 'spark' that lies waiting inside every single one of them – and encourage it and gently nurture it until it can burst into flame. Be mindful of noticing strengths instead of just noticing faults, as most teens are consumed by their flaws and faults and have a daily battle with a crushing sense of worthlessness. Also, remember the hunger and yearning for intimacy and genuine connectedness. There are many experts writing about how today's teens seem more connected but that the connections are much shallower than in previous generations. I would say it's not just the younger generation, as I heard the wise relationship expert Esther Perel express on a podcast that she has thousands of followers online and no-one to feed her cat. Experts are concerned that many teens are struggling with hidden anxiety from the lack of meaningful human intimacy. True resilience comes from human connectedness and many of today's teens' systems of connection are virtual and not real. So much of what they really need cannot be purchased with AfterPay or with credit or on eBay. It only comes from positive human interaction.

Something that can be incredibly helpful is for you to be a sower of hope and positivity in their world. Avoid the doomsayers who are always criticising our teens and find stories of those making the world a better place. Just recently in my local community, four young teenage boys rescued a family from drowning in a dangerous rip. There are teens who volunteer in their local communities and many teens volunteer as umpires in weekend sporting fixtures. Keep reminding your teen about how fabulous adolescents can be and are. They just don't feature in the media as often as the badly behaving ones.

A longitudinal study that follows the same families for many years explored the influence of having positive views of teens and adolescents versus those who took a darker, more negative view in general. The research showed that those families who had more negative views about adolescence in general were more likely to report that their teens were having more conflict with their parents and were more likely to choose to spend time with a riskier crowd. **Your children are listening to your perceptions and expectations all the time.** Just the same as with teachers, when you hold high, positive expectations kids tend to live up to them. When the opposite is happening, they tend to live down to them. So, speak positively about the upcoming teen years, and you will be surprised that it can really make a positive difference. As a high-school teacher, I enjoyed being around teens, with all their ups and downs. I not only liked them, I understood them way more than I did my toddlers when they arrived. I welcomed all my boys' mates and friends into our homes, really loved my nieces and nephews, and I loved coaching their basketball teams. At some deep, fundamental level, I still miss being in that classroom!

Letting go

Letting go of your teen happens in two ways. First, we have to let go of each of our children as they cross the threshold to adolescence and start that bumpy ride to adulthood. At that time, we wish they could stay children in the sanctuary of our homes away from the harsh reality of the world and that they will keep listening to our good advice. Secondly, we have to let them go again as they leave home to follow their own path to wherever it may take them.

> 'Remember, our children are meant to leave home. Sometimes they boomerang back, and they can sometimes pack you to the rafters.'
>
> – Maggie Dent, *Black Duck Wisdom*

Allow your offspring to go and live their own lives, not live your lives through their lives. When my oldest three sons completed their studies and started working as independent young men, I breathed a sigh of relief. It was a very deep breath in the knowledge that boys are 75 per cent more likely to die from accidents, trauma and suicide than girls under 25.

I know most parents breathe a sigh of relief after their teens leave high school, thinking the worst is behind them. Sadly, that is not always the case as statistically the years 18–25 years are still an incredibly risky time. However, by that stage, most teens have reconnected with their parents, after pushing them away through the early years of high school. Remember when you couldn't look at them, you breathed too deeply, you ate too loudly, you didn't know anything, and all you seemed to do was nag and criticise? The good news about the continual myelination of the brain is that they start to review the way they see their parents and often you will feel them 'coming back'.

Sometimes, that just makes the letting go even harder.

Your job as a parent is to raise your children to leave home so they can go and live their own lives. No, it really is!

I am the proud mum of four sons who are now all dads themselves. For around 20 years, I cooked, cleaned, ran around after, laughed with, cried with and worried about these wonderful boys in every permutation possible (now I am doing all those things with my grandkids!). When it came time to let the boys go in adolescence, though, as they moved to the city to study, my head had told me this would be easy, but my heart did not listen. Every son was hard to let go, and each time it upset me. I pretended to them at times I was fine, and other times I told them I missed them. I saw them as still unfinished and yet knew they needed space to stand on their own. It was hard. I knew they had to work out how to manage money, food and the rigours of university without me beside them. It was hard. It was before smartphones so I couldn't even text them, I had to call the landline! I wanted to call them so often just to remind them of things or to check how they were going, and I resisted. It was hard. Instead, I looked forward to *their* calls and *their* visits back home.

Letting go is difficult, yet it is the greatest act of love we can give our teens.

There were many challenges in their bumpy ride after the safety of home: failed exams, crashed cars, funerals for mates, deaths of cousins, cars vandalised, sporting injuries, knee reconstructions and frequent mismanagement of money. In a perfect world, when a teen struggles and a parent seeks professional help, it would be available and affordable for everyone. However, that is not happening and is unlikely to change any time soon. My hope and my wish is that this book will empower mums and dads everywhere, and the lighthouse figures in our teens' lives – the aunts, uncles, grandparents, coaches, a friend's parents, teachers, neighbours, family friends and community members – to know you can offer so much more than you may have realised. Please keep the metaphor of the lighthouse at the back of your mind, because when things are really dark for our teens, they simply need light. Light in the form of good humans who can allow them to feel seen, heard, accepted, valued and still loved. This is what our teens need the most – good humans who can lean in with compassion, and act as a safe base and a place for them to regroup, to replenish, to renew, to recover and to grow.

Remember – every teen matters, no matter what.

Maggie Dent

Former troubled teen, high school teacher, counsellor,
basketball coach, mum of four sons and lighthouse
to so many tweens and teens over the last 45 years and
hopefully for many more years to come. Also devoted
nanny to eight grandchildren who will be
teens before we know it!

Acknowledgements

Once again, I need to begin my acknowledgements page with a serious thank you to the wonderful Ingrid Ohlsson, who is the director of publishing at Pan Macmillan Australia. She has such incredible faith in me and is incredibly patient because I really had thought that *Girlhood* was my last book.

I have had two wonderful editors from Pan Macmillan working on this book. The first is Belinda Huang, who was my structural editor, taking the raw Word document and taming it and shaping it into a book. Then I was lucky to have Samantha Sainsbury step in and work her magic. I have worked with this word genius on a previous book and I knew I was in good hands. Thank you both so much for working on my tenth book baby. I am truly so grateful.

I have been supported in the writing of this book by some of the most trusted and respected experts in the teen space and I would like to acknowledge them upfront. Thank you so much to Professor Mat Coleman, Dr Vanessa Lapointe, Lisa Damour, Brad Marshall, Allison Davies, Michelle Mitchell, Claire Orange, Karen Young,

Sharon Witt, Claire Eaton and Dr Yael Perry and the whole team from the Telethon Kids Institute.

My fabulous friend and researcher, editor, publicist and my right hand Carmen Myler has again tamed my apostrophes and helped shape my writings into something half decent and has helped me search for research that matters. As always, Carmy, I couldn't do this without you so thank you from the bottom of my heart.

Another one of my long-term supporters and extra editor Lou Shannon has again helped to get the manuscript ready for the publishers close to the deadline. What is extra special is that Lou is now working in this space and her own boys are now teens and I knew them when they were little.

I always like to acknowledge Team Maggie because the reason I have time to write and research is because they cover so much for me. My PA, my gorgeous niece Laura Browning, thank you for all the organising behind-the-scenes of my seminars and conferences. You are absolutely brilliant. Hayley Metcalfe and Kate O'Donnell look after so much of my online activity so that I don't drown in emails. Tilly Wylde also helps keep up with my socials so that I have concentrated time writing. Will Ambrose helps me create, collate and sort all the surveys, and also makes sure the website keeps ticking over. Kelly Skinner, thanks again for helping with copyright permissions. Katharine Middleton, who was my graphic designer for close on 30 years, thanks for being such a creative genius in my life and helping my work look better.

My good bloke and husband Steve has survived yet another birthing of a book. I keep telling him it's the last book and this is the tenth one and I think that's a great place to stop. As always, he ensures that I am well nurtured with endless cups of tea, drinks of water and allowing me to be as noncommunicative as I need to be when I am deep in book writing. Thanks, babe.

My growing family are really the wind beneath my wings as they bring the most profound joy into my life. As I step back from being quite so busy, I am getting to spend more time with my nearest and dearest, and I reckon being a Nanny is quite simply the best role ever on earth.

To every teen who completed the surveys and shared their truths and their worries with me, I am profoundly grateful. I hope I have kept your voices strongly throughout the book, and I wish I could have included every single one of you. I sincerely hope that this book will help you be better supported by the grown-ups in your life. Remember, nothing is ever too big to tackle – please reach out, there really are good humans who will support you.

My very last and special thanks goes to all those who have purchased my books – thank you. If you have come to one of my seminars or attended one of my conferences, thank you. If you have been a part of one of my webinars, or listened to either of my podcasts, *Parental as Anything* or *The Good Enough Dad*, I thank you too.

I still find it hard to comprehend how a little girl who grew up on a farm in the wheat belt of Western Australia can have the wonderful opportunities I have had as a parenting educator and author. And of late as a podcast host! It may have been an accidental journey, however, it has certainly been something I am deeply passionate about and hope to continue until my last breath.

Appendices

I hope you find these sample letters helpful in guiding you to write your own well thought out, heartfelt letters to the teens you love in your life.

Appendix 1: The parent letter

Example 1

Dear ....

Please take a few moments to read this letter. I know you think I am always worrying, and I try too hard or I am a try-hard (?) but I am your mum/dad and that's part of what parents are meant to do.

Just lately something is different about you and yes, I am worried. You haven't smiled for weeks, and you are struggling to get good sleep. You are spending much more time than usual in your bedroom and your friends haven't been around for ages. You really seem down and I am worried.

I have been online and checked out some youth websites and some of these things are listed as being a sign that you may be struggling.

There is just so much pressure on you kids these days – and too much stress can make you sick. I also know that you won't want to worry me – and that you might think you will be okay soon – and yet my mum/dad radar is ringing loud bells.

Can we have a chat? If not me, my love, can you please have a chat with some other adult?? If you want to chat to Dr . . . ., I am happy and I will let you go without me if that's what you want. Or maybe a school counsellor or someone anonymous online through one of the support services that are out there.

I really want you to let someone listen to you and see if there's anything we can do to help you ride out this bumpy bit.

I have printed off some of the fact sheets and would love it if you could glance through them.

If you really are okay, maybe we could just go for a coffee or a hot fudge sundae, do some window shopping or take a walk on the beach. Massage? Hot bath with bubbles? Swim with dolphins? Holiday in Monaco or Italy? Okay, maybe not the last one.

I am happy if you just write me a note – that will be a great start.

I guess I just want to know – how can I help? Can you please give me three clues on how I can help you at this time?

Remember that adolescence is a time of intense turmoil and confusion, and it will one day get better when your brain finishes growing.

I love you with every fibre in my being.

Mum/Dad

Example 2: Letter to Bring Up the 'S' Topic

Dear . . . .

This is one of those things that parents find really hard to talk about to their kids, especially when you are an adolescent.

I need you to know that at times you get told things by your friends about sex and stuff and just like when I was an adolescent, not all of it is true. I remember being told by someone that all the girls in our high school had been having sex! I thought she was telling me a fact and I felt a bit like a loser. I spent ages trying to work out who I could have sex with so I wouldn't be a loser anymore. Luckily my cousins came for a visit and when I told them what had been said – they laughed and said, 'That is rubbish!' I was so relieved! But I often wonder what would have happened if they hadn't come for a visit.

I know how easy it is to be able to watch porn and statistically many of our boys and girls are watching it. Porn is not how I want you to learn about how to be sexually intimate with another human. Porn is about power and dominance and is definitely not about sharing your body with someone else, respectfully and joyfully.

I am giving you a book about puberty and the physical changes that are happening soon if not now – and I want you to check it out. A really good site to check out that includes videos is www.sexedrescue.com.au. Then if you have any questions – I hope you will come and ask me rather than rely on your friends.

I totally get that this chat can be really awkward and so we could do it in the dark if it would be easier?

Please remember that having sex is a big step that needs much thought and preparation. I want you to leave it until you are **much older**, as it can impact you mentally, emotionally, as well as physically. No, not everyone is doing it and don't believe what people tell you! Telling fibs around the topic of sex is common. Staying safe while being sexually intimate with another person is also important and it's not just about avoiding pregnancy, it's about avoiding sexually transmitted infections (STIs).

Please also remember that alcohol and drugs can make it easy to be taken advantage of – and they can make you do things you may regret. Having genuine consent from whoever you are being sexually intimate with is incredibly important and yes, partners can change their minds and withdraw consent.

And always always remember that I will come and collect you from anywhere anytime you don't feel safe – NO MATTER WHAT. And I will do that for any one of your friends as well. No lecture – no cold shoulder – just safety!

Hope this is not too 'cringy' and uncool – this is important stuff and I would like you to know that we CAN have conversations about sex and stuff anytime you want.

Love you heaps, always.

Mum/Dad

Appendix 2: A letter to someone special in my life

I am writing this to show you how valuable you are in my life. Firstly, I'm going to list five things I love about you:

1. ____

2. ____

3. ____

4. ____

5. ____

Now I want to tell you about something I'll always remember about you. This is a memory I want you to know that I keep with special memories deep in my heart:

____

____

I also want to thank you for:

____

All my love always and forever.

Appendix 3: The truth letter

Sometimes we can resolve issues with people by writing an honest letter to them – and it is usually best if we do not even need to give them the letter, but the mere process of acknowledging what troubles you is enough to resolve it inside yourself. Use this template to help you express your feelings on paper. It is best to symbolically destroy it – tear it into tiny pieces and bin it or burn it safely. It suggests to your unconscious as well as your conscious mind that it is complete and finished.

Dear . . . .

I am writing this letter to release my resentment and negative emotions and to discover and express any positive feelings that I might have towards you.

ANGER

I don't like . . .

I feel angry . . .

I hate it when . . .

I can't stand . . .

I resent . . .

HURT

It hurt me when . . .

I feel hurt that . . .

I feel sad when . . .

I feel awful about . . .

I feel disappointed about . . .

FEAR

I'm afraid that . . .

I feel scared when . . .

I'm afraid . . .

I get afraid of you when . . .

REMORSE, REGRET, ACCOUNTABILITY

I'm sorry that . . .

Please forgive me for . . .

I'm sorry for . . .

I didn't mean to . . .

WANTS

All I ever wanted . . .

I want you to . . .

I want . . .

I deserve . . .

LOVE, COMPASSION, FORGIVENESS, APPRECIATION

I understand that . . .

I appreciate . . .

I forgive you for . . .

I love you because . . .

I love you when . . .

Thank you for . . .

Adapted from Jack Canfield,
1997 Self-Esteem Seminars,
Santa Barbara, USA.

Appendix 4: Twelve agreements for teens around tech

Rather than a letter, this is an agreement you sit down with your teen and negotiate.

1. No computer or device in your bedroom – without permission – especially overnight
2. Be actively engaged in outside-of-bedroom/home-based activity that builds emotional and social competence at least twice a week – preferably group activity
3. Be engaged in some form of sport/surfing/music/skating/dancing/martial arts/swimming at least three times a week
4. Complete normal chores around home
5. Ensure school grades are maintained
6. Be at family meal times (without devices) and have an agreed bedtime (again, without devices)
7. Have a friend visit or go to visit a friend IRL (in real life) weekly – and have time offline together
8. Be responsible for any excessive data expenses
9. Do not disable the parental controls that are in place and ensure you maintain privacy controls on your accounts
10. Avoid porn sites and viewing MA 15+ or R 18+ material or showing anyone else. [Please stress they are NEVER to show this material to anyone even if they ask.]
11. No offensive language while gaming
12. Any consequences for breaking the agreements start small, e.g. they lose half an hour of recreational technology time. Future misdemeanours gradually increase.

Allow some flexibility if your teen negotiates small changes occasionally. This encourages cooperation and fairness rather than resentment and rebellion.

Resources

For an even more detailed list of resources from Australia and overseas, a reference list and endnotes for this book, as well as some special advice from experts who work with teens, visit maggiedent.com/HelpMe/extras. I will be updating that page as I come across new things I'd like to recommend.

Helplines – for immediate support

Remember, if someone's life is in immediate danger, you should call the emergency number 000 (in Australia – if you are elsewhere, please dial the appropriate number).

There are many Australian support services, helplines and websites for adolescents who feel they need to connect with someone to help them feel safe, accepted and heard. Many offer email or web counselling and live chat if you prefer not to call. Also don't forget your regular GP can be a helpful starting point if you want to talk to someone and would like to set up some ongoing counselling.

Kids Helpline
Call anytime for any reason or visit their website for more instant help.
1800 55 1800
kidshelpline.com.au

Suicide Call Back Service
24/7 telephone and online counselling to people who are affected by suicide.
1300 65 94 67
suicidecallbackservice.org.au

Lifeline
24/7 phone crisis support for suicide prevention.
13 11 14
lifeline.org.au

ReachOut
Australia's leading online mental-health organisation for young people and their parents.
au.reachout.com

Headspace
Australia's national youth mental health foundation. They have a great function on their home page for parents or adolescents to quickly find tailored information, online support, work and study support or a local headspace centre.
headspace.org.au

Youth Beyond Blue
Helping young people respond to anxiety and depression.
www.beyondblue.org.au/mental-health/youth

13YARN
For Aboriginal and Torres Strait Islander people who are going through a tough time and feel like having a yarn.
13 92 76
13yarn.org.au

1800 RESPECT
A service if you or someone you know is experiencing sexual assault or domestic and family violence (all ages).
1800 737 732
Online text chat – 1800respect.org.au

Some respected and much-loved teen experts

Lisa Damour, clinical psychologist, author, speaker, researcher
Claire Eaton, author, speaker, youth mindset coach
Andrew Fuller, clinical psychologist, author, ambassador for Mind Matters
Dr Vanessa Lapointe, author, parenting coach
Dr Andrew Leech, GP with special interest in teens
Dannielle Miller, CEO of Enlighten Education
Michelle Mitchell, author, speaker, educator
Claire Orange, co-founder, Best Programs 4 Kids, founder of DiGii Social
Tina Payne Bryson, researcher and author
Dr Jo Prendergast, psychologist and author
Nancy Reynolds, author at Raising Teens Today
Daniel J Siegel, M.D., researcher and author
Lyn Worsley, psychologist and creator of The Resilience Doughnut
Karen Young, psychologist and founder of Hey Sigmund

Mentoring organisations and Rites of Passage programs

Youth Off the Streets
Raise Foundation
Youth Focus, Western Australia
Sister2Sister, Sydney
Zero2Hero, Perth
The Rites of Passage Institute
The Rite Journey
Fathering Adventures
The Fathering Project
True North Expeditions

If you type 'rites of passage' into the search at maggiedent.com, you'll see an even longer list recommended by my community.

Apps

There's a good list of apps for teens at: au.reachout.com/tools-and-apps

Resources for specific concerns

When is a moody, grumpy teen a depressed teen?

Resources

You can visit your family doctor or GP to get a referral to see a psychologist wherever you live. In Australia, when your teen sees a GP, they may be able to access a Mental Health Care Plan, which is funded by Medicare to allow your teen to access up to 10 subsidised sessions with a psychologist, accredited occupational therapist, or social worker. Each state also has a dedicated child and adolescent crisis line, which teenagers can access, usually called the Child and Adolescent Mental Health Services (CAMHS). This can provide valuable local support.

Also, there are comprehensive lists of helplines and support services throughout Australia at emhprac.org.au/resource/digital-mental-health-for-young-people/ and at au.reachout.com/tools-and-apps. Here are some key ones that may help

- kidshelpline.com.au
- au.reachout.com
- headspace.org.au
- beyondblue.org.au/mental-health/youth
- brave4you.psy.uq.edu.au
- coolkids.org.au
- headtohealth.gov.au
- andrewfuller.com.au/free-resources
- zero2hero.com.au/youth-resources
- heysigmund.com
- raisingteenstoday.com
- cci.health.wa.gov.au/resources/looking-after-yourself
- moodgym.com.au

Podcasts and apps

- Smiling Mind app
- Headspace app
- Mello app from Orygen (to help with 'stuck thinking')
- *Not Alone* – A Beyond Blue podcast
- *Well, Hello Anxiety* podcast with Dr Jodi Richardson (especially episodes 73, 84, 85, 86, 87)
- *Minding Your Mind* podcast with Professor Ian Hickie & James O'Loghlin
- *Better Than Yesterday* with Osher Günsberg
- *This is Normal: A Podcast About Youth Mental Health*
- *Dear Hank & John* hosted by John and Hank Green, authors and YouTubers. (You may recognise John Green as the author of YA bestselling novel *The Fault in Our Stars*.)
- *Speaking of Psychology* – the American Psychological Association podcast has some good episodes on adolescent/teen psychology.

Books

Lisa Damour PhD, *The Emotional Lives of Teenagers* and *Under Pressure: Confronting the Epidemic of Stress and Anxiety in Girls* and *Untangled: Guiding Teenage Girls Through Seven Transitions Into Adulthood*

Maggie Dent, *From Boys to Men*

Jonathan Haidt, *The Anxious Generation*

Katie Hurley, LCSW, *The Depression Workbook for Teens: Tools to Improve Your Mood, Build Self-Esteem, and Stay Motivated*

Dr Ginni Mansberg & Jo Lamble, *The New Teen Age: How to support today's tweens and teens to become healthy, happy adults*

Michelle Mitchell, *What Teenage Girls Don't Tell Their Parents*

Michelle Mitchell, *Parenting Teenage Girls in the Age of a New Normal*

Dr Jo Prendergast, *When Life Sucks: Parenting your teen through tough times*

Daisy Turnbull, *50 Questions to Ask Your Teens*

What to do when you find a vape in your teen's bag (or worse, that they are addicted to vaping)

First, remember that your teen *may* need the support of a doctor/general practitioner to come off vaping if they are addicted to nicotine.

Websites

Wherever you are in the world, the following websites have information, fact sheets for parents and teachers and tips for talking with teens about vaping and supporting them to stop.

- darta.net.au – search 'vaping'
- positivechoices.org.au
- In UK – search 'vapes' at talktofrank.com and the NHS Better Health websites
- In Ireland, search vaping at the Heart Foundation website: irishheart.ie
- au.reachout.com – search 'how to talk to your teen about vaping'
- The US CDC website, cdc.gov – search 'electronic cigarettes'

- In Canada, you can get some good advice and support links by searching 'vaping' at the Canadian Government site: canada.ca
- Vaping lingo dictionary – Truth Initiative. This is an interesting dictionary of popular phrases, products and general language used in relation to vaping which may help you better understand them.

Podcasts

- Paul Dillon's *Doing Drugs with Paul Dillon*. Also check out Paul's podcast for young people called *The Real Deal on Drugs with Paul Dillon* – he has an episode on vaping there. You can get both on Spotify and Apple Podcasts.
- *Parental As Anything* episode on vaping
- *RCH Kids Health Info* episode – 'How harmful can vaping be?'
- *Ask Lisa: The Psychology of Parenting* with Lisa Damour and Reena Ninan, podcast episode 103 – 'How do I talk my teen out of vaping?'
- *The Generation Next Podcast with Andrew Fuller* – 'Current Trends of Substance Use in Young People'

More resources on quitting nicotine

- Hooked on Nicotine Checklist – search for this at health.nsw.gov.au
- The US Government's site smokefree.gov and they have two apps: QuitGuide and quitSTART
- The Australian Government's Quitline site and hotline: 137 848
- Many country's health departments have equivalents to Quitline so search 'quit smoking' to find the site most relevant to you.
- Read *The Conversation* article, 'My teen is addicted to vaping. How can I help them quit and manage their withdrawal symptoms?'
- My QuitBuddy app
- UK – FRANK – Text 82111, phone 0300 1236600 or find a support centre/ email via talktofrank.com
- Some good resources at lung.org, search 'helping teens quit'. They also have an online Not On Tobacco® (N-O-T) program for teens aged 14–19 to help break their dependence on nicotine, whether that come from vaping, smoking or using other tobacco products. notforme.org

What to do when you find out your teen is sexually active

Websites

(Search 'sex' on the sites below that are not specifically dedicated to puberty and sex education.)

- au.reachout.com
- raisingchildren.net.au
- talkingthetalksexed.com.au
- sexedrescue.com
- anatomyforkids.com
- drlisadamour.com
- michellemitchell.org
- dads4kids.org.au
- scarleteen.com

Books

Chanel Contos, *Consent Laid Bare*

Vanessa Hamilton, *Talking Sex: A Conversation Guide for Parents*

Dannielle Miller and Nina Funnell, *Loveability: An Empowered Girls Guide to Dating and Relationships*

Michele Mitchell, *A Guy's Guide to Puberty*

Michele Mitchell, *A Girl's Guide to Puberty*

Peggy Orenstein, *Girls and Sex: Navigating the Complicated New Landscape* and *Boys and Sex: Young Men on Hook-ups, Love, Porn, Consent and Navigating the New Masculinity*

Collett Smart, *They'll Be Okay: 15 Conversations to Help Your Child Through Troubled Times*

Andrew Smiler, *Dating and Sex: A Guide for the 21st Century Teen Boy*

Yumi Stynes and Dr Melissa Kang, *Welcome to Consent* and *Welcome to Sex* (Some of the stuff in this book may be confronting. I suggest you check it out yourself before passing it onto your teen).

Podcasts and videos

- *Parental As Anything* episode on talking to kids about sex
- *Speaking of Psychology* episode on 'How to talk to teen boys about dating and sex', with Andrew Smiler, PhD
- Peggy Orenstein TED talk – 'What young women believe about their own sexual pleasure'
- *Help! I Have A Teenager* with Dr Ginni Mansberg and Jo Lamble – episode called 'So . . . You Just Found Out Your Teen is Having Sex'
- You can also find some great podcast chats about talking to your teens about sex by putting some key experts' names into your podcast app: Peggy Orenstein, Vanessa Hamilton, Dr Melissa Kang, Cath Hakanson.

What to do when your teen 'comes out' or is confused while exploring their sexuality or gender

Helplines/web support

- QLife LGBTQIA+ phone and chat counselling and info service, phone 1800 184 527 (3 pm–12 am every day) or go to www.qlife.org.au
- eHeadspace: headspace.org.au/online-and-phone-support/connect-with-us/talk-about-mental-health/phone
- ParentLine: 1300 1300 52
- Suicide Call Back Service available 24/7: 1300 659 467
- Non-urgent mental-health support is available through Headspace on 1800 650 890.
- au.reachout.com (search 'LGBTQIA+ support services' for a great list of services across Australia. They also have a great list of culturally diverse LGBTQIA+ support services and groups.)
- Transcend Australia (transcend.org.au) has resources for trans, gender diverse, non-binary and gender-questioning teens and their families.
- Rainbow Families (www.rainbowfamilies.com.au).

- Minus 18 – champions for LGBTQIA+ youth (minus18.org.au)
- GLSEN – a US network to make schools safe and supportive for all students (glsen.org)
- Safe Schools Program (vic.gov.au/safe-schools)
- Sam Killermann's 'The Genderbread Person' – google this model for a useful explanation of sex, gender, sexual orientation and gender expression.
- Rainbow Door (rainbowdoor.org.au)
- Parents of Gender Diverse Children (pgdc.org.au)
- Kids Helpline has useful tips on gender identity (search kidshelpline.com.au)
- The Trevor Project – US (thetrevorproject.org)
- The LGBT National Hotline – US (lgbthotline.org)
- In Canada (with French translation), schools.healthiertogether.ca has useful tips on talking with kids about sexual and gender diversity

Podcasts

- *Parental As Anything* episode on 'Kids and Gender'
- Telethon Kids Institute *Embracing the Mind* episode on gender diverse and trans young people's mental health
- *Just Breathe: Parenting Your LGBTQ Teen*
- *Help! I Have A Teenager* with Dr Ginni Mansberg and Jo Lamble has a couple of episodes on gender and sexuality including 'How to Talk to Your Teen About Their Sexuality'

Books

Robyn Fausett and Molly Fausett, *The Kids Will Be All Right: A guide to raising teens in a complex world*

Dr Ginni Mansberg and Joe Lamble, *The New Teen Age: How to support today's tweens and teens to become healthy, happy adults*

Dr Jo Prendergast, *When Life Sucks: Parenting your teen through tough times*

There is a good list of books for LGBTQIA+ teens and their parents available at rainbowfamilies.com.au

parenthoodbliss.com also has a good list called 'Top 8 Best Books For Parents Of Gay Kids'

What to do when you find a bong, some weed or a small plastic bag with random pills in it

More resources

In Australia, we have the National Alcohol and Other Drug Hotline – 1800 250 015. The hotline will automatically divert you to the Alcohol and Drug Information Service in your state or territory. These services offer support, information, counselling and referral to other services.

Also it's a good idea to get your teen to download and learn how to use the Emergency+ app, which uses GPS to help a Triple Zero (000) caller provide critical location details to emergency services.

Websites

- au.reachout.com
- positivechoices.org.au – this site has fact sheets, webinars, videos, apps and games to educate about making safe choices
- adf.org.au – Alcohol and Drug Foundation
- DARTA blog 'Doing Drugs with Paul Dillon' at darta.net.au
- Paul Dillon and I did a masterclass on 'Alcohol, Drugs, Parties & Teens'. You can find it online at commonsenseparenting.com.au
- UK – FRANK – Text 82111, phone 0300 1236600 or find a support centre/email via talktofrank.com
- US – Substance Abuse and Mental Health Services Administration (SAMHSA) National Helpline on 1–800–662–4357 or samhsa.gov

Podcasts

Paul Dillon has two podcast series. I also highly recommend that you listen with your teen to get up-to-date balanced information at any time. You can find them at darta.net.au/podcasts.

- *Doing Drugs with Paul Dillon*
- *The Real Deal on Drugs with Paul Dillon*

The Australian Government *Student Wellbeing Hub* podcast has an episode on 'Drugs and the Teenage Brain'. Also check out the *Parental As Anything* podcast episode called 'Is It OK to Let My Teen Drink Alcohol?'.

Books

Paul Dillon, *Teenagers, Drugs and Alcohol*

Robyn Fausett and Molly Fausett, *The Kids Will Be All Right: A guide to raising teens in a complex world*

Dr Jo Prendergast *When Life Sucks: Parenting your teen through tough times*

What to do when your teen comes home seriously drunk

More resources

If you are ever worried while your child is drunk or after, you can get free and confidential advice about alcohol and other drugs from the National Alcohol and Other Drug Hotline – 1800 250 015. The hotline will automatically divert you to the Alcohol and Drug Information Service in your state or territory. These services offer support, information, counselling and referral to other services.

Again, if you know your teen's now drinking, it's a good idea to get them (and you) to download and learn how to use the Emergency+ app, which uses GPS to help a Triple Zero (000) caller provide critical location details to emergency services.

Websites

- drinkwise.org.au
- positivechoices.org.au
- adf.org.au – Alcohol and Drug Foundation
- DARTA blog 'Doing Drugs with Paul Dillon' at darta.net.au

- Paul Dillon and I did a masterclass on 'Alcohol, Drugs, Parties & Teens'. You can find it online at commonsenseparenting.com.au

Books

Paul Dillon, *Teenagers, Drugs and Alcohol*

Robyn Fausett and Molly Fausett, *The Kids Will Be All Right: A guide to raising teens in a complex world*

Dr Jo Prendergast *When Life Sucks: Parenting your teen through tough times*

Podcast

- *Help! I Have A Teenager with Dr Ginni Mansberg and Jo Lamble* – episode on 'Parties, Drinking And The Problem with "Giving Up" On Your Teen'

What to do when your teen is experiencing significant bullying, including cyberbullying

Websites

- esafety.gov.au
- digiisocial.com
- safeonsocial.com
- stymie.com.au
- bullyingnoway.gov.au
- dollysdream.org.au
- alannahandmadeline.org.au

Counselling and helplines

The eSafety Commissioner website has a comprehensive list of support sites here: esafety.gov.au/about-us/counselling-support-services

But here are a few key ones:

- Kids Helpline: kidshelpline.com.au or call 1800 55 1800 (5–25 years)
- ReachOut: au.reachout.com (under 25s)
- SANE Australia: sane.org or call 1800 187 263 (18+ years)
- eHeadspace 1800 650 890 (available 9am to 1am, every day, for young people between 12 and 25)
- Lifeline 13 11 14 (available 24/7, for all ages)
- qlife.org.au, 1800 184 527 (available 3pm to midnight, every day, for all ages)
- 1800RESPECT 1800 737 732 (available 24/7, for all ages)
- MensLine Australia 1300 78 99 78 (available 24/7, for men of all ages)

Podcasts

- *Parental As Anything* episode on cyberbullying
- SBS has a podcast series called *Harmful*, which interviews specialists in mental health, behaviour and education provide insights on how we can better tackle bullying
- *The Generation Next Podcast with Andrew Fuller* has a couple of helpful episodes on bullying

- *Help! I Have A Teenager* with Dr Ginni Mansberg and Jo Lamble has a couple of episodes on bullying including one on what to do if your child is a bully

Books

Claire Eaton, *ROC and Rise: The teenager's guide to building resilience, optimism and confidence needed to level up at school, in relationships and life*

Robyn Fausett and Molly Fausett, *The Kids Will Be All Right: A guide to raising teens in a complex world*

Dr Ginni Mansberg and Jo Lamble, *The New Teen Age: How to support today's tweens and teens to become healthy, happy adults*

Sharon Witt, *Wise Guys* and *Girl Wise* (guides to school)

What to do when your teen's phone use becomes problematic

Websites and help

- unpluggedpsychologist.com
- drkristygoodwin.com
- Download my social media reminder graphics at maggiedent.com

Books

Robyn Fausett and Molly Fausett, *The Kids Will Be All Right: A guide to raising teens in a complex world*

Dr Kristy Goodwin, *Dear Digital, We Need to Talk: A guilt-free guide to taming your tech habits and thriving in a digital world*

Brad Marshall and Lindsay Hassock, *How To Say No to Your Phone*

Johann Hari, *Stolen Focus: Why You Can't Pay Attention*

Jonathan Haidt, *The Anxious Generation: How the Great Rewiring of Childhood is Causing an Epidemic of Mental Illness*

Mari Swingle, *i-Minds: How Cell Phones, Computers, Gaming, and Social Media are Changing our Brains, our Behavior, and the Evolution of our Species*

Podcast

- *Parental As Anything* episode on teens, smartphones and how to deal with it

What to do when your teen's gaming becomes problematic

Some resources for more help

- I recommend Brad Marshall's book, *The Tech Diet for your Child & Teen* as a guide, as it's full of great suggestions and insights, and if you follow him on Instagram and Facebook, he has lots of 'bite-size' tips around this topic.
- He also has a parent tutorial video series at unpluggedpsychologist.com.au
- Raisingchildren.net.au has a recorded webinar on 'Gaming: how to make the most of it in your family', for families of 11–16-year-olds who want to learn more about their adolescent's gaming and how to make the most of it. Also check out their page on 'gaming & gambling'.
- If you're in Australia and your child is at the more severe end of use, and/or you would like an expert opinion, you can make a referral to The Screen &

Gaming Disorder Clinic for assessment by a professional. Search the clinic name to connect with them.

- You can visit your family doctor or GP to get a referral to see a psychologist wherever you live. Some sites (like, here in Australia, the Australian Psychological Association) allow you to search for counsellors that specialise in addictions/compulsions in whichever country/area you live in.
- Brad Marshall mentioned resetsummercamp.com has an online digital detox roadmap that may be helpful.
- A few years back, Kids Helpline teamed up with some of Australia's best gamers to run a Twitch session (that's where you watch others game and commentate while they do so) in which they talked about mental health. Could be a useful entrée for a gaming teen. Google 'Truth 'n' Loot' and Kids Helpline and you'll find it.
- Gamequitters.com is a global support community for gamers and families with members from 95 countries. It has an informal quiz parents can take to determine if their child may have an issue. They also have a podcast called *Gaming the System*.
- The 12-step program is not for everyone but Gaming Addicts Anonymous has an online self-test for gaming addiction and a section for family and friends that may be useful for you to check out as a parent: gamingaddictsanonymous.org

What to do when your teen hates their body and you suspect their eating habits might be disordered

Resources, websites and support

- Butterfly – for eating disorder support. Phone 1800 33 4673 (1800 ED HOPE) or visit butterfly.org.au
- Butterfly's Body Pride Resource Hub has resources specific for LGBTQIA+ adolescents and adults
- Among other resources, the Eating Disorders Alliance of Australia has a great fact sheet on 'how to start the conversation' (search at nedc.org.au)
- The National Eating Disorders Collaboration has some great resources for families, supports and those with lived experience, and they come in several languages (nedc.org.au)
- The WA Centre for Clinical Interventions has some self-help resources for body dysmorphia and disordered eating at cci.health.wa.gov.au/resources/looking-after-yourself
- Eating Disorders Families Australia (edfa.org.au)
- Size Inclusive Health (www.sizeinclusivehealth.org.au/find-a-provider)
- InsideOut Institute (insideoutinstitute.org.au)
- Internationally, F.E.A.S.T (Families Empowered and Supporting the Treatment of Eating Disorders) is a global support and education community of and for parents of those with eating disorders. Website: feast-ed.org and forum: aroundthedinnertable.org
- The Be Real Campaign on Instagram @be_real_campaign
- Healthline.com has a list of the best eating disorder recovery apps

Podcasts

- *Parental As Anything* episode on 'Teaching Your Kids Body Positivity'
- Butterfly's *Let's Talk* podcast: this podcast has four seasons of great chats about body image and eating disorders
- *The Generation Next Podcast with Andrew Fuller* – 'Eating disorders in young people'

Books

edfa.org.au has a list of the top 30 eating disorder books for parents and carers, so I recommend you start there

2023 Australian of the Year Taryn Brumfitt's book *Embrace Yourself* and her documentary *Embrace* could be an inspiring watch/read

Dr Jo Prendergast, *When Life Sucks: Parenting your teen through tough times*

What to do when you discover your teen is intentionally self-harming

You can visit your family doctor or GP to get a referral to see a psychologist wherever you live. Some sites (like, here in Australia, the Australian Psychological Association) allow you to search for counsellors that specialise in self-harm in whichever country/area you live in. There are some specialised units at some large city hospitals. In addition to the apps/programs already mentioned in the chapter on self-harm (page 283), here are some more resources:

Websites

Search 'self-harm' at

- kidshelpline.com.au
- orygen.org.au
- headspace.org.au
- youngmindsmatter.telethonkids.org.au (a Telethon Kids Institute website)

Consider training in Mental Health First Aid (MHFA). Mental Health First Aid Australia has an 'ALGEE' action plan that includes:

A – approaching, assessing and assisting with any crisis
L – listening non-judgementally
G – giving support and information
E – encouraging appropriate professional help
E – encouraging other supports.

Podcasts and apps

- Listen to the *Parental As Anything* episode on 'what to do if your child is self-harming'
- *Well, Hello Anxiety* with Dr Jodi Richardson episode 104 on understanding self harm.
- Telethon Kids Institute's *Embracing the Mind*
- *Raising Teens* with Collett Smart

- *Speaking of Psychology* (The American Psychological Association podcast) – 'Anxiety & Teen Girls' episode with Lisa Damour
- *Family 360* episode with Michelle Mitchell on 'Self Harm: Why Teens Do It and What Parents Can Do To Help'
- Calm Harm is an app that provides tasks to help distract you from self-harming.

Books

Michelle Mitchell, *Self-Harm: why teens do it and what parents can do to help*

Dr Jo Prendergast, *When Life Sucks: parenting your teen through tough times*

Janis Whitlock and Elizabeth Lloyd-Richardson, *Healing Self-Injury: A Compassionate Guide for Parents and Other Loved Ones*

What to do when your teen's school grades suddenly plummet

Websites

- headspace.org.au has a section dedicated to work and study with online resources, peer group chats weekly and a monthly professional led group chat
- claireeaton.com.au – check out Claire's blog
- My Learning Strengths™ with Andrew Fuller: mylearningstrengths.com
- rebeccasparrow.com/school-study-resource/
- raisingteenstoday.com (I like the blog article 'Hey Mom I don't think I can do it')
- organisingstudents.com.au has some good blog articles, learning and motivation app recommendations, plus a page of resources and products to help kids be more organised.

Books

Claire Eaton, *ROC and Rise: The teenager's guide to building resilience, optimism and confidence needed to level up at school, in relationships and life* and *The Organised Teenager* (Claire also sells some audio 'pep talks' for teens on her website.)

Dr Ginni Mansberg and Jo Lamble, *The New Teen Age: How to support today's tweens and teens to become healthy, happy adults*

Collett Smart, *They'll Be Okay: 15 Conversations to Help Your Child Through Troubled Times*

Sharon Witt, *Wise Guys* and *Girl Wise* (guides to school)

Podcasts and videos

Podcasts, audiobooks and videos have opened a whole world of learning and inspiration for our teens so help them find content that feeds their spark.

- *Stuff You Should Know*
- There are some great TED talks about learning and motivation (check out John Green's 'The nerd's guide to learning everything online' and search 'learning' at TED.com for more)

- Claire Eaton has been interviewed about teenage mindset on the *Bossy Bitch* podcast and about helping teens have resilience, optimism and confidence on the *Digital Families* podcast
- The Victorian Parents Council's *Parent Podcast Series* has some good episodes on helping kids at school.

What to do when your teen's anxiety becomes problematic and prevents them from doing things that matter

Your family doctor/ GP may help your teen access a Mental Health Care Plan, which, again, is funded support for up to 10 subsidised sessions for your teen to get counselling support. You/they can also call your state's dedicated child and adolescent crisis line, usually called the Child and Adolescent Mental Health Services (CAMHS), to access local support.

Online resources

- Beyond Blue has some great tips on their anxiety resource page (beyou.edu.au/fact-sheets/mental-health-issues-and-conditions/anxiety)
- Black Dog Institute's Bite Back free program is a self-guided online program for young people aged 13–16 years old (biteback.org.au)
- MOST – most.org.au. A digital mental-health service created by Orygen Digital, the technology division of Orygen, Australia's Centre of Excellence in Youth Mental Health.
- Mello – mello.org.au. Created by Orygen, this is the world's first clinically designed app to address rumination, aka 'stuck thinking'.
- Headspace (headspace.org.au) has a great function on their home page for parents or adolescents to quickly find tailored information, online support, work and study support or a local centre about mental health
- Brave Program is an interactive online program for the prevention and treatment of child and adolescent anxiety. Also has programs for parents, designed by The University of Queensland (brave4you.psy.uq.edu.au/teen-program)
- AT Parenting Survival is a US-based site with courses to support children and teens with anxiety and OCD (atparentingsurvivialschool.com)
- *Hey Sigmund* is an excellent blog that has useful evidence-based articles, strategies, videos and books to support children and teens with anxiety (www.heysigmund.com)
- The WA Centre for Clinical Interventions has some great self-help resources for various mental-health problems at cci.health.wa.gov.au/resources/looking-after-yourself
- Moodgym.com.au is an online tool that's like an interactive self-help book which helps you to learn and practise skills which can help to prevent and manage symptoms of depression and anxiety.
- There are some online cognitive behaviour therapy (CBT) courses and some of these will give you free access if you get a referral from a GP. One example is the 'This Way Up' Clinic, which has a teen worry and sadness program (thiswayup.org.au).

Consider training in Mental Health First Aid (MHFA) Australia, which has an 'ALGEE' action plan that includes:
A – approaching, assessing and assisting with any crisis
L – listening non-judgementally
G – giving support and information
E – encouraging appropriate professional help
E – encouraging other supports.

Podcasts

- *Well, Hello Anxiety* – Episodes 73, 84, 85, 86, 87
- *Parental As Anything* episode on 'Do you have an anxious child?'
- *Ask Lisa*
- *AT Parenting Survival* (covers anxiety and OCD)

Apps

- Smiling Mind
- Headspace meditation app
- Insight Timer
- Calm app
- Breathe2Relax

Books

Lisa Damour, *Under Pressure: Confronting the Epidemic of Stress and Anxiety in Girls* and *The Emotional Lives of Teenagers*

Dr John Duffy, *Parenting the New Teen in the Age of Anxiety*

Jonathan Haidt, *The Anxious Generation: How the Great Rewiring of Childhood is Causing an Epidemic of Mental Illness*

Michael Grose and Dr Jodi Richardson, *Anxious Kids: How children can turn their anxiety into resilience*

Madonna King, *Being 14: Helping Fierce Teens Become Awesome Women*

Daniel J. Siegel, M.D., *Brainstorm: The Power and Purpose of the Teenage Brain* and *Mindsight: The New Science of Personal Transformation*

Collett Smart, *They'll Be Okay: 15 Conversations to Help Your Child Through Troubled Times*

Daisy Turnbull, *50 Questions to Ask Your Teens*

Sarah Wilson, *First, We Make the Beast Beautiful* and *This One Wild and Precious Life*

What to do when your teen experiences a significant loss experience or a death

If you or anyone you know is in need of crisis or suicide prevention support, please call Lifeline on 13 11 14 or visit www.lifeline.org.au/gethelp.

Helplines and resources

- GriefLine – 1300 845 745 from 8 am to 8 pm: 7 days (AEDT) or visit griefline.org.au
- Grief Australia (grief.org.au)

- Australian Child & Adolescent Trauma, Loss and Grief Network (earlytrauma grief.anu.edu.au)
- Lionheart – a children's bereavement program supporting grieving children between the ages of 5 and 12 (lionheartcampforkids.com.au)
- Grief Connect (griefconnect.com.au)
- Headspace, ReachOut and Beyond Blue all have good resources on grief (head to their pages and search 'grief')
- Canteen – support for young people dealing with the impacts of cancer in their family or with a diagnosis of their own (canteen.org.au).
- whatsyourgrief.com
- allianceofhope.org (for those grieving loss after suicide)

Books and articles

Lynne B. Hughes, *You Are Not Alone: Teens Talk About Life After the Loss of a Parent*

Article on 'How to help a grieving teen' adapted from the book, *Helping Teens Cope with Death* by The Dougy Center (dougy.org)

'Addressing Grief: Facts and Tips.' Find via the National Association of School Psychologists at nasponline.org

Teenagers and Grief by Australian author Doris Zagdanski. Her website allaboutgrief.com also has some fact sheets for parents on supporting teens in grief

I have written an ebook called *Death and Loss Through the Eyes of a Teen* available from maggiedent.com plus there are many articles and videos about death and loss.

Podcasts

- *Teen Grief* podcast
- *Grief Out Loud* podcast from Dougy Center – personal stories from other teens, kids, and adults grieving a death
- *Navigating Parenthood* with Rebecca Sparrow – Episode 5: Grief and Resilience

What to do when your teen experiences sexual harassment or sexual violence

Helplines and resources

If you are in crisis and require assistance 24/7, please call:

- 1800 RESPECT (1800 737 732) – national sexual assault, family and domestic violence counselling line. They also have support (and a list of other support services) at 1800respect.org.au
- 1800 FULL STOP (1800 385 578)
- Kids Helpline – 1800 55 1800
- Lifeline – 13 11 14
- 13YARN – 13 92 76
- Police Link – 131 444
- QLife (LGBTQIA+) offers support from 3pm to midnight 7 days a week – (1800 184 527)

- Blue Knot (for adult survivors of child sexual abuse) – Call 1300 657 380 Monday – Sunday between 9 am – 5 pm AEST/AEDT or email helpline@blueknot.org.au
- Australian Childhood Foundation – counselling for children and young people affected by abuse and trauma. Phone 1800 176 453 or visit childhood.org.au
- The Alannah & Madeline Foundation offers care programs, prevention programs and advocacy work to support children who have experienced or witnessed serious violence, and to prevent violence and advocate for children's safety and wellbeing (alannahandmadeline.org.au)
- Childsafety.gov.au – has a good article on how to respond to a child's sexual abuse disclosure (and a list of support services).

ReachOut Australia has an excellent, comprehensive list of sexual assault support services on their website, which you can find if you head to au.reachout.com and search 'sexual assault support'.

The Raising Children Network page on 'sexual assault and teenagers' has some excellent further advice and support services listed (raisingchildren.net.au).

Another excellent organisation to contact is Bravehearts – 1800 272 831.

Podcasts

- *The Generation Next Podcast with Andrew Fuller* has an episode on preventing sexual violence that may be of interest.
- Chanel Contos chatted on *The Imperfects* podcast in an episode called 'Consensual Healing', about consent and rape culture.
- *On Boys* podcast episode: 'Empowering Boys to Challenge Rape Culture'.
- *Parental As Anything* episode called 'My teen is hassling for nudes'.

What you need to know about supporting your neurodivergent teen through the challenges of adolescence

Websites

- autismawareness.com.au
- allisondavies.com.au
- yellowladybugs.com.au
- kristyforbes.com.au
- christinakeeble.com
- squarepegroundwhole.com.au
- understood.org
- thriveautismcoaching.com (search their list of 10 mental-health resources for neurodivergent teens and adults)
- icannetwork.online

If you go to maggiedent.com and search 'autism', 'ADHD' and 'dyslexia', you'll find three different resources that contain community-suggested resources on supporting kids and teens across these neurotypes.

Books

Puberty guides: Heather Anderson, Fay Angelo and Rose Stewart, *Puberty and Special Girls/Special Girls' Business* and also *Special Boys' Business*

Megan Ashburn and Jules Edwards, *I Will Die on this Hill: Autistic Adults, Autism Parents, and the Children Who Deserve a Better World*

Grace da Camara, *Fridays with Tristan: Understanding ADHD from a Mentoring Perspective*

Grace da Camara and Madalena Bennett, *What Lies Beneath Matters* workbooks (one for tweens and teens with ADHD, the other for their parents), published by UWA Press

Robyn Fausett and Molly Fausett, *The Kids Will Be All Right: A guide to raising teens in a complex world*

Dr Emma Goodall, *The Autism Spectrum Guide to Sexuality and Relationships: Understand Yourself and Make Choices that are Right for You*

Chloé Hayden, *Different, Not Less: A Neurodivergent's Guide to Embracing Your True Self and Finding Your Happily Ever After*

Kay Kerr, *Love & Autism*

Jenera Nerenberg, *Divergent Mind: Thriving in a world that wasn't designed for you*

Susan Pinsky, *Organizing Solutions for People with ADHD*

Dr Jo Prendergast, *When Life Sucks: Parenting your teens through tough times*

Dr Devon Price, *Unmasking Autism*

Dr Sharon Saline, *What Your ADHD Child Wishes You Knew*

Desiree Silva & Michele Toner, *ADHD Go-to Guide*

Sonny Jane Wise, *The Neurodivergent Friendly Workbook of DBT Skills* and *We're All Neurodiverse*

Yellow Ladybugs, *Supporting Autistic Girls and Gender Diverse Youth: An essential neuro-affirming guide for parents, teachers and allies*

Podcasts and videos

- *How to ADHD*, explainer videos on Youtube
- *Too Peas in a Podcast* by Mandy Hose and Kate Hose
- *I Have ADHD* podcast
- *Square Peg Round Whole* podcast
- *ADHD Alien* (comics)
- *Parental As Anything* podcast has episodes on parenting autistic kids, and kids with ADHD and dyslexia

What to do when you are worried your teen may be considering suicide

If someone's life is in immediate danger, please phone 000 (Triple Zero) or the appropriate emergency number in your country.

For immediate support, visit the HELPLINES list on page 373.

Helplines and resources

- Lifeline's Beyond Now safety planning app may be worth exploring together
- CALM's suicide prevention (Connect. Ask. Listen. Monitor.) has three apps:
  - o Be Safe app for a potentially suicidal person
  - o Be Calm app for a person providing care to the suicidal person
  - o Care Calm app for the person in need of immediate care.
- Orygen's #chatsafe program at orygen.org.au
- Suicide Prevention Australia has a best practice directory on their website too
- Beyondblue.org.au
- Mental Health First Aid Australia (mhfa.com.au)
- Standby Support – call 1300 727 247 (24/7) for anyone impacted by suicide at any stage of life
- The National Indigenous Postvention Service – 1800 805 801 (24/7 support to individuals, families and communities affected by suicide or other trauma that is culturally responsive to their needs)
- Youthsuicide.com

Podcasts

- *Parental As Anything*, 'How to Talk About Suicide'
- *Raising Teens with Collett Smart*, S5 Ep 04: 'Dealing with Family Suicide' and S6 Ep 05: 'Supporting a Suicidal Teen'
- *The Wonder of Parenting* – episode on suicide
- *Not Alone* – Beyond Blue podcast
- *Holding Onto Hope* – Lifeline podcast
- *Teen Grief* podcast – Suicide series

Index